THE

DAYS

OF

MY

LIFE

POETRY BY MACDONALD CAREY

BEYOND THAT FURTHER HILL
THAT FURTHER HILL
A DAY IN THE LIFE

THE
DAYS
OF
MY
LIFE

Macdonald Carey

ST. MARTIN'S PRESS

NEW YORK

DESIGN BY BARBARA M. BACHMAN

Library of Congress Cataloging-in-Publication Data

Carey, Macdonald.
    The days of my life / Macdonald Carey.
        p. cm.
    ISBN 0-312-05410-6
    1. Carey, Macdonald. 2. Days of our lives (Television program)
   3. Actors—United States—Biography. I. Title.
    PN2287.C268A3   1991
    791.45′028′092—dc20
    [B]   90-49230
                                     CIP

First Edition: February 1991

10 9 8 7 6 5 4 3 2 1

For
Ted and Betty Corday
and
my brothers,
Charles and Gordon Carey

ACKNOWLEDGMENTS

My everlasting thanks to Mark Rosin for his editing and for his work and expertise in getting this book together.

My thanks to Toni Lopopolo of St. Martin's Press for her editing and for her incisive suggestions and my thanks to Ruth Cavin for her help in getting a finished manuscript.

I also want to thank the people who have assisted me in writing this book: Joyce Rosenblad, JoAnn Stambler, Mike Carey, Ken Corday, Richard Sale, Alvern Wendel, Juliana Everist Schust, NBC, and all the people at "Days Of Our Lives." And for refreshing my memory: Norma Dauphin, Lois Kraines, Frances Reid, Betty Carey and all my children—Lynn, Lisa, Steve, Theresa, Mac, and Paul.

I wish to express my eternal gratitude to AA for turning my life around.

PROLOGUE

January 8, 1991, My "Ninth Birthday"

My name is Mac and I'm an alcoholic. This is my "ninth birthday." I can't believe I am where I am now from where I was nine years ago, sweating and shaking and saying for the first time, "My name is Mac and I'm an alcoholic." Nine years ago, on January 8, 1982, I was as disengaged with life as a man can be and still be alive. A lot of you told me on that night that I didn't look like I was going to live much longer. I was barely functioning spiritually, mentally, or physically. I was just as withdrawn from my TV job as Dr. Tom Horton in "Days of Our Lives." I was still doing the show but wasn't in every episode. The writers had just given my character a stroke on the soap opera so I wouldn't have so many lines to forget. The audience didn't have as much time to examine me very closely, thank goodness, as my own life had also gone to pot. I'd been divorced and was not close to my children, a love affair with an attractive woman had not worked out, and I was in danger of losing the friendship of another lovely woman who had been tolerating my companionship for nine years.

Here I am, however, nine years later. I am getting letters from fans asking, "What is your secret? How did you get yourself cured? You don't shake anymore—you must no longer have Parkinson's disease." This year, I am closer to my six children than I ever was in my life. My former wife, Betty, and I are on friendly terms. I'm a published poet—three times! I am back in the Catholic church with a vengeance, as they say, an usher, a lector, and a Eucharistic minister who takes Communion to the sick, the elderly, and shut-ins. I serve on the Board of the San Fernando Valley Mental Health Center, and I am happy at seventy-seven, more alive and into life than I was when I was thirteen years old in Chicago, meeting the Queen of Romania.

As a member of Alcoholics Anonymous, the fourth step in our twelve-step program asks for a complete and honest inventory to be taken of one's past life, including the sins of commission and the sins of omission. This book is that inventory. It is a soap opera in itself.

Like a character in a soap opera, my life has been filled with narrow escapes from reality into alcoholism and similar addictions and obsessions. In the soaps, characters never seem to be cured. Years pass and they are still making the same mistakes while the audience is still asking, "Why doesn't Mary tell Jack that she is hooked on tranquilizers?" or "Why doesn't Jack tell Mary he's the father of Helen's child and that's why he's acting distant, which makes Mary so nervous she has to take tranquilizers?"

My story tells how long it took me to find out all the facts about myself—things that everyone else knew, apparently—and how I was finally able to discover my shadow and look at it. Carl Gustav Jung, the Swiss psychologist, divided the human personality into persona, anima, and shadow: the persona is the archetype, the person that the world sees; the anima (or animus) is the soul or spirit that moves your being; and the shadow is the part of the human personality that the individual never sees but that everyone else sees. There were countless signposts, flags dropped along the way of my life, that should have told me the reasons for the problems I was having. But like a character in a soap opera, no matter how blatant the warnings, no matter how clearly others could see, I ignored them. As an actor, you know how your character is motivated; you analyze his problems. In playing my character, I didn't think I had to prepare. I'd been playing my part since the day I was born.

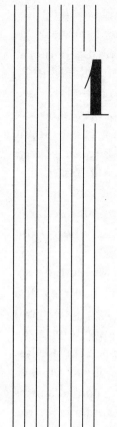

I am a boy again, about two years old. It is
Sioux City, Iowa, 1915. I'm walking beside
my father near Central High, "the Castle on
the Hill," as it was called because of its tur-
rets and ramparts, all in a rough-hewn black
stone, everything but a moat. We stop for my
father to talk to someone I will ever after
remember: the high school principal, who
has a carriage with a baby in it. Everybody is praising the
infant. My father lifts me up to see the baby and I'm encouraged to kiss it. I bite it. I bite the baby. The baby doesn't
cry. I am roughly reproved and set firmly on the ground at
my father's feet. I've gained nothing, in fact, I've lost a little
esteem, but I've declared myself and feel a little more sure
of myself.

I won't positively say that this is an analogy of my life—
asserting myself, overplaying it, and being chastened—but it
comes close.

There are other little scenes I remember from my childhood, like skating on the ice even when it—and the snow—

are melting, trying to savor and squeeze the last bit of joy out of winter, but in my mind they are all silent movies.

The next time I feel myself threatened is at my home at 2711 Jones Street in Sioux City. I am four years old. Mother is in the hospital. The household is upset; two baby boys are brought into *my* house. I am hurt. I am angry. I feel ignored, abandoned, unimportant. A nurse, Mrs. Bronger, is brought in to take care of the new boys, Charles and Gordon; a cook, Florence, has also been hired. The whole world has turned against me until my father takes me aside and tells me that these small boys are helpless without me. I am put in charge of them. It becomes my world again, my house, where I am still top man.

Of course, my father is really top man, but everything revolves around me. I am spoiled, but not as much as Jim Thorndike across the alley, who has a buzzer and light rigged to the fourth step leading up to his room. When you hit it, he knows you are coming. And of course there are the Kellys, half a block away, who own the *Sioux City Tribune*, but I'm still the guy who brings the bat and ball to the games across the street. I have the best hockey stick of anybody in the neighborhood, and as I grow up, there is a constant basketball game in my backyard because we have a backboard and hoop there.

Also there's Uncle John; when he moves from Rock Rapids, he becomes managing editor of the *Sioux City Journal*. Grandfather has a good library. Dad has sixteen silver tennis trophies in a glass case behind the head of the dining room table and there are loving cups all over the house. He's been the singles and doubles champion of the Missouri and Mississippi valleys for twelve years.

When I'm eight, I am supposed to see him play the 1921 world champion, Bill Tilden, at the Boat Club. The day of the match, I have to stay late at school to make up homework.

6

I'm afraid I will miss the match, so Dad comes to pick me up at school to make sure that doesn't happen.

We go to the tennis match, which is just an exhibition game that Tilden strings out to make Dad look good—but the champion wins in the end. What I really remember most about the day is the root beer float, with vanilla ice cream, that Dad buys me on the way home. Many years later in Hollywood, I see Tilden giving tennis lessons at a public tennis court down on Franklin Avenue. The glamour is gone from his name, a sad ending for someone who was everybody's idol at one time.

Nevertheless, when my father plays the exhibition match with him, Tilden is in his heyday. Afterward, my father tells me of another match he once played that he couldn't possibly win. It was in Des Moines, Iowa, on another clay court. It had rained the night before and the court was soggy. Dad's opponent had kept him waiting for three hours and then had appeared on the court wearing shoes with heavy cleats. When they changed courts, as one does in a tennis match, it was like playing in a plowed field. My father lost that one, too.

The Careys are a close family and they were always telling each other how special they were. There was lots of positive stroking, which we instinctively felt was necessary as we liberal Catholic Careys were growing up amidst the alien corn. Every Thanksgiving, we went to Uncle Alvern Wendell's farm in Bronson. Even though he was Dutch and not Scottish-Irish Catholic, he was all right. He was married to Aunt Loretta, Dad's sister and the president of the Grange, the national farm women's organization; they had a son, Alvern, Jr., who was about my age. The John Careys drove in from Rock Rapids. The Ed Careys drove in from Cedar Rapids. Of course, there was Uncle Perc McDaniel and Aunt Dool, Father's other sister. With all the children, there were about thirty-seven of us in all.

The children always put on a show for the grown-ups. Until the twins were old enough, I was relegated to pulling the curtains. My cousin Alvern tells me that I forced the twins to do whatever menial work I could think of as soon as they were physically able. He remembers sitting beside me in our backyard as we supervised the two boys digging a tunnel under our garage to store the films I showed to the neighborhood kids.

Films and performing were always in my life. Before my father presented me with a film projector when I was twelve, I had a theater first in our parlor and then in the family basement at 2711 Jones, where I did magic tricks and recitations on an impromptu stage while the twins stood on their heads on either side of the stage to form a proscenium arch. How they did it, I don't know, with all that blood rushing to their heads, but they stood on their heads that way for five to ten minutes at a time. Mercifully for them, we would close the show at this point with the movie.

What is left behind is irretrievable
But continues like a melody whose logical and grieving
progression nothing can halt

—John Ash

Grieving? No. Looking back, there's a lot to regret but a lot that becomes rich in the remembering.

Stories about my Grandfather Carey, who came from Limerick, Ireland, started when he was twenty-one as a traveling salesman with the firm of Carson, Pirie and Scott. Based in Galena, Illinois, the home of Ulysses S. Grant, he traveled the countryside on horseback wearing a Lincolnesque stovepipe hat. According to a family story, one day a farmer plowing his field waved my grandfather to a stop. It was April, a fine spring day. "Sir," the farmer said, "you look like a man from the city. Who won the election last November?" "Abra-

8

ham Lincoln," Grandfather answered. Communication was a little different then than now.

Look what we've done with it. As I write this, a full collection of Lincoln's speeches has just been published. People are marveling at his eloquence, his wit, and his ability to communicate, especially as contrasted with the "news bite" eloquence we've become used to from our public figures.

By the time Grandfather Carey had gone to work for Carson, Pirie and Scott, he was already married to my grandmother, Julia Anasthasia Mahoney. They had four sons in Galena before moving to Sioux City. Their first, Lawrence, died at eighteen months. Their oldest surviving son, my Uncle Edward, went into the mercantile business and eventually had his own dry goods store. Uncle John, the next oldest, had his own newspaper in Rock Rapids and then returned to Sioux City when he became the managing editor of the *Sioux City Journal* and editor of a column called "The Rear Seat." O. O. McIntyre and the Algonquin Round Table's FPA (Franklin Pierce Adams) were his peers, and they published each other's stuff in their respective columns. My father, Charles, the youngest son, was in business management and banking in Sioux City.

After Grandfather and Grandmother Carey had moved to Sioux City, they had two daughters: Loretta, who married Alvern Wendell, and Marie (nicknamed Dool), who married a grocery salesman named Perc McDaniel.

The ambience my father grew up with is mirrored in this letter my Uncle John wrote on December 16, 1939, to their older brother. It's a lengthy epistle but more evocative of the times and of my family background than anything that could be written secondhand. The letter sounds as if it could be the beginning of the script for *Meet Me in St. Louis*:

Dear Ed,

Do you remember way back when the Careys and the Rochfords lived in the big brick house on Bench Street in

9

Galena, and we could look out our second story front windows and see the Grant home atop a high hill on the east side, and the horse drawn purses from Calderwood's and Hunkin's Livery stables used to lead funeral processions up the steep winding roadway to the Catholic graveyard and evenings you and I used to look out the same windows and count the lights as they would appear in other windows one by one and Mother would light our own old-fashioned gas jet as soon as we could report a count of ten other lights, and when E. Carey of W. J. Quan and Company would come home from Chicago, he would bring us a bag of commies [the cheapest, the common denominator of marbles] and a box of candy and there was a picture of a young man and a dog hanging in our sitting room and Father said the young man was Johnnie Spillane, and in Unnie Rochford's room there hung a picture of General Sherman (after whom Unnie had named his own first son) ... and all the little folks were afraid of "Crazy Maria" because grown-ups had told them she toted a butcher knife under a plaid shawl, and McCarty, the Ice Man, wore whiskers and a red flannel shirt, and long, lanky Dan Ryan was town marshall and carried handcuffs and Tom McDermott was in the midst of a more-than-fifty-year service with the Illinois Central and lived over the Depot and Bish Hughes ran an Illinois Central switch engine with a smokestack almost as bulgingly big as the engineer's car itself and "Old Uncle John" Mahoney sported a high hat and carried an umbrella (rain or shine) and read the *Chicago Times* and served mass and went to all the funerals (whether or not he was acquainted with the corpse) and lived in the dugout on Upper Spring Street, and Big Mississippi River steamboats came up the Galena River and when the whistle blew, all the boys in town (including the Careys) would scurry down to the black bridge to help turn it and at night the big steamboats, tied up at the levee, would be ablaze with vari-colored lights and music and song would fill the air ... and going to Dubuque (to visit the Macdonald family) was a genuine adventure (with the trip through the East Dubuque Tunnel as highlight #1) ... and Galena and the I.C. [Illinois Central railroad] brakeman pulling into Galena from the west would always call it GAY-lena so the passengers for Lena would not get off by mistake; ... and the town was full of folks who boasted of their close friendship to the Grant family and December 17, 1874, was a red letter day for Galena with E. Carey passing the cigars in celebration of the arrival of his first child and namesake-to-be, the future merchant prince of little old Cedar Rapids on the Cedar? Happy Birthday to you.

Signed,

John (The Humble) Second Born

I wasn't all that conscious of my middle-class roots, again as Auden says, "as most citizens are not conscious of their citizenry." There was a bleakness, a black-and-whiteness, about Sioux City, Iowa. Not recognizing how deep my roots were, how much Sioux City was a part of me, my fondest dream—I think the fondest dream of all of us, Bill Kass, Harold Decker, all my friends—was to escape and go to a more rarified and bohemian atmosphere where music, the arts, and theater were the only subjects discussed: a utopia that still let you move with the best of society. I empathized with Uncle John Carey; his job as a newspaperman was romantic and, because of his wit, he was the toastmaster general of Sioux City. Unfortunately, his circle of friends included types my friends and I looked down on, like Edgar Guest, who was the Hallmark card type of poet of the day.

Even though I am a Carey, my middle name is Macdonald; my first name is Edward, both for the requisite saint's name for a Catholic child and in deference to my Uncle Ed, the eldest brother of my father and Uncle John. Macdonald had become sort of an imaginary family crest for the Macdonalds, and they always passed that name down in the families into which they married. Mother's favorite cousin, for example, was an Englishman, Basil Macdonald Hastings, whose son was called Mac, as I am. Basil was a writer of some note during the 1920s. One of his short stories, "The Ghost Goes West," was made into a 1935 movie by producer Alexander Korda. He also had many successful plays to his credit, including *Victory* with Joseph Conrad and *If Winter Comes.*

My maternal grandfather, John Macdonald, had come to America from Scotland with the Northwest Tea Company and owned stores in Chicago and Dubuque, Iowa. He was a dealer in hides and fur and, in the beginning, he prospered. I have a letter he wrote his bride-to-be, Miss Eliza Powers, saying he was sending her a piano as an engagement present. They married and settled in Dubuque, where, among other interests, he helped build "the first high-level bridge across the Mississippi." Galena, where the Careys lived, was fairly close, and when the two Catholic families met, they became friends.

After twenty years, Grandfather Macdonald moved my grandmother and their daughters—my mother, Elizabeth, and my aunt Evelyn, budding young ladies by this time—to Ravenswood, Illinois. I have a newspaper clipping that begins, "We take great pleasure in introducing Mr. Macdonald to the people of Ravenswood. He comes here not with flying colors or sounding trumpets, but with the best of bank references."

My grandfather later was in the grocery business and finally retired to run the Macdonald Hotel in Belphi, Indiana. His last years were spent with my mother and father, and me, of course, in our home at 2711 Jones in Sioux City, but I remember visiting the Macdonald Hotel as a child. It must have been about 1920. I was given a bowl of corn flakes that

I trust did not come from my grandfather's grocery store because my first spoonful of cereal held a wriggling worm. I was seven at the time and the trauma was lasting. It was years before I could eat cereal again.

As young women, Aunt Evelyn and my mother were teachers at the Chicago Music Conservatory. Mother taught fiddle and my aunt taught piano—they were a good source of my musical genes. They both had girlhood crushes on their cousin Basil, whom they visited in England when they were in their teens. Aunt Evelyn married Edward Pasmore, whom she had met through the Chicago Little Theatre, the first such theater in America. Later, they were among the founders of the Chicago Playwrights Theatre. Aunt Evelyn and Uncle Ed never had a child, and I became her adopted son of sorts.

Grandfather Macdonald wrote in 1926: "Macdonald is getting to be quite a society man." I was only thirteen at the time, and I assume what he meant was that I had already begun on my lifelong course as an extremely social being, with things to do or people to see every hour of the day. Further evidence of my rigorous social schedule showed up in a letter he wrote to Aunt Evelyn in 1927, where he observed: "Macdonald is having a great time. He delivered an address last night at the Hobby Fair at the Auditorium [this was Sioux City] and was selected to deliver Lincoln's Gettysburg Address at the Floyd Cemetery on Monday. He also plays the big drum in the procession at the head of the Boy Scouts. I think he will be pretty tired to deliver his address." I remember the day well, and I remember I wasn't tired at all. The march had taken the edge off my nerves and I didn't have the usual stage fright. Saying Lincoln's wonderful words to people as if they were my own words gave a strong boost to my latent desire to act.

Whenever I visited Chicago, Aunt Evelyn always took me

1 3

all over. She and Uncle Ed knew many people in Chicago's art, music, and theater world, and later they helped nurture my talents and got me the right introductions. Even when I was a child, Aunt Evelyn was my window to the world of the arts. In my scrapbook, I have an engraved invitation from 1926 to the South Shore Country Club in Chicago to meet Marie, the Queen of Romania. I am only thirteen. She is stunning, but no more attractive or stately than my aunt Evelyn. I am not surprised to meet a reigning queen; it is just another part of the unfolding of my life. This response to new experiences is a constant. Brought up on fairy tales and literature, I expected the unexpected; queens are part of this world.

I learned that day, by inference, the connection between publicity and attracting a crowd, that it takes more than a name and good looks to draw an audience together for your performance. Marie, the Queen of Romania, had a great advance man. She was in the United States to raise money for her country, something most Americans were not ready to grant her. Hence the saying, "Who do you think you are, the Queen of Romania?" Despite my diffidence, all this is pretty heady stuff for a thirteen-year-old Sioux City, Iowa, boy, especially on the heels of an art exhibit that features Marcel Duchamp's *Nude Descending a Staircase*. Parties in artists' studios and visits to real theaters and to society events hold up tempting visions of both the bohemian and the social worlds that were always to be conflicting utopias in my life.

As I grow up, the middle-class, merchant class Carey side and the artistic, musical, and theatrical Macdonald side are mirrored in my two groups of close friends. One group is represented by Bill Kass, who writes and with whom I discuss philosophy and the literary world, and Harold Decker, with whom I sing in choirs and in operettas and quartets, and who is devoting his life to music. The other group includes Bland Runyon, Bob Conner, and my Minnesota friends, who represent a more social life. Of course, the two groups are not that clearly defined—one spills over into the next, and the neighborhood boys are always good for pickup basketball, hockey, baseball, and football games.

As I am writing this, little scenes keep appearing, flashbacks that seem to illuminate moments in my past. Is it symbolic that at the age of twelve I dropped the big Bible as I moved it from one side of the altar to the other? (In the old Mass, the altar boy had to do this.) The way the family tells it, when I dropped the Bible, the pages flew everywhere and I scrambled in front of the altar to put them back in place. I see it now as sort of symbolic of my later fumble with my drinking; I dropped my own life and am just now, at seventy-seven, getting it back on course. Is it also symbolic that I used to go swimming naked in the creek on Uncle Alvern's farm in Bronson? The creek, which is called "The Big Whiskey," ends across the road in a trickle, where it is called "The Little Whiskey."

I get a chance to visit the farm often. My cousin Alvern would herd the hogs back to their pens, yelling "Sooey." I try to imitate him with no success while I keep asking, "What do I say to them?" My lousy command presence followed me through life. I remember getting another unwanted laugh as I made my first practice talk to my pretend troops in Officer Training. "All right men, orientate yourself," I demanded.

Since I was born on March 15, a Piscean—supposedly indicative of a double personality—and since I have two last names, Macdonald and Carey, there has always been a duality in my nature. All my life, I have swung between the poles of introvert and extrovert, sensitivity and hardheadedness. It was rumored that both grandfathers—Macdonald and Carey—had drunk away their businesses, but it's more than rumor that all the Carey men and the Macdonalds had some sort of weakness for alcohol. Uncle John, the newspaperman, was the only one who recognized this and was a lifelong teetotaler. Uncle Ed and Charlie, my father, despite their success in business, loved to drink.

When I am growing up, it is Prohibition and everybody drinks. The rite of passage for a boy in Sioux City in the twenties is being able to drink twelve bottles of spiked beer sequentially without passing out. The recipe for spiked beer is to take one bottle of near beer, drink off the contents of the bottle's neck, fill that with white or A (straight alcohol), put your thumb on the opening, tilt the bottle until the alcohol mixes with the near beer, and then swallow the whole thing. That's one-and-a-half ounces of straight alcohol per bottle, the equivalent of two shots of vodka. Is it any wonder most of my friends and classmates have been long dead and gone?

Alcohol is on everyone's mind then. I remember hearing the highest praise for a priest of the church, one Father Savage of Le Mars, not for his piety or his learning but for his cellar of rare wines. The main thing I remember about Grandfather Macdonald and Grandfather Carey is that neither can drink any alcohol. We are told it isn't good for them, but it is wonderful having Grandfather Macdonald around because he is a great audience for me; that's certainly what I want.

As I get older, besides the twins, Charles and Gordon, my father also gives me Mother to take care of. In 1924, Grandfather Macdonald writes Mother's sister, Aunt Evelyn, in Chicago: "I am very troubled about Bess. She gets so many setbacks and the headaches are very hard on her. She doesn't seem to gain strength." This is seven years after the birth of the twins and about six years after what is referred to as Mother's "nervous breakdown." She went back to Chicago at the time to visit Aunt Evelyn and to rest up from giving birth to the twins. Today, what she experienced would be diagnosed as postpartum depression and would be properly treated. When Mother returned home from Aunt Evelyn's, she found the house had been taken over by her husband's sister, Aunt Dool, and Mother feels left out. From this point on, she is always treated by the Carey family as some sort of fragile vessel. The home, the nest she has created, has been taken away from her in some sense, which adds to her feelings of depression and isolation.

What happened to Mother's position in the family is an example of the Careys' tendency to see things just in black and white. I can only guess at how she must have suffered from the Careys' perception of her as "an oversensitive artist" who just couldn't cope. Her "nervous breakdown" is a natural reaction to the physical and emotional stress of childbearing—twin boys, what's more, and to the oversolicitousness of the Carey clan. The Careys don't just help out, they take over. Aunt Dool is already ensconced in her place when Mother gets back from the hospital. Thereafter, Mother is discouraged from doing anything extra, including going to the Lady's Club. Since she always had an aversion to small-town women's clubs, her "nervous breakdown" and the family reaction to it becomes an excuse not to do the things she doesn't want to do anyway. This is the only side benefit of being considered delicate.

Everyone coddles her, and even Dad is heard to say when he wants her to sleep with him (in the Biblical sense, I mean), "Oh, come on, Bess. It'll do you good. Best thing in the world for your bowels." Of course, I'm not supposed to hear that, but I do. I remember, too, that Mother and Dad were good Catholics who practiced the "rhythm method" in its strictest form—intercourse just a couple of days a month, another factor to keep a woman in a stressful state.

I am sort of protective of Mother as well. Because she's not preoccupied with women's clubs, I see more of her than other children do of their mothers, and we become close. She is something of a loner. Although she is no longer teaching music, her heart is in the arts, and she encourages my musical development with years of piano lessons, violin lessons, drum lessons, and singing. Being so close to her, I identify with her more than I realize at the time. Even though I am very outgoing, my ultimate kinship is with her and her sensitivity.

When I get my driver's license, if Mother goes anywhere during the day, I always drive her. I do this during moments between my characteristic frenzy of activity. Besides all my music lessons, I am in the Boy Scouts, I take ballroom dancing and tap dancing, and, by the time I get to high school, I am playing drums in a little jazz combo. Every Saturday morning, I have French lessons from Professor Greynald. In the winter, I play hockey; each spring and fall, there is a constant basketball game in our backyard. Poor Grandfather complains in 1927 that the backyard is as white as the street. He should complain. We trample the grass flat and his garden is long gone.

I play on the high school ice hockey team and for years am also heavily involved in collecting stamps. In junior high school, I had organized a stamp club, gotten myself elected president, and conducted my own auctions at the end of each meeting. Harris and Company of Philadelphia sold me mail-order sheets of post–World War I stamps for a nickel up to a dollar for a sheet of one hundred. I bought wholesale and sold retail in the auctions that I had organized. I would sell single stamps from each sheet of one hundred.

I don't know how I had time to read during this period, but read I did, greedily and copiously. Grandfather Carey and Dad have provided me with a great library and I read everything I can: Dickens, Stevenson, Twain, Longfellow, Whitman, Burns, Keats, Shelley, Byron, Wordsworth. Still, I was always interested in show business. This took various forms. I had a chemical set and several Gilbert magic sets. In grade school and in junior high, I gave shows in our basement to pretty good houses, sometimes twenty people on weekends, particularly after Dad gave me the movie projector. I bought or rented Mack Sennett and Keystone comedies starring Buster Keaton, Lloyd Hamilton, Charlie Chase, and Charlie Chaplin, along with occasional feature movies. Entrepreneur that I was, I charged the neighborhood kids a dime or fifteen cents admission.

This merchant instinct I inherited from both sides of the family. What makes it so wonderful for me is that the product is the thing I love—movies and the theater. That's also what makes it terrible in a way, however, because there is a tinge of prostitution in it; I am selling what I could give away. Greed and reality temper my guilt, though it's always there in every actor's heart: "Will somebody catch on today that what we're doing is really fun and we don't have to be paid for it?" Being preoccupied with the arts is a reward in itself. You always feel it's an extra bonus to be paid for doing what you enjoy.

On the other hand, the money I took in from the movies that I showed as a child, I spent on the movies, going downtown on the streetcar to the Star and to the Bijou to see *The Silver Bullet*, a serial with Wallace Reid, a leading man of the silent screen who plays a race driver, and *The Perils of Pauline* with Pearl White as a heroine who many times is literally left tied to the railroad tracks or hanging on a cliff (this is how the term "cliff-hanger" was coined) at the end of each episode. Thus, I am early indoctrinated, if not injected, with the essence of the soap opera.

Besides these theatrical activities in Sioux City, every summer from 1920 to 1930—when I am seven to when I am seventeen—my father sends us to Lake Alexandria in Minnesota for three to four months while he stays home and works. At Lake Alexandria, I again participate in some version of show business: I do pageants and dance dramas with my cousin Liz from Cedar Rapids. Liz, who was born in March, three days earlier than I was, was a child prodigy

1 9

dance teacher and choreographer. In her teens, she was already teaching and dancing professionally, and today she runs the children's theater in Cedar Rapids.

My last year in junior high school at Sioux City, I played the lead in the senior class play, George M. Cohan's *A Prince There Was*. In the last scene, I was supposed to kiss the leading lady, who is played by Elizabeth Passman. She had garlic for dinner the night of the performance. You would think I'd learn something from that experience. But no. Years later, garlic does to my breath what it did for my junior high leading lady's—only the love scene I eat garlic before is in *Take a Letter, Darling* (1942), my second movie for Paramount; my leading lady is Rosalind Russell.

Further proving Grandfather Carey's remark that I am getting to be quite the society man, I was always going to parties with my teenage friends. There was always something vaguely erotic about those parties; many of them ended up being kissing parties. I remember one at Mary Van Dyke's house. A year before, Mary was my first real steady girl. I was mad enough about her to take photographs of her photographs and then more photographs of them. I literally couldn't get enough of her. Our mock engagement was short-lived, though, and by the time the parties started, we were just good friends. Mary's house had a circular tower; on its top floor, there was a sort of banquette, a built-in couch around the circle. We sat there in a circle, boy-girl, boy-girl, and played a game we called "Pass It On." The boy kisses the girl on his right, who kisses the boy on her right, and so on.

When we are a little older, and in high school, it is necking in the backseats of cars. Up to that time, in our innocence, we never pass on anything worse than bad colds. From the first game of "Spin the Bottle" in grade school through kissing games at the house that my younger brother Gordon deplores, I remain quite virginal and just on the fringes of sex. Of course, sex is on my mind. I masturbate like every other young boy. When you hit your teens, it's hard to avoid being sexually aroused by the oddest things. Everything, as a matter of fact. Like every other boy, I am looking for erotica in whatever I read but usually find nothing more provocative than the *National Geographic*'s bare-breasted natives.

Besides going to parties and playing basketball, football, and hockey—and looking for erotica—my friends and I do a lot of singing. Against local Catholic church doctrine, I am in a choir that sings in every church in town and even a synagogue. My friends and I are also very busy finding out who we are, not only in the games we play, the songs we sing, and the things we study in school but in the endless bull sessions we have. Bill Kass, Harold Decker, and I are always debating where we are going with our lives. We are in rebellion against the insularity of the Midwest, Sioux City, of course, in particular. Just to sing in churches other than Catholic is a rebellion of sorts. The very Irish Catholic strain that at the time dominates this part of the American Catholic church frowns on our doing this. Bill and I argue about Schopenhauer and Wordsworth and we write and look at each other's writing. Bill espouses artistic achievement, art for art's sake. Harold and I think artistic achievement can be combined with worldly success.

I always instinctively gave more than equal time to my social life, which revolved around a different circle of friends—not only going steady with Mary Van Dyke or Julianna Everist but palling around with Bland Runyon, whose doctor father, during Prohibition, provided us with a gallon of Templeton Rye one summer to be sure we drank good stuff, or with my friend from Omaha, Bill, Willard Deere Hosford, an Exeter and Yale man I emulated. His grandfather had invented the John Deere tractor. Though I knew in some vague way I was a step below the Hosfords socially, like Gatsby I was mixing with the swells in East Egg, little realizing that one day I would be playing Gatsby's only friend in a movie based on Fitzgerald's book.

Along with my social aspirations, I always felt the influence of my family's social conscience and their commitment to the arts. My father, though a banker, had been a spear-carrier for the traveling opera and theater troupes that came to Sioux City in his youth. On my mother's side, music and the theater were life itself. Both sides of the family keep social consciousness alive in me. Uncle John, the newspaperman, was a liberal Catholic. The Ku Klux Klan smashed his presses and burned his house while he lived in Rock Rapids. Uncle Ed, who has his own department store in Cedar Rapids and who was the oldest and richest of my father's brothers, always kept not only the *Wall Street Journal* on his coffee table but also the *Daily Worker*.

Any anti-Semitism or racism floating around in Iowa at the time—and there was plenty—never rubbed off on me. My father and my uncles were not prejudiced and made a point of teaching the children to guard against that. On my most recent visit to Sioux City, Saul Landsburg, the boy I grew up with next door at 2711 Jones, spoke to me about my father. The Landsburgs are Orthodox Jews. Saul says my father taught him that there are people besides Jews who believe in tolerance and civil rights. I remember how pleased my father was that in high school I got Lester Wilkinson, a black schoolmate, into the Civic Society, which had been my father's high school fraternity. This was a first for Sioux City Central High, where the Friedman twins (now Abigail Van Buren [Dear Abby] and Ann Landers), who lived across the street from us on Jones, were kept out of a sorority because they were Jewish. Anti-Semitism and racism just never happened in our family.

It seems to me that acting was always a driving force in my life. When I went to high school, I planned to start really learning more about it, but I was not quite mature enough to know what singleness of purpose really is, and I was hardly together as a human being yet. In Mother's old papers, I found a piece written by me just before my seventeenth birthday:

The Futility of Life
The rest of my time on earth can be nothing but tedious repetition. God might as well take me now. It is too bad that "God has set his canon against self slaughter."

Who did I think I was? And who did I think would believe me?

With all that false Weltschmerz, no wonder my high school English teacher, Laura Belt, thought I was a smartass, even though English was my best subject. When I have the whole front row of students cross their legs in unison, she says, "That's enough, Macdonald" and at the end of the semester gives me an F, which makes it impossible for me to be in any of the school plays—another example of my asserting myself, overplaying it, and being chastised.

The punishment makes me put all my energy into music, and Iowa is one of the most musically literate states in the United States. We had voice and instrumental contests in grade school, in junior high, and in high school, then city contests, county contests, district contests, and finally state contests. If we survived this far, we would then go on to a National Orchestra and National Chorus. I win bass for Iowa my last year and am sent to Chicago to be in the National Chorus. I remember being smitten by Elizabeth Gammon, a soprano from Birmingham, Alabama. We never got beyond the necking stage as the rooms at the Stevens Hotel where they put us up are too supervised.

Of course, we never tried to make serious passes at "nice girls." In Sioux City, certainly in the 1920s, you just didn't do that. All those kissing games are pretty harmless, and though we always longed for girls who aren't in the so-called "Sioux City Social Register," we remained pretty snobbish about our girlfriends. There were two kinds of women: those who do and those who don't. We want desperately to know what sex is like firsthand but we are told—and we believe—that we can't be sexual with any of the girls we know, and any of the girls we can be sexual with, we really shouldn't know.

To put it briefly, I was horny and confused.

My complete fall from grace didn't come until after my freshman year at Wisconsin.

My English teacher's punishment turned out to be a reward. I ended up graduating from high school early because of my extra music credits. I wanted to go to Dartmouth, the school my cousin John had graduated from, but Dartmouth wouldn't accept the music credits, so, following in the footsteps of Bill Hosford I went east to Phillips Exeter Academy to get the credits I needed for Dartmouth.

Hesitant but inwardly eager to enter this new environment, I am pleased when the dean invites me to his quarters and tells me that because of my own poise and sophistication, I've been chosen to take as a roommate one Harry Hubble, a brilliant student in physics who needs breaking in socially. This immediately makes me feel on a par with everybody in the world, which, of course, right now is Exeter. Harry later became a renowned mathematician who worked on the atomic and hydrogen bombs.

I did well at Exeter, particularly in French—because of my early lessons at home from Professor Greynald—winning a French prize and also a prize in drama for reciting Cyrano's "Thank You" speech. (French remained my second language until much later, when I did a picture in Spain and learned Spanish. Now only a few French phrases linger in memory but my Spanish remains pretty passable.)

I remember going to Boston for a weekend outing and waiting in the living room with two of my classmates while another one has sex with a married woman in her bedroom. She is not a prostitute but rather one of my schoolmate's conquests. We are meant to envy him but all I recall is a sense of unease. Afterward, all of us—except the married woman—go out to a tea dance at the Copley Plaza.

As it turns out, Exeter is the nearest I get to an Ivy League school. I am about to take my college boards when I receive a letter from my father, written on yellow notebook paper, saying there is no money for Dartmouth.

I was devastated but not destroyed because these things were happening to everybody. It was 1931, the Depression. I was happy that I could at least go to the University of Wisconsin. Once there, I emulated Cousin John, at least by joining his fraternity, Alpha Delta Phi. Its political and theatrical attraction was that it was the fraternity of both Franklin Delano Roosevelt and Fredric March, the movie star. The itch for the theater is as strong as the literary itch, but I learned that Wisconsin, under the progressive education policy of its president, Meiklejohn, doesn't allow freshmen to do any acting. All first-year classes must be traditionally academic.

I moved out of the Alpha Delt house almost as soon as I moved in. It was too conservative and expensive. Along with some other freshmen, I formed a dramatic club to produce our own plays. Our first production was so weird it never materialized. It was to be one act of Maeterlinck's *The Blue Bird*, Gilbert and Sullivan's *Trial by Jury* and an act of e. e. cummings's *Him*.

In fact, lots of things were weird about Wisconsin. While Prohibition was flourishing, so were a few of the old Wisconsin breweries—at least their rathskellers.

The first night of Rush Week, I am wearing my new camel-hair coat and riding in the rumble seat of somebody's car. We drink endless beers all night. On the way home, the rain pours down. I am soaked, drenched to the skin. My new coat turns into a wet rag. My bladder is filled to overflowing and when I go to bed on the sleeping porch of my room, which is on the lakeshore, the rain keeps falling, keeps splattering all night, and I wet my bed. The next night, the landlady puts a rubber sheet under my bottom sheet and I am never able get her to remove it the whole time I live in the boarding house. She is convinced I am a bedwetter.

I don't stop drinking beer, though.

For the first few months, I was on the freshman crew. The coach swore he can tell how many beers any of his oarsmen have drunk the night before by the way they pull their oars. He finds me out early and after three months I'm dropped from the crew. I pay no attention to this warning sign that I am drinking too much beer. Drinking is much more integral to my life than being on the crew and I write off the coach as overly demanding.

William Ellery Leonard, a poet you don't hear about anymore, was the resident muse while I was at Wisconsin. He'd written a book called *The Locomotive God* and an epic poem called "Two Lives," which were acclaimed in at least the Wisconsin literary community. Even more than for his poetry, he was famous for his agoraphobia. He lived a block from the campus and was never able to walk beyond this block, which contained his classroom.

Despite Leonard's weirdness, or perhaps because of it, all this excites me, as does the graduate class I am allowed to take in French poetry from the *Chanson de Roland* through Alfred de Musset and Baudelaire to the moderns. The teacher was wonderful. He'd written a stream-of-consciousness novel emulating Joyce and Proust. He taught well, but he never looked at the class, always over our heads or out the window or turning around to the blackboard behind him. Poetry and literature are still somewhere near me, even though I'm not writing myself. Everything, I feel, is grist for the mill of acting.

This idyll of a year ends in my return to Sioux City. The money has really dried up and there is nothing but time to spend. That summer, I feel I have to become a man the quickest way possible and I go to a whorehouse on Pearl Street. I drink enough to get my courage up and pay my $20 (inflation has changed this, I understand). I should have the memory of that "first time," but my mind has erased it.

There is also one boozy night at the Martin Hotel. I am let into a dark room where a nameless girl is waiting for me on the bed, a nameless girl whose face I never see. We couple in the dark and before long I'm in the hotel corridor, weaving homeward. I still have nightmares about that night, and I think of the other boys or men who were also let into that room.

One of these experiences—I don't know which—left me with a dose of clap. This became about the most traumatic thing that happened to me in my development, affecting my attitude toward everything: sex, women, my father, my self-image, my writing, and my acting.

When I tell my father I think I have the clap, he sends me to a doctor for treatment. As I vividly remember, it consists of passing a long steel rod covered with silver nitrate into the opening of the penis. It is as chilling an experience as it sounds.

The infection cleared up for a while, but when I came back from San Francisco—a trip I've yet to tell you about—the doctor said it had flared up again, so I continued the treatment and again I became celibate.

After a year or so, the doctor told me my father had told him to keep my penis irritated to teach me a lesson, but by this time, the irritation is self-perpetuating. I'm furious at my father but keep it to myself. Years later, after he's gone, I finally realize he never would have done such a thing. It wasn't in character. Today I believe that the doctor told me this to cover up his own incompetence and because he, not my father, judged me puritanically.

Nevertheless, that resentment of my father lurked in my subconscious for those many years. Because of it, I never credited him with all the sacrifices he made for my mother, for my brothers, and, most important, for me. My pulling away from him as I got older and never telling him why must have hurt him deeply. I know it haunts me.

Listening

I never sat down and wrote this before.
    I never
Knew how to say it—ever. But I guess I
    never tried
Before, either.
But nothing—there is nothing to stop me
    now. No excuse,
Nothing between us now but time, not even
    regret. Time's
Rubbed that out. Time's rubbed out shame.
I never told you I loved you dad. And even if
    I'd said
The words, which I didn't, I wouldn't have
    convinced you.

The last look I saw on your face after you
    had opened
My door in the hotel at LaJolla to

say goodnight.
I had broken my leg after too many
    breakfast martinis
And my squadron was leaving for overseas
    the next week.
You opened the door and almost hit the girl
    who was
Hiding behind it.

I've forgotten many things about you but not
    that look.
That look on your face. That last look. It
    wasn't shock.
It wasn't disbelief. It was just a look
    of acceptance
Of finality.

But there are other things I haven't forgotten too.
The careful way you carved roast beef during
    the only
Moments of silence at the table that
Held mother, the twins, grandfather
    and always
A guest and me—when you'd ask me if I
Wanted the fairy toast. I always got it because
I was the oldest boy.
Just another way you tried to make me feel
Wanted, since I felt the twins, my
    younger brothers,
Had taken my place in the nest.

After we'd eaten we'd all talk at once till
You'd quiet us somehow and say,
"Nobody ever listens to me"
But some part of us was always listening.

I kept listening even though I was way too
Grown up for them by then—listening when
    you told
The same dumb fairy tales to the twins.
They must have traveled deep into me
Because the first night I was in Ireland
    staying in
The Yeats suite at the Old Conna Inn
I took a walk in the evening mist and I swear
I saw the fairies.

And you fed me more than roast beef and
    fairy tales.
You fed me books. My reward after any
    sickness or spanking
Was always a book. I read Mark Twain,
Stevenson, The Rover Boys, The Motion
    Picture Boys, Tom Swift,
The Oz Books, The Horatio Alger Books,
    Detective Stories,
Weird Tales, Dickens, Thackeray, Edgar Allen Poe
And *Captain Billy's Whiz Bang.*
And you let me fill my room with all the smells
in the world. Before I collected stamps
    I collected
Chipmunk and squirrel skins and rocks and
    marbles and
Cigar bands. I remember Mother saying,
    "Charley, that's
Too much. You are a banker, you know."
    That was
When you'd come home at night with a
    cigar band
For me you'd picked up in the gutter on
    5th Street

In front of the Pierce Building where you had
    your office.

You never came to Minnesota with us in the
Summer though you'd sent us there.
    You stayed
Home in Sioux City and worked through
    the summer
So we could go. Just as you'd stayed
    home from
College though you'd won a scholarship.
    You'd turned
The money over to your sisters so they
    could go.

You died that first year I was overseas
And I never told you I loved you
And that I listened to you.

Loved you and listened to you.
Listened to you.

Listened to you.

At least my father lived to see me get a Broadway hit and a
movie contract, a kind of realization of his own theatrical
yearnings. Thinking back on it, it was small enough reward
for the childhood he'd given me. Besides all the French and
dance and music lessons, all the support for college, he gave
me something that is hard to describe; if something unpleasant ever happened to me, it wasn't just that he said, "Pretend
it never happened"; he taught me that wishing does make it
so. Through him I learned there was always a link between
wishing, pretending, and praying. They were all of a piece.
    The trouble was, I mixed up what my father taught me

3 2

about pretending with drinking. That got mixed up with the fact that drinking rubbed out guilt and, in turn, created more guilt. To show you how confused I became, when I drank as I got older, I never felt I was being unfaithful to the girl I was with if I went to bed with another. It was my version of the old elemental double standard. When I was in my teens, I was taught one copulated with nameless sexual beings but one made love with nice girls and married them. I extended this false theory into my relationship with my wife, believing that if I went to bed with someone I didn't know when I was drunk, it didn't count. Drinking further helped me to rationalize these things this way: I was going to bed with the dress the girl wore because that is what I most remembered afterward; not the act, not the girl, but the dress.

All this is ahead of me. That summer after my freshman year of college, I have lost my virginity, acquired the clap, cured it (for the time being), and now need to find a way to earn money. Four of us, Scott Hunt, Bill Callaghan, Bill Kass, and myself formed a quartet. Most of the time, we discussed philosophy and writing and the work ethic, which we heartily believed in but weren't getting a chance to practice because there were no jobs. We sang at the ballpark in Sioux City between innings for five bucks a night. We also sang in local speakeasies for all the bootleg beer we could drink.

Scott Hunt had his AB (able-bodied seaman) papers and he got a job on a steel freighter, the SS *Bessemer City*. The three of us who remain in Sioux City sang together, now a trio, for a few months more and were offered a contract by KSCJ, the local radio station, to sing for Montgomery Ward. Instead of taking it, we all decided to join Scotty on the SS *Bessemer City*.

My father, who had retired from the bank, knew a vice president of the Chase National Bank, who was also a vice president of U.S. Steel, which owns the SS *Bessemer City*. He got the man to give us jobs as work-a-ways. This meant we would be paid one cent a month. The bonus is that we would be learning the merchant marine trade and, after a few months, we would be able to apply for our ordinary seaman papers. There is another bonus, too: the ship was going around the world. Part of our objective was to follow in the footsteps of Jack London and Eugene O'Neill, two of our writing idols; we were taking this trip for the experience, to see the sea, and to become writers ourselves.

There was no money for me to pay the fare to New York, where the SS *Bessemer City* was docked, so my father, through his poker buddies at the Sioux City stockyards, got me a free ride on the caboose of a freight train as chaperon of a car of hogs. I was there to see they were fed once a day. In reality, the food was already there and they ate without me. They were pigs.

My friends and I get aboard the freighter, leave New York, go through the Panama Canal to San Diego, then on to Los Angeles. Our quartet has been reunited, but we have little chance to sing or to write. We don't even get to see very much of the sea because we do nothing but chip rust off the bilges below decks or scrub the decks topside. Though we keep thinking about Jack London, Eugene O'Neill, and our own desire to become writers, we don't keep diaries. We are too tired and too busy. I still don't know how London, O'Neill, or any of the writers who kept sea diaries did it. They must have done all their writing ashore after a voyage. The only peril I encounter on this trip is the cook, who keeps invading the shower room when I am taking a shower. He keeps wanting to scrub my back. I keep telling him I don't need it. I complete the trip with my virtue intact.

When we hit San Diego, we go ashore and almost miss the boat because we are partying when the ship starts to move out of the harbor. A Coast Guard cutter takes us out to the freighter in choppy water and we catch the SS *Bessemer City* just as she's about to leave the harbor. I remember that climb up the ladder to the deck.

We got off in Los Angeles, again, and this time we really missed the boat. We knew we had several days before we had to be in San Francisco to catch it there, so we rented an apartment on Yucca Street in Hollywood. Scott has been in Hollywood before, and he picked up a girl, who moved into the apartment with us. We stayed four nights and she slept with a different one of us each night. On the fifth day, we all checked out, the girl disappeared, and we rented a Ford to drive up to San Francisco.

It is nighttime when we get near Bakersfield and a big Cadillac races past us on a curve. As we round the next curve, we see the car piled up on the side of the road. Three people stand forlornly beside it. The woman has a cut on her face, and we take them into town and get a doctor. The three people turn out to be the screenwriter and playwright Dan Totheroh, the actor Melvyn Douglas, and his wife, the actress and Congressional representative-to-be, Helen Gahagan Douglas. I recognize Douglas as Melvyn Hesselberg, which was his real name, from Wisconsin, where he'd been leading man in a stock company whose performances I used to go to. I talk to them about my ambitions, and Totheroh, whose impressive career includes screen credits for *Yellow Jack*, *The Count of Monte Cristo*, and *The Dawn Patrol*, and *Distant Drums* on which the Lerner and Loewe musical *Paint Your Wagon* is based , tells me, "If you really want to write, if you really want to act, go back to your state university, go back to the University of Iowa."

By the time we arrive in San Francisco, none of us wants to continue the voyage. We get our clothes from the freighter. Scott and the two Bills started a throwaway newspaper for a grocery store. Embarrassed as I was to do it, I was spoiled enough to overcome my shame and I wired my father for

3 5

train fare back to Sioux City. When it came, I bought in Chinatown an Amida Buddha painted in oil on sutra, which I still have. That left me with bus, not train, fare and money for three oranges and three chocolate bars. I arrived back in Sioux City hungry but with my buddha and a dime for a streetcar ride home to 2711 Jones Street.

I worked for a while in a grocery warehouse, sorting out cans whose contents have botulism or incipient botulism. They are "bloaters"—cans that are swollen at both ends. These were thrown away. The "flippers" were cans whose contents have just started to turn and are swollen on one end only; when you push, they flip out on the other end. These were saved in special boxes to be given to the Indians—one of my first experiences with the "generosity" of the white man to his red brothers. The remaining good cans went to the regular market. The Food and Drug Administration was a long way off. It's amazing my generation lived at all. If alcohol didn't get us, the canned goods would.

I spent part of the year at Morningside College, and one of my classes was under a marvelous English teacher who happened to be a full-blooded Indian—a strange coincidence after the job I'd just had.

About this time, the nation's newspapers published pictures of a steel freighter, the SS *Bessemer City*. It had split in two in bad weather off Wales. As I remember, a few hands were lost. But for the grace of God and Buddha . . . !

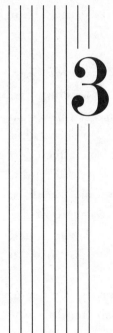

3

The next summer, in 1933, I followed Dan Totheroh's advice and went to the University of Iowa. It turned out to be the best advice I'd ever been given.

In order to enter in the fall as a junior, I had first to go to summer school to make up for the credits I'd missed in my sophomore year at Morningside. I got a job waiting tables at the Kappa sorority house, and that lasted through my three years at Iowa. All of us waiters at the Kappa house were considered to be a lesser breed, a slightly lower class, though most of us were dating or engaged to girls in other sororities. Since I was playing the role of a servant, I expected to be treated that way anyway; it didn't bother me. My life was principally consumed by the theater, so there was no time for romance, and the clap, which I had thought was in remission, reappeared, sadly making me no fit candidate for a love affair.

That summer, B. Iden Payne, who had earlier started the theater at Stratford-on-Avon in England (and who later started the Stratford theater in Canada), was at Iowa on loan from Carnegie Tech, teaching Shakespeare and directing Dekker's *The Shoemaker's Holiday.*

I play the juvenile lead. I'm finally acting. I also play Posthumous in *Cymbeline* for Payne. He starts by teaching me how to read and speak Shakespeare's lines, getting me to shed the "actorish" affectations I'd associated with reading the Bard. It wasn't that my ordinary speech was affected— it wasn't—but when I read a Shakespearean line, I'd read it differently from the way I'd read an American playwright's. I wasn't an affected young man. I was always one of the boys; I did a lot of my drinking to ensure that I was. I just thought that's the way Shakespeare's lines were supposed to be spoken.

On hearing me read Shakespeare, however, B. Iden said, "Carey, your English accent is more English than an Englishman's."

I blushed but I was there to learn and I figured that if I couldn't take direction I was in the wrong business anyway.

"Just read each line as if it were prose," he tells me. "Let the idea and meaning of the line carry the line. The commas at the end of the line are where you breathe. The phrase itself draws your breath for you."

I'm glad I listened. It is a wonderful introduction to Shakespeare.

When the regular school year started, the head of the University of Iowa Drama Department, E. C. Mabie, who once had headed the drama department at Dartmouth (this being as close to Dartmouth as I ever get), only let me be cast in small character parts. This did not fit my self-image. It had never occurred to me to be cast as anything but a leading man. I was the head man at home. I am a good-enough singer. With my friend Harold Decker, I believed in the success ethic. I believed in all the Horatio Alger stories. It was just *natural* that I would get success, that I would get leads. Unfortunately, Mabie thinks I am a lightweight because I am always off to Cedar Rapids thirty miles away, beer partying with my cousins.

"You'll have to give up the beer if you want bigger parts," Mabie tells me.

Unlike my response to the Wisconsin crew coach, this time I did swear off the booze, not just for my acting but for the additional reason that beer was irritating the lingering urinary tract infection. I went to the urology department at University Hospital regularly to irrigate the infection with potassium permanganate. One of my beer drinking buddies at Iowa was an intern and got me in to do my own treatments for free. Later, he married Mary Van Dyke, the girl I used to date in Sioux City when I was growing up. Even though in a few months the infection was no longer contagious, I never do more than casually date girls. I was always afraid of the possibility of infection, and I had a lingering guilt about my "social disease." This self-induced repression is a prolongation of the trauma of getting the clap to begin with; in my mind, I still have it. It is no doubt an extension of Catholic guilt: I am being punished by God for my transgressions. I've confessed, but only the church has given me absolution. I haven't given it to myself.

By my last year, I've forgiven myself enough to become quite taken with Toady Yarnell, a little blonde from California, Pennsylvania, who is likewise taken with me. The fact that I never try to sleep with her she falsely attributes to the purity of my intentions. I don't really know what I want in my relationship with her. I keep dating Toady while staying at a distance. I plead poverty and lack of time. The only passion I indulge is in the arts of the theater. I am passionate enough to convince Mabie I am serious about acting and he begins to give me leads.

My medical condition, besides affecting my sex life, interfered with my acting. It stopped me from completely giving myself to a character and to a dramatic situation. Putting myself in the moment was very hard for me. Mabie freed me enough to act and act freely. He helped me to be in the center of a character and in the center of the moment so that the character's inner voice would be my own. My first big part under his direction was as George Washington in Maxwell's Anderson's *Valley Forge*.

Working with Mabie was a revelation. He zeroed in on Washington's first appearance, a speech to one of his men in Valley Forge who is about to leave the army and go back to the farm. Mabie worked with me until I could talk to this character as I might want to talk to one of my younger brothers, admonishing him and reasoning with him as he's about to leave.

In the drama department, we were as consumed with the theater as the interns in medical school were with medicine. The theater was ours and we were the theater's, twenty-four hours a day. We studied plays and the history of the theater. We wrote plays. We directed. We designed sets, built and painted sets. We lit the productions. We produced them. We acted. If there is any weakness in such a regime, it is that we actors didn't just act all the time, but there was never a day in Iowa when I was not rehearsing or performing. We worked at nothing that is not related to the theater, and it was never dull. It is never dull today. Any weekday that I'm not taping my soap or playing in something, I'm taking a singing lesson or some other kind of lesson. I'll be in school forever. There's always something to learn and it feels good to stretch.

When I am twenty-three and about to take my orals for my master of arts degree, I am offered a job with the Globe Theatre. It comes through B. Iden Payne, the man I always felt would hold the key to my professional future. It is 1936 and the Globe, the creation of Payne and American Shakespeare authority Thomas Wood Stevens, has been a big hit at the Chicago World's Fair. There will be jobs in three Globe

4 0

companies: one for a fair in Cleveland, one for San Diego, and one for the Texas Centennial in Dallas. The actors are to come from the University of Iowa, the Cleveland Playhouse, the Goodman Theatre, and Carnegie Tech. Everybody is young. The plays are to be performed in a reconstruction of the Old Globe in London in Shakespeare's time, but they are streamlined, cut to a little under an hour, with the exception of *Hamlet* and *Lear*, which run two hours. They are performed with pace as they must have been performed originally, when they were just another midway attraction in London in competition with the bear pits and the cock fights.

I am chosen for the Dallas company. When I leave the University of Iowa and embark on my first professional acting job, I go with no baggage except an eight-year plan that I've laid out for myself. Of course, my eight-year plan is stolen from FDR's four-year plans and Russia's five-year plans. Russia is always extending its five-year plan to another five years, so I give myself a more practical eight years. If in eight years I haven't made it—and made it big—I'd go into some other business. E. C. Mabie had already promised me a doctorate and a career as a teacher if I want it.

I was hired by the Globe in Dallas as a juvenile and bit player, but there were two other juveniles in the company already, so I was a bit player, period. Until one night Carl Benton Reid, who was one of the best character actors in American theater and who was the leading player with the Globe, approached me during the mob scene of *Julius Caesar* and said, "Get up in Brutus tonight. I'm leaving tomorrow morning."

I took the streetcar home to the YMCA in Dallas, stayed up all night, and played Brutus the next day with only one fluff. In the scene in which Cassius is urging Brutus to join the conspirators, instead of replying, "What you would have me do, I have some aim," I said, "What you would have me do, I have some." It was such a highly charged performance, however, that no one noticed.

I hadn't just inherited the role of Brutus; Reid was the biggest name in the company, and when he left, I got all his roles. It was a real leap ahead for me, and I was deliriously happy.

Before Reid left (he later starred in the original production of Eugene O'Neill's *The Iceman Cometh*), I'd already gotten some wonderful advice from him. "Mac, you never can be sure you've given a good performance. At best, you will do well twenty-five percent of the time. At best." He went on to tell me that a good rule of thumb is when you think you were great, you weren't. The best you can do is follow the rules of preparation you have learned, concentrate, and lose yourself in the moment. You already know who you are (your character, that is). You know what your character's goal is in the scene. You try to live in that moment.

The externals have to do with what kind of actor you are. In Hume Cronyn's words, "You're either someone who throws open his arms and figuratively says to the world, 'Here I am—take me' or the kind that peeps out at the world from behind the hands he holds over his eyes or the veil he wears around him." In my case, in the first appearance I made on a stage that I remember, I played Simple Simon in a junior league nursery play. Julie Everist was next to me playing Miss Pussy. My fly was open and Julie reached over and buttoned me up. Ever since, the first thing I always do before I go on is to feel if my fly is open. Every male actor has recurrent nightmares all his life that he'll be caught on stage with his fly open. This is worse than dreaming you are suddenly naked on stage.

Psychologists have said we dream to escape, to let off steam from life's pressures. The actor has lived in dreams since childhood, perhaps for that reason. Any child with imagination plays "pretend" at one time or another, and being a professional actor just means you can go on pretending, like the little rich boy who always gets a game because it's his bat and ball. Of course, the actor doesn't need any *things*; he can play pretend with no props at all. Every day I go to work, I say, like any other actor, "Here I am again. They haven't caught on to me yet. They're still paying me to do this."

But there are the nightmare times when you're not paid and you can't get a job and the just-as-real nightmares when, for instance, you start listening to your own voice. David Janssen, whose series "The Fugitive" I was on once, told me he was hearing his voice all the time and couldn't stop it. Was it by chance that he died so soon after that? Sherrill Milne, the opera baritone, says, "If you listen to your voice when you sing, you can't hear it the way it sounds to other people." He sometimes rehearses in the subway when a train is speeding through so he can't hear himself and can't even try.

In the summer of 1936, getting Carl Benton Reid's parts at the Globe was another step up in my eight-year plan. In Dallas, the work ethic that I had gotten into full force at the University of Iowa continued to rule my life. One of the ingenues, Nora Doyle (née Nora McGillicuddy), and I would get to the theater at 10:00 A.M. to rehearse scenes from Noel Coward and Philip Barry, to make sure all this Shakespeare we were doing—six shows a day and seven on weekends and holidays—didn't spoil our touch for the modern theater.

Theater was everything to us. When we were not rehearsing or performing, we were watching. I remember sitting in the audience for a performance of *Midsummer Night's Dream*, one of the plays I wasn't in. Sitting next to me are a mother and her young son. The boy laughs at a joke in the play; the mother slaps his arm and hisses, "Don't do that. It's not polite to laugh at Shakespeare." Thank God the rest of our audiences didn't have such strange inhibitions.

In *Twelfth Night*, I had an elaborate makeup as one of the sailors, a mustache and goatee, which my fellow actors call "my crow's nest." One night, a movie scout sent word back that he wanted to see me with the idea of testing me for the movies. When he met me after the show and my goatee and mustache were off, he said "I'm afraid you'll never do. I thought you were more mature."

I say, "I'm an actor, remember?"

He says, "You're too young."

I wrote the whole thing off and interpreted it as a compliment to my makeup. I'm not ready to think about pictures yet, anyway. They come later in my plan. Right now, I still have too much to learn.

When the Globe closed in Dallas, we had a two-week hiatus before going on the road in the Midwest. Naturally, I made a beeline for New York to catch up on the shows. I also wanted to see Toady Yarnell, my University of Iowa girl-friend who had gone there to break into the theater. Although the irritation had healed and I no longer had to be celibate, I still was. It would be good to see Toady now that there were no restrictions.

My first night in New York during that 1936 Christmas trip, I left my hotel to see Toady at the Royalton, where she was having two of her best friends over for drinks before dinner.

As drinks and dinner and the evening progress, so does the ardor of Toady's friends for each other. They decide to run off to Maryland that night to get married by a justice of the peace. They want Toady and me to make it a double ceremony. Things are moving too fast. I remind Toady that, as a Catholic, I only want to be married in the church; she knows from Iowa that no matter how bad the hangover, I never miss Mass.

"Well," says Toady, "I have a surprise for you. I've become a convert."

Now I had never slept with the girl, I'd never proposed to her, and I am certainly not solvent enough to get married.

At the thought of her converting on my behalf, I am speechless. Toady doesn't notice this. She is too busy seeing the other couple off.

"The priest who gave me instruction will talk to us after Mass tomorrow morning," she tells me.

I'm so nervous I don't drink any more that night; I want to be stone cold sober and steady as can be to handle this properly in the morning.

Sunday dawns. I am in the pew of the church thumbing through a missal when I notice the whole service is in English. It is 1936, remember, and the Mass is still only in Latin. Toady has converted to the "wrong" religion. She is now an Episcopalian, not a Catholic. It is St. Mary's Church on 49th Street, a high Anglican church but not a Catholic church. I don't want to embarrass Toady or, perhaps, as usual, I want to avoid confrontation. Maybe it's just cowardice, my usual flight from reality. I sit through the service, rush through a friendly good-bye to Toady afterward, and leave it to the priest to tell her of her mistake about the religion to which she had converted.

I'd planned to see a few more shows in New York but instead I left for Chicago. The whole incident didn't really end for me until six months later, when Toady's attorney father called on me in my aunt's apartment in Chicago, fixed me with his jury eye, and demanded I state my intentions toward his daughter.

I say I have none. I have my career to think of—to say nothing of the need to make a living. So that's the way it ends; not with a bang but a whimper. I feel a little guilt, but mostly relief, and within a year, Toady marries the owner of a hardware store and lives happily ever after.

Soon after, our company started on its road trip. The places we played varied only in their oddness. We were on what is called the Redpath Circuit, famous in the Midwest during the Depression years. You never knew where you would be booked: in school auditoriums, schoolrooms, tents, old civic auditoriums, or theaters. You hit all the small towns for one-night stands. I remember one engagement in Flint, Michigan. The theater must have been built in the late 1800s. The stage was raked at a thirty-five-degree angle. We kept sliding down into the audience. We had to nail the chairs and tables down. We also played the new University of Iowa theater, which was fabulous—flies, wagon stages, a revolving stage, your tickets color coordinated with lines on the floor that led you to your seats, a lightboard that was an electrician's dream. I've never played in a better house. One night, we played *Hamlet* in a blizzard in Yankton, South Dakota. Not only did most of the audience not get there, our scenery didn't arrive. It was snowbound, too. Our set was kindergarten furniture, and I don't think my Claudius the King was very regal sitting there with his knees around his head. From Yankton, we were to play a number of dates in Indiana when a flood hit the state. We had to close.

As usual, I accepted this in stride.

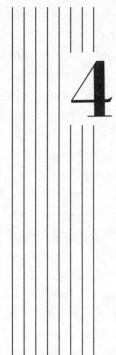

4

It is early 1937 and Chicago is the hub of
the radio universe: more radio shows come
from there than New York and Los Angeles
combined. So when my company of the
Globe folds, I decide to go to Chicago, move
in with Aunt Evelyn and Uncle Ed, and try
out for radio. Once I'm there and concen-
trating on radio, everything falls my way.
My voice and my training in speech at Iowa bring me good
luck.

At my first audition, I won the part of Lincoln in a popular
half-hour national show called "Behind the Camera Lines"
at WGN. I then tried out for the part of the First Nighter on
NBC's "The First Nighter"—a show that all radio America
listened to. I used as audition material George Washington's
speech to the troops from Anderson's *Valley Forge*, the part
E. C. Mabie had coached me in at Iowa. C. L. Menser, the
first vice president of NBC, liked my voice. I got the part and
they signed me to a contract. Don Ameche got his start on
that show as the running lead in the radio play we do each

week; when I came aboard, Don had just left and Les Tre-mayne was taking his part. My part as the First Nighter was to introduce the play and serve as a surrogate host to the radio audience. I was also the acting host for the studio audience and, as such, every Friday night I dressed up in tails and gave a little speech to warm up the studio audience before we went on the air.

The almost two years I spent in Chicago were wonderful. I was always working and happy. I went to the Goodman Theatre for speech and dialect lessons from Mary Agnes Doyle, a friend of my aunt and uncle's who had been with the Abbey Players in Dublin, and I took singing lessons from Hannah Butler at the Chicago Conservatory. Hannah, who is also a friend of Aunt Evelyn's, had among her singing pupils a beautiful blonde niece named Marcy Westcott. The West-cotts lived near my aunt and uncle on the near north side. It was a charming home to visit, which I did frequently; not quite as charming as it could have been, however, as Marcy's mother, Flossie, and her husband were on the point of sep-arating. I was very taken with Marcy but still traumatized from my long siege with my venereal past. Healed though I was, I hadn't the confidence to pursue her. In the back of my mind, there was still residual guilt over my transgressions.

Luckily, there's too much going on in the way of career and music to worry about my sex life—or lack of it. A bunch of us radio actors form our own stock company, the Little Theatre Off Bughouse Square, in Hecht and MacArthur's Old Dill Pickle Club in the part of Chicago that today is called Old Town. Art Peterson, the star of the radio soap opera "Guiding Light," is our own guiding light in this venture. He produces and directs our plays. It is one feast day after an-other. Chicago is full of jazz clubs. I spend every night I can at the Three Deuces with Art Tatum or Nellie Lutcher at the piano bar and Roy Eldridge playing in the inside room or Earl "Fatha" Hines in the Silver Slipper on the south side.

If it's summertime or fall, I'm drinking nothing but vodka and tonic because that seems to assuage the hay fever that plagues me; the rest of the time, my drink is scotch and water.

In my radio life, while Friday night was a dress-up night for me, Wednesday night was the real excitement. We did a show called "Lights Out," for which we used Studio E, the largest studio at NBC, in the Merchandise Mart. This is before tape and tape delays, so "Lights Out," like all radio shows, was live. The show, created and written by Will Cooper and Arch Oboler (who later became the first director/writer/producer of 3-D movies), was a precursor of "The Twilight Zone" and "One Step Beyond." Oboler and Cooper in fact, created the genre.

NBC made every effort to provide an eerie atmosphere for us to act in. When we were on the air, all the lights were out except for the sound man's and a lamp by the mike in the center of that vast studio. After two hours of rehearsal, we did the show for the East Coast at 11:00 P.M.; then we went out, ate at Ricket's on Chicago Avenue and came back at 1:00 A.M. for the second show, for the West Coast. What a fabulous time it was for actors. I played kiddies, teenagers, old men, Frenchmen, Germans, Spaniards, heroes, villains, anything they wrote. I played a headless Chinese man in "Lights Out" one night who runs around saying, "Where iss my haid?"

The Depression continues, of course. FDR is in his second term. There are countless strikes, the Spanish Civil War, and Picasso gives us *Guernica*; Stalin is in charge of purges in Russia; Mao Tse Tung and Chiang Kai-shek start to argue. We radio actors start to organize our own union, the American Federation of Radio Actors (AFRA). The Screen Actors Guild also forms. Joe Louis beats Jim Braddock for the 1937 world heavyweight championship. The abdicating Duke of Windsor marries his Duchess. Amelia Earhart is lost at sea. Bessie Smith dies. The *Hindenburg* goes up in flames, and the

Nazis are taking over in Germany. Most of us are unaware of the implications of this; we only know that, like today, we are living in a volatile atmosphere, a time when anything can happen and does.

In 1937, I feel, as always, a blind faith; it was hard for me to articulate then, as it is for me now, how sustaining that blind faith was and is. It served me then and it serves me now.

Ars longa, vita breva est: art is long, life is short.

Although the Depression is still on, I'm on, too. I'm working. I get my first soap opera in 1937, "Women in White." I play a young doctor, Lee Markham, in a script by Erna Phillips. Then NBC gives me my own soap opera, "Young Hickory," in which I play another young doctor. This time it's a young *country* doctor. At the same time, I also appear in a lot of other Chicago radio shows—shows like "Betty and Bob" on CBS.

One night, I go back to my aunt and uncle's apartment to find Alec Templeton, the blind English jazz pianist, having cocktails with them.

"Hello," I say.

Before they can introduce me, he responds: "You're Macdonald Carey. I'd know you anywhere."

"What do you mean?" I say.

"Well, you're not only the First Nighter, I've heard you on daytime shows."

This, of course, is the accolade of all time for me. I am such a fan of his that I can't believe he actually knows who I am. Such, however, was the power of radio.

As a member of the NBC stock company, I continue doing "Lights Out," "The First Nighter," and any other show on which they have a part for me. One of these, for Zenith, is done with Duke University, and we try ESP experiments on the air. I hold two cards in my hand, for example—say the jack of clubs and the seven of hearts—and I just think about them. The radio audience is asked to call in and say what cards I'm holding. A surprisingly high percentage of callers are correct. These experiments always follow some dramatic playlet about a famous psychic or metaphysical writer.

Radio would try anything in those days—and so would I. At the end of 1938, I treated myself to a Pullman berth on the Twentieth Century and headed back to New York to take a serious crack at Broadway. That was because of a fortunate meeting with Katharine Cornell, a meeting that occurred through my Aunt Evelyn and Uncle Ed.

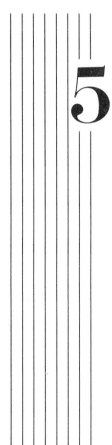

In the late 1930s, while radio and motion pictures were exploding, the days were coming to an end when stars of the magnitude of Cornell, Otis Skinner, Walter Hampden, the Lunts, Nazimova, and Eugenie Leontovich would tour the country with a troupe of actors and appear in such star vehicles as *Cyrano, Hamlet, Macbeth, Kismet*, and *Merchant of Venice*. We were also living through the last days of a profusion of road companies—second companies of Broadway shows that played every town no matter how small. But there were still stars of the theater in 1938—people who could take any kind of company on the road and draw a full house—and Katharine Cornell was one of them.

McKay Morris was an actor friend of my aunt and uncle, famous for playing the lead in Robert Sherwood's first big Broadway hit, *The Road to Rome*, a satirical comedy about Hannibal. He visited Chicago twice with touring companies while I was living there. The first time, two years earlier, when I was rehearsing Shakespeare with the Globe, McKay came into town starring with Eugenie Leontovich in Henrik Ibsen's *Ghosts* and in Jacques Deval's *Tovarich*. The second time, he was starring with Miss Cornell in Shaw's *Candida* and Maxwell Anderson's *The Wingless Victory*, an adaptation of *Medea* set in 1800 in Salem, Massachusetts. A big, strapping guy, McKay was that rare commodity in the theater: a handsome, masculine-looking matinee idol who could really act. Some years later, he died in a mental institution. Apparently, he had a constant inner battle with his homosexuality, but when I met him, I knew none of this. I admired his acting and was grateful when he and my aunt and uncle introduced me to Katharine Cornell, whom I regarded with great awe.

Miss Cornell promised to mention me to her husband, Guthrie McClintock, who was then one of the most famous producers on Broadway. McKay Morris also wrote a letter of introduction for me to the great man. It was good timing: McClintock is casting a new play by Dubose Heyward, *Mamba's Daughters*, a melodrama about three generations of a black family, the killing by one daughter of her daughter's seducer, and of her own subsequent suicide. Soon I hear there is a part of a young white man for which I might be right. Memories of my disastrous 1936 Christmas trip behind me and visions of Broadway stardom before me, I am again in New York, I meet McClintock's casting director, and read for him. I am told I will get the part if I come back the following week and read once more—just a formality.

But never be sure of anything in show business until you've already got it, had it, and done it. That goes for life, too.

There is another reason for committing myself to New York in 1938, and that's Marcy Westcott. By this time, I realize that although her aunt Hannah did introduce me to Marcy, I can also thank Hannah for some bad singing habits. One of her exercises involved holding your tongue to get certain sounds. Supposedly, this frees your throat. The more

I practice these exercises, however, the more I tie up my throat. Marcy, at nineteen, is a talented and natural soprano and her throat is made of stronger stuff—or maybe she just does the exercises correctly—but she sounds as lovely as she looks.

While we were studying with Hannah, I sang Debussy, as did Marcy, and she was to my mind's eyes and ears Melisande. Alas, she didn't seem to realize I was her Pelleas. At the end of my stay in Chicago, Marcy has made a hit in New York in the musical *Two Bouquets*, which is how I know she is there. *Two Bouquets*, written by Eleanor and Hubert Sargeon, is a pastiche of Offenbach and Gounod, directed by Marc Connelly. It had run one hundred weeks in London; it lasts seven weeks on Broadway. It closed before I got there. According to George Kaufman, who collaborated with Connelly on *Dulcy, Beggar on Horseback*, and *Merton of the Movies*, more people came to the rehearsals for *Two Bouquets* than to the performances, even though Brooks Atkinson called it "a nosegay of a musical." But it does introduce Marcy Westcott to New York—and I'm figuring that if I get a part on Broadway in a Guthrie McClintock production, I'll not only be advancing my career, I'll be near Marcy.

New York in 1938 is an exciting and disturbing place. The Depression isn't over yet. Fascism is on the move everywhere. Every now and then, we read about it but most of us don't pay enough attention, though there are some concerned enough to join the Abraham Lincoln Brigade and fight with the Spanish government against Franco's Fascists. Hitler is beginning to annex country after country. We hear he has just moved into Austria. A perfect symbol of the time's confusion is Douglas ("Wrong-Way") Corrigan, so named because when the U.S. refuses him permission to fly his plane solo over the Atlantic to Europe, he does it anyway, ending up in Ireland and explaining that he really set out for California but his compass was off. As Andy Warhol would later say, sooner or later everyone has fifteen minutes of celebrity. (In fact, Wrong-Way Corrigan has more than fifteen minutes. His nickname passed into the language as an epithet, in particular for one hapless football player who mistakenly ran the length of the field and scored a touchdown for the opposing team.)

In 1938, New York is at its peak as the cultural hub of the world. The Empire State Building, just completed in 1931, is the tallest building in the world; Manhattan is the Empire City in the Empire State. It is also the crystallization of America's emotional and political feelings. Crystallization is perhaps the wrong word because everything is in such flux. Reality keeps nagging for our attention, but, like alcoholics, we keep insulating ourselves in fantasy. Europe is on the brink of war and people are jumpy. Orson Welles broadcasts *The War of the Worlds* on CBS Radio and the whole nation panics. A new comic strip hero is created—Superman. Nobody faces reality.

I'm used to taking things in stride, of course, with my own interpretation of my father's advice: if something unpleasant happens, or if I make a mistake or fail, I put it out of my mind and tell myself it never happened. Since it's 1938 and I think I'm a big boy now, give me enough drinks and there's nothing I can't put out of my mind.

When I get to New York for my callback, *Mamba's Daughters* is already in rehearsal and Jose Ferrer has "my" part. With my philosophy, this is no problem. There are worse things than being stranded in New York with no job and $297. I have promised myself eight years to make it in show business, which for me meant starring on Broadway and in Hollywood and all the perks that go with it—a beautiful wife, a big, happy Catholic family, and walking off into the sunset forever, with a complete wardrobe. Since *Mamba's Daughters* has fallen through, I am in New York with five years to go on my eight. I know because of my success in radio soap opera in Chicago that I won't starve. Broadway may not be ready for me, but there is still radio, there is still soap opera.

The brownstone on 53rd Street into which I move is next to the Rehearsal Club, the famous boarding house full of young women trying to get started in the theater. The Rehearsal Club had been the model for Edna Ferber and George Kaufman's 1936 play, *Stage Door*, which, as a 1937 movie, became one of the early successes for Katharine Hepburn, Lucille Ball, and Ann Miller. For a young actor, the Rehearsal Club is also a good source for dates—if you have the money for a date. Most of the money I make I spend on just maintaining myself in a datable-looking state. It isn't enough to spill over into much of a social life, but my confidence is coming back.

It enchants me to know that the much-married and much-publicized actress, Jessie Royce Landis, lives at 35 West 53rd Street, my building. However, during my entire tenure at that address—tenure may be overstating it a bit since my roost there is a tiny room that was my first fumbling attempt at a foothold in New York—I never even glimpse the notorious Jessie Royce Landis in the elevator.

The real reason I move onto West 53rd Street, however, is Marcy Westcott. Fortunately for me she is living there; unfortunately for me, with her mother, Flossie. As in Chicago, Flossie is always around and always letting me know I am much too old for Marcy. Of course, Flossie is obviously angling for a better catch for her daughter; Marcy is only nineteen, after all, while I am a doddering twenty-five. I also like my drinks a little too much to suit Flossie. I drink scotch and water with her whenever there are cocktails or highballs, as they used to call them, after dinner. When I move in next door to her, Marcy is starring in Rodgers and Hart's *The Boys from Syracuse*, singing the two hit songs, "Falling in Love with Love" and "This Can't Be Love." But most weekends, she, along with other Broadway ingenues, is in the country at dancing parties with George Abbott, who, when he isn't dancing, is writing, producing, and directing hits on Broadway.

"Freedom Week," I find out, is what Mr. Abbott's week of country entertaining is called, and it takes place at Sands Point, Long Island, with Abbott, Jack Baragwanath, and William Rhinelander Stewart as the hosts. George and Will are bachelors. In fact, Will is one of the most socially prominent and sought-after bachelors on the eastern seaboard. Baragwanath, who has mining holdings in South America, is married and gives his uncommonly liberal wife, Neysa McMein, the week off. Hence, the name "Freedom Week."

Neysa McMein deserves a paragraph for herself, if not a whole book, which she already has (aptly named *Anything Goes*). For Neysa McMein, life was a freedom week. Dorothy Parker said that for Neysa, "home was any room where you could lay your hat or the husband of one of your best friends." Neysa married Baragwanath and spent her honeymoon in Europe without him but with critic Alexander Woollcott, concert violinist Jascha Heifetz, Marc Connelly, Arch Samuels (who was the editor of *Harper's Bazaar*), and Ferdinand Touhey. The honeymoon was described by journalist Herbert Bayard Swope, the then-editor of the *New York World*, as "A new groom sleeps clean." The odd-woman-out at the Algonquin Roundtable—odd because Neysa never had lunch with the others at the Algonquin but received them later in the day at her studio, where she did covers for *McCall's* and *Saturday Evening Post*—she had what were then euphemistically called "romances" with several of the regular Roundtable members, including Franklin P. Adams and Harpo Marx, all of whom were in love with her. Woollcott's love, though platonic, was undying. It's no wonder she gave her husband freedom.

George Abbott had bought the Sands Point house from

Neysa McMein and Jack Baragwanath. For "Freedom Week," a limo would pick up three girls in New York and take them for a night and day with their gentlemen dates: swimming, cocktails, dinner, parlor games, and the limo back to New York after lunch the next day. What happens in bed depends on the girls. Marcy Westcott told me recently that they had the nice girls out on the weekend and the "broads" during the week. After I married, I was surprised to learn that my wife, Betty, her roommate, Marian O'Brien, and Marcy Westcott had together been on one of those "Freedom Week" weekends in Sands Point.

In 1938, at age twenty-five, I think of Abbott, Baragwanath, and Stewart, who are all in their fifties, as so old that the weekends can be nothing but platonic, and everyone assures me they are. Flossie makes sure my weekdays anywhere near Marcy are equally platonic.

This leaves most of my evenings free to hang out at our local bar, the Gotham—so dark it defies description—on Sixth Avenue between 52nd and 53rd streets. The whole neighborhood, mostly actors and actresses, meets there every night to discuss their careers. Frank, who owns and runs the bar, is Italian and fond of telling us how much better things are in Italy now that Mussolini has the trains running on time. No one pursues Frank's comments into any political argument or inquiry. We are actors and we are interested in jobs and we don't happen to be working for the Group Theatre, many of whose productions are politically oriented. Instead of talking politics, we just talk theater shop and radio shop and drink beer.

Often your greatest strength is also your greatest weakness. I have always been a Catholic, I never seriously lapse, and I "keep the faith." But I use it and abuse it. I drink to excess, confess the error of my ways, and drink to excess again, excusing it all on artistic grounds. I can quote you chapter and verse on Edgar Allan Poe and John Barrymore. Drink was their muse, I tell my friends at the Gotham or anywhere else I happen to be drinking. By going to a different confessor every Saturday—New York is a big town and has lots of churches and lots of confessionals—I avoid recognizing the serial nature of my life: a drinking, confessing, drinking, confessing merry-go-round. Also, while working on radio soap operas—as I quickly begin to do—I never experience my hangovers with my whole body and mind. In radio, I am a disembodied voice.

Being so young, I have considerable stamina, too. During these early days in New York, besides taking singing lessons, acting lessons, dancing lessons, and studying French, I keep up my tennis and work out at the Y, occasionally boxing with a former pug named Tommy McLaughlin. I particularly like training with Tommy because he says we both should have a sherry with an egg in it before every workout. I regularly go down to the Village for fencing lessons from Giorgio Santelli. I also take judo lessons from Nadgi, Giorgio's Hungarian assistant.

All of this keeps me in pretty good shape, though it's hard for me now to say exactly what I looked like at twenty-five. In my experience, it's not easy to describe yourself physically in an accurate manner. You don't even recognize the sound of your own voice when you hear it played back after it's been recorded for the first time. I remember that in 1941, after seeing the rushes of my first movie, *Dr. Broadway*, I went out in the alley and threw up. It's not that I wasn't as handsome as I thought I was—I knew I was no Arrow shirt type—but it was hard to see myself for the first time on the screen, see how I must look to other people. It's like that first horrible time you try on a suit and see yourself in that glaring three-way mirror. You only see your faults, magnified and reflected endlessly into infinity.

Who Is That Masked Man?

You can go years
without realizing
Other people know things
About you
That you don't

You could walk down
The street and
Pass yourself
Without knowing who
It was
You passed

It's hard enough
To catch up
With yourself

And then it doesn't
Do you any good
Because you don't know
Who it is
You've caught up with

All I can tell you is that I have always been taken for a detective when I walk into strange bars or strange railroad cars.

Maybe this is why, in 1939, Marcy's mother prefers that Marcy get engaged to a famous photographer called Sarra rather than to me. Who knows? Within months after my arrival in New York and my starting to work on the New York radio soaps, Marcy does get engaged to Sarra, and, with nothing more for me at 53rd Street, I move to 54th, where I can nurse my heartbreak a block away from Flossie's watchful eye.

Ironically, only last year I saw Marcy again. She is now divorced from Sarra and when I finally tell her what my intentions were in those days, she says, "Pity. I always thought Momma had a hankering for you." Life is a French farce after all . . . only sometimes you have to wait fifty years for the punch line.

At 64 West 54th Street, another young actor, Stefan Schnabel, son of the famous pianist, Arthur Schnabel, has the big room on the first floor and his own bathroom. We both rent by the week. I never meet him; his friendship is as unattainable as his front room. The weeks I'm flush (at $44 a radio episode, I can make up to $300 per week and more if I pick up a commercial for Royal Crown Cola or Betty Crocker), I live upstairs in a big room in the back; the weeks I'm poor, I live in a small room in the back. The small room has nothing but a door and a window, and a bed you fall into as you walk in the door. Not even a closet. Those poor weeks, I live on peanut butter, whole wheat bread, and onions. The peanut butter gives me vitamin B, the onions vitamin C, and the bread vitamin E. The peanut butter makes the onions sweet and the onions take the stickiness out of the peanut butter. A five-gallon tin of peanut butter, an occasional fresh loaf of bread, a few onions a couple of times a week, and I am set dietetically and economically for months.

I still love this combination and I recommend it to all income groups.

My income fluctuates terribly and my social and love life fluctuate correspondingly during this period. However, the latter is generally in the "disaster" column or "meets an early death." The young woman I date might be a Rockette, for instance—the Radio City Music Hall is the new rage and it's only a block from the Gotham bar—but my Rockette always lives in the Bronx, Brooklyn, or Queens, and I'm stuck with an endless and costly cab ride. The subway is beneath me in every sense—or so I like to think. The nights I do go out, I want to go first-class even if it means I'll be broke for the rest of the week. I don't seem to be able to handle being a grown-up in society, but I don't worry about it because it's the temper of the times. Everything's uncertain. It would be foolish of me not to live foolishly, that's what I say to myself.

To give myself some sense of order, I program my drinking slightly: Before dinner, I have either martinis, manhattans, or old-fashioneds; if I have anything with dinner, it's a scotch, as I can proceed with that later on in the evening—and I often do. This is not usually done alone. I can always find a drinking companion, especially if I'm buying.

Somehow my moments of extravagance never worked out the way they should have. I bought my first expensive over-coat and wear it when I take a fellow actor's woman friend out on the town. He set us both up. He told me she was sexy, attractive, and stagestruck. I had been healthy and celibate for a long time and I had a new coat, so I was overjoyed to take her out.

I decide on Don the Beachcomber's for dinner. I knew the drinks were deadly if the right ones were chosen, and the ritual of choosing them would soon replace the desire to go anywhere after dinner. The first part of the evening goes exactly according to plan. After eating, we simply go to the bar and order zombies. As the second zombie arrives, however, she says, "One of my teeth just fell out." It had landed on the floor amongst the popcorn. After a lengthy search with the bartender's flashlight, I find the tooth and hand it to her. She starts to put it in her mouth and I say, "Let's sterilize it first" and delicately dip it into the zombie in front of me. I hand it back to her, she puts it in her mouth, and says, "This doesn't fit. It's the wrong tooth" and drops it on the floor, back amidst the popcorn.

My date is already obviously loaded and beyond playing

any love scene with me. I somehow get her in a taxicab and we start the trip to her hotel. With the cab's first lurch, she gets sick on my new overcoat. I have to leave it in the waiting cab while I get her past the hotel desk and up to her room. When I come down again, the cab is gone and so is the overcoat. As far as I'm concerned, the driver is welcome to it.

The moral of this story escapes me.

I am obviously not yet ready to cope with the real world, but that's not where I'm spending my time. There is always radio, there is always soap opera.

At this time, because of antitrust laws, NBC Radio is divided into two networks, the Blue and the Red, which operate from contiguous floors in the RCA Building in Rockefeller Center. Shortly after the *Mamba's Daughters* fiasco, I had made contact with Bob Smith, vice president of the Blue Network. Bob was a friend of George Voutsas, the head of the music department at NBC Radio in Chicago, where I had worked under contract. Bob Smith had what must have been one of the greatest collections of records in the world at his house in Connecticut.

An avid record collector myself from my high school days, I was fascinated by the richness of Bob's collection, and it was a kick for me to get out of New York for the weekend when he invited me to his Connecticut house. It became the thrill of my life when Grace Moore also arrived. She is one of the few opera stars who made successful movies. She was also a beautiful woman. I had seen her in *New Moon* (1930) with Lawrence Tibbett, the famous baritone from the Metropolitan Opera, and in *One Night of Love* (1934) with Maurice Chevalier, which had been a real hit. By the time I met her, she was famous not just for her voice but for her talent in comedy, which she demonstrated on Broadway in the operetta *DuBarry*. In that show, as she quaintly put it, her "underpinnings were prominently displayed."

Grace Moore already had been where I am hoping to be:

Broadway and Hollywood. When she appears in Bob Smith's house in Connecticut that weekend, she is accompanied by a bevy of brothers who are all six-foot-nine giants. Grace herself, while well-proportioned, is no petite miss. For me, an opera enthusiast, it is a visitation from a Valkyrie, but I get more than a breath of Valhalla from Bob. He helps me get a running part on "Stella Dallas" as Dick Grosvenor. Not grand opera, but soap opera.

"Stella Dallas," I find out, is based on the Barbara Stanwyck movie of the same name; "the world famous drama of mother love and sacrifice" is how the handbill distributed by the radio network describes it. In the radio show, Stella is always protecting her daughter, Lolly-Baby, from a fate worse than death. Once she commandeers a submarine to rescue Lolly-Baby, who has been kidnapped by a lustful sheik. Another time she lands a crippled airliner to save my character, Dick Grosvenor, from the psychotic millionairess, Ada Dexter.

I play the part for three years and, because I have hay fever, I am written out every August 12 until the first frost. Every time I am written out, my character commits suicide, once by jumping out a window, once by poison, and once I forget how. Each October when my hay fever is over, I am miraculously revived. From October through August, my life, as well as Dick Grosvenor's, is an active and exciting one.

As I marked time pursuing my radio career—while simultaneously showing up at every producer's and agent's office in New York, angling for a Broadway play—AFRA was really coming into its own. At one well-attended meeting at the Astor Hotel, I am excited when Gypsy Rose Lee appears to demonstrate that the variety artists are with us as we pledge our support of the screen actors striking on the coast against the producers who, we are told, are somehow in cahoots with, or being shaken down by, the mobsters.

By this time, Gypsy Rose Lee is a legend. I have seen her

strip in Chicago and I think of her as the ultimate sex queen. Later I find out that she is a very modest woman and that when she performs she always makes sure there is no audience behind her or on either side of her. What she does to be sexually provocative is pure illusion. She never strips down to anything less than two bows on her breasts and a G-string, and these you see for only the most fleeting of moments, although you swear you've seen more. The major portion of her act is a reverse strip—she puts on her clothes rather than taking them off—but she does this so suggestively that what she's doing is sexier than what she's not doing. You're so mesmerized that you don't know the difference.

As part of my New York life, I go to Minsky's, where Gypsy used to strip, whenever I can. I know burlesque is dying and as an actor I want to see it while it's still around (in fact, New York Mayor Fiorello La Guardia closes it down in 1939). The added bonus for me, of course, is the little sexual thrill the "joke-book reader" in me gets from seeing the act of stripping. (There's an old saying in burlesque and circus life that you play to the "joke-book readers"—the hayseeds, the rubes—and since I'm from Sioux City, Iowa, I qualify.)

On Broadway and 45th, Minsky's was a legend itself by the time I came to New York, and it had a continuous show from noon to midnight.

One afternoon, I come in and line up with other patrons in the Standing Room Only section behind the orchestra, waiting for the first show to break. As usual, people are leaving at intervals. We are roped off, waiting for our turn for seats. The usher takes the ropes down and a few of us start down the aisle to get a seat before the rush. The usher trips the two guys ahead of me and all three of us fall stacked up in a pile; we then slink back in line.

Minsky's had a totally different atmosphere from Radio City Music Hall, I observed. It is a question of air and attitude: the air and costumes were musty at Minsky's, to put it kindly, the usher was more of a bouncer than an usher. But the material onstage was basically the same and I soon found that the burlesque skits were also the basic material for vaudeville and musical comedy. Later I saw them reappearing in television sitcoms.

For me, New York is an adventure day and night. Every minute I'm not working on a soap opera, I am going for an audition for another soap opera or for a play, traveling from casting office to casting office. I sometimes alternate Minsky's with the Metropolitan Opera House, where I stand in my overcoat in the "gropatorium" SRO section—one buck for the poor like me. I remember hearing Lotte Lehmann in *Der Rosencavalier* and slapping away the hand of someone beside me who wasn't clapping.

I have weeks where I work every day, every hour, on a different radio show. I finish "Stella Dallas" at 4:25 in the afternoon and run from NBC in Radio City to CBS at 52nd and Madison, where I am on "Young Widder Brown" at 4:40.

"Young Widder Brown" is about "a woman as real as her friends who listen to her." She is actually the most fickle woman on the airwaves, with a new admirer every year; including Dr. Peter Turner, Herbert Temble, and Dr. Anthony Loring. With the prospect of marrying the young widow Brown, Dr. Anthony Loring is, to quote one critic, "faced with the horrible possibility of finding happiness at last. He chooses agony instead—an evil woman woman named Millicent."

"Young Widder Brown" is one of many soap operas written by Frank and Anne Hummert. It is directed by Martha Atwell, who directs numerous shows for Blackett, Sample and Hummert, an advertising agency that controls more than half of radio soap opera, including "Stella Dallas." I play various roles on "Young Widder Brown" just as I do on "Just Plain Bill" and "Mr. Keene, Tracer of Lost Persons," two of Blackett, Sample and Hummert's other series, both of which are also directed by Martha Atwell. I also play on "Backstage Wife," which is about Mary Noble, the wife of matinee idol Larry Noble. Mary's problem is fighting off the large percentage of American womanhood who lust after her husband.

The radio soap opera industry was a big sausage factory that ground out link after link of serial soaps. By 1938, the airwaves carried at least sixty soap operas every day, a minimum of three every fifteen minutes from nine in the morning until five in the afternoon. Most soaps were about lonely women facing terrible odds and the crisis, or even the possibility, of approaching forty and being single. These themes hit home all the harder because these were the Depression years. Millions of people listened to forget their own troubles, and soap operas became a regular part of everyone's daily life. There's a built-in addictive quotient. Like the first movie serials, you can't wait for the next episode. With the listeners' daily exposure to the characters' troubles, joys, and travails, the characters become as real as the people they know, as the people they are.

The scriptwriters were writing twenty-four hours a day. As an actor, half the time you picked up your script for the first time just before you went on the air and you did it on the spot. Most producers and directors knew you, they knew what you could do, and they called you in when an appropriate part came up, though usually there were auditions the day before. The great appeal for me is that I get to do a wide variety of roles, characters of all different ages and dialects, a pattern I first established in college and at the Globe Theatre and that I later maintain in the movie industry.

As a footnote, theater actors in New York at the time viewed radio actors with suspicion, first because the radio actors were working more and also because of the radio actors' facility in first readings. The theater actor claimed these readings were only superficial. For me, the truth lies somewhere in between. As a theater actor who went into radio, that envied facility was not easily obtained. To get truth in your acting, radio or theater, you must approach it from all sides. If you have the time—as you do in theater—you move slowly into the framework of emotion and character that the part demands; in radio, you must develop a recognition of emotion and character that is immediate, even as you read the material for the first time. You are in a way improvising and recognizing the moment immediately. It is a tremendous challenge. This radio actors' ability has too often not been recognized for the talent it requires.

My feeling is that acting is acting; rehearsal time is devoutly to be desired, but in the commercial world of entertainment, it's a luxury the actor doesn't always have, particularly when he receives a script the night before or only hours before his performance, which often happens today in television and in movies. I didn't realize at the time how much training radio soap operas were giving me for my future.

A certain kind of concentration is required for doing a radio soap. If you weren't in the studio at the time, you wouldn't realize what can go on. When I did "John's Other Wife"— "the story of John Perry, his wife Elizabeth, their kids, and their beloved Granny Manners"—Elizabeth was played by Erin O'Brien Moore, who dropped each page of her script on the floor as she finished it during the playing of a scene. We had to walk and stand very carefully in that sea of paper. Perhaps she was making a comment on the transitory nature of the script.

The more soap operas I do, the more real life gets mixed up with them. A friend of mine, Craig Giroux, the husband of Janice Kelley, a girl I'd grown up with in Sioux City, is accused of stealing some furs from the Greenwich (Connecticut) Country Club during a luncheon. Since Craig was having lunch with me in New York the exact day and the exact hour of the luncheon, I am his alibi, and I take a train to Ossining, New York, where Sing Sing Prison is also located, to bear witness at his trial.

I am put on the stand in court to attest to our luncheon date's time and place, and my date book is introduced as evidence. When the prosecutor sees the page for July 6, he begins questioning my morals, reviling me as a rake, a Casanova, and I don't know what else. "Eleven-thirty," he reads to the court, "Mary Foster, the Editor's Daughter; twelve-thirty—lunch with Craig; two-thirty, Young Widder Brown; three-thirty—Stella; and"—he pauses dramatically—"4:15 —John's Other Wife." To add to that, I had made the date in the Gotham bar a week before and "lunch with Craig" was written in lipstick, which I had borrowed. Of course it takes much longer for me to explain all of this to the court than it does to tell this story. The case against Craig is dropped. He goes free.

Now that I have been in New York for several months, it seems that the whole country is immersing itself in the Hollywood dream, perhaps because the world is becoming increasingly nightmarish. The New York World's Fair opens April 1, 1939, with the theme "Progress and Peace," but everyone knows Europe is on the brink of war. *Gone With the Wind* (1939) and *The Wizard of Oz* (1939) are winning applause. The soaps are reaching unprecedented popularity with listeners, and the newspapers' headlines proclaim: NATION'S EARS GLUED TO RADIO SERIALS. Women working at home hear an average of 6.6 soaps a day; amnesia, terminal illness, and forbidden romance are the main fodder. By the end of the year, the war has begun.

When Hitler attacks Poland in 1939, I am in Wilkes-Barre, Pennsylvania, with my friend and fellow actor Mike Ellis, visiting his family. Mike has a very cute sister. He and I sleep in adjoining beds in the same room. Before we get to bed, we have lots of beer and I make repeated trips to the john. Mike gets very little sleep. Whenever I get up, he is always awake, watching to see that I don't wander into his sister's bedroom. Of course, no such thought ever crosses my mind. Not with Mike awake.

The declaration of war didn't make the emotional impact on me that it should have, perhaps because its inevitability had long been assumed. The act itself was only the long-expected dropping of the other shoe. Again, this was all a part of the feeling of the times, a reigning unease and a gnawing fear that war would engulf our lives sooner or later. The extent of the atrocities for which the Nazi regime is responsible was never spelled out for us, the American public. Most of our lives went on as before.

One day in the middle of 1939, Paul DuPont, an old friend of my aunt and uncle from their Playwright's Theatre days in Chicago and a new friend of mine, introduces me to Cheryl Crawford. At this time, Paul, who later will become head designer for Eaves, the biggest costume designer in the world, is designing costumes for the Group Theatre. Cheryl Crawford, with Lee Strasberg and Harold Clurman, runs the Group Theatre and produces for them.

On meeting Cheryl, I'm struck by her uniqueness. She dresses in suits, her hair cut like a boy. She has a tough, no-nonsense manner, but I soon discover that despite her mannish appearance, she is warm and sentimental at heart, a Midwestern girl from Ohio who enjoys having meals at home and old-fashioned songfests around the piano. She is a sensitive, bright, compassionate woman with a strong sense of moral values. Her lesbianism, like Paul DuPont's homosexuality, makes no difference to me. I had known gay people at Iowa and in the Globe Theatre, and I'd inherited from the Macdonald side of the family—my mother and my aunt Evelyn—the sense that one's sexual preference is one's own business. By the time I'm twenty-six years old and am introduced to Cheryl, I feel comfortable with her dry Midwestern voice, her no-illusions laugh, and her utter directness.

While Cheryl is a real folksy, 'one-of-the-boys' girl, she is also a canny commercial and artistic producer. (Later she produced, among other landmarks in American theater, Tennessee Williams's *The Rose Tattoo*, Lerner and Loewe's *Brigadoon*, and the acclaimed revival of *Porgy and Bess*.) We spend nights just sitting around after dinner and singing at her apartment, and one gala night I go dancing with her and the cast of *Porgy* at the Savoy Ballroom in Harlem. I love to dance, and I love being just another dancer on the huge floor of the ballroom, where nobody seems to care whether I am black or white.

I am making better money now because I have a regular spot on Helen Menken's "Second Husband," a nighttime radio show that pays more than AFRA scale. Miss Menken has been a star for the Theatre Guild, playing Queen Elizabeth to Helen Hayes's Mary in *Mary of Scotland*, and she has starred in the play based on Edith Wharton's *The Old Maid*. Working with Miss Menken is a special challenge. She circles the microphone with both her hands so that as you face her, her script is between you and the microphone. Then she waves her script at you in a steady beat, in time with some inner rhythm she has. You have to say your lines and quickly dodge back or you'll get hit. It is a kind of boxing match the customers in the studio are treated to—the show is done in front of a live audience.

Now that I have the money, I move to 34 Beekman Place, across the street from Cheryl's apartment. If you lean out the window at 34 Beekman, you can see the East River. Lots of actors live at 34 Beekman, but I see more of them in casting offices and at Walgreen's lunch counter on Broadway in the theater district than I do at home. For one thing, we're hardly ever home; we're either looking for work or, preferably, working. In between reading for parts, we hang out in casting offices so that casting directors will get to know us. We also hang out at Walgreen's in between hanging out in casting offices. And when we go to the theater ourselves, it's usually as much to be seen as to see the play.

At 34 Beekman, I rented two rooms for $70 a month. For the first time, I decorated my apartment, painting three walls of the living room chocolate brown and doing the fourth wall with gold marbleized paper. It looked pretty good. Paul DuPont has helped me with the interior decoration. I have long ceiling-to-floor drapes made of tan burlap sacking and a yellow felt cover on the living room couch. I have an Ansley phonograph, a good collection of records, and a closet with a hot plate, a tiny icebox, and one bottle each of gin, vodka, vermouth, and Angostura Bitters. I am in business as a New York bachelor. I am ready for anything—but those few hours I'm home, friends from other parts of town keep dropping in. I am advised by Dane Clark to answer the door naked with a fountain pen in my hand, as though I've been interrupted composing a sonnet. He assures me that will put off constant callers.

But now that I have the location and the proper setting, the occasion of sin rarely occurs as almost immediately I meet the girl I am to marry. Also, Bill Kass, my best friend from childhood, shows up to make his way in the big city and wants to move in with me. How can I say no? Especially since I'm almost never there myself. I'm working regularly now, not just in radio but also in theater.

Dane Clark, Henry Jones, Clancy Cooper, and I are in a group called the Actors' Repertory Theatre. We have a sort of epic drama; we do readings of called *These Were the Times*. It is an eclectic arrangement of vignettes from various hit plays. One night I am reading one of George Washington's speeches from Maxwell Anderson's *Valley Forge*. This is a lucky piece for me in every sense. When E. C. Mabie had directed me in it at Iowa, he had somehow finally opened me up to what acting could be, and from then on, I always tried to be "in the moment," unself-consciously in the moment I am playing. I'd used the piece again successfully as audition material for the NBC stock company in 1937. The night I did it for the Actors' Repertory Theatre, Cheryl Crawford was in the audience. She liked my work and introduced me to the people in the Group Theatre. She also hired me to work in several of her plays in her summer theater in Maplewood, New Jersey.

I worked with good people there. In the little more than two years of its existence—from 1940 to 1942—Oona O'Neill, Jacqueline Susann, Robert Ryan, and William Bendix gave their first professional performances at Cheryl's theater. Ethel Barrymore, Helen Hayes, Ingrid Bergman, Paul Robeson, and Tallulah Bankhead played there, too. Cheryl got as many stars as she could for each production. My work with stars in radio kept me from being overly awestruck in such company.

My own first play in Maplewood is Clare Boothe's *Margin for Error* with, among others, Sheldon Leonard. There are two things I remember about that production, both connected with Sheldon. One night, he came onstage with his fly unbuttoned. Since his character is onstage most of the play, he had to find a way to button up his fly without the audience seeing him do it. He managed to do it so masterfully, with such sleight of hand, that even though I was onstage with him, I didn't know how in the world he did it. The other thing I remember is a weird conversation I had with Sheldon over drinks, when he advised me about the proper way to conduct a secret affair with a married woman—how to be *sure* not to be found out. This advice is: "Never have lunch or dinner in a hideaway. Always take the lady to a public place. Then no one will notice you." Both memories—the fly and the advice about an affair—seem to be connected in some subliminal way, both having to do with private parts and public places.

We also did S. N. Behrman's *No Time for Comedy*, which takes place during the Spanish Civil War. The play is about a comedy writer who feels the world is far too seriously troubled with the homeless, with civil wars, and with cities being bombed for him to do his work; in other words, no time for comedy. He meets a woman who is very serious about causes and about him. The writer's wife, I remember, tells the other woman, "Sleep with him if you must, but for pity's sake, don't ruin his literary style." I played the Englishman, Pym.

After doing *No Time for Comedy* in Maplewood, we take it to Atlantic City. In both towns, Francis Lederer plays the leading role of the comedy writer and Larry Fletcher, a marvelous character actor, plays the supporting role of a critic. Before coming to Maplewood, Francis had worked in Hollywood and had made several movies. And before that, he had come from the European theater, where you have to fight to keep your name in lights and anything you do onstage is fair. He brings this tradition with him, I discover. In Maplewood, Larry gets a hand after his first long speech about the Spanish always fighting civil wars, so on opening night in Atlantic City, the minute Larry finishes his speech, Francis claps onstage, thereby killing any chance of Larry getting a hand from the audience. Francis also doesn't powder his greasepaint and he rubs his makeup off on the black dress of his leading lady, Claudia Morgan, during their first love scene. Francis has not endeared himself to at least two of the cast.

In the same year as our production of *No Time for Comedy*, Francis had a big hit as a Nazi in the movie *The Man I Married*. In the picture his lover finds him out and scrawls "Heil Hitler" on his bedroom mirror. Our second night in Atlantic City, Claudia gets to the theater first and on Francis's dressing room mirror she scrawls in lipstick the legend "Heil Heel."

He shrugged it off. He felt he was only experiencing the

antipathy that theater actors have for anyone who carries the stigma of movie star.

Later on that season, Kurt Weill came to Maplewood to see Edna Ferber during the production of her *Royal Family*. He told Cheryl they were looking for someone to play the part of the advertising manager opposite Gertrude Lawrence in the new musical he and Ira Gershwin were doing. Moss Hart was directing, Sam Harris was producing. They are looking for "someone sort of plain-looking," Weill says, "on the style of Charles MacArthur," Helen Hayes's husband. Cheryl recommends me.

I go to the Music Box Theatre and read with Gertrude Lawrence for the whole crew. I am nervous, of course, but sight readings are the best thing I do; I'm a radio soap opera actor. They thank me and I leave. I later hear Sam Harris thinks I am too young. I forget about it. It's only another death in the family, and life in the theater is a series of little deaths.

A week later, I am walking down 43rd Street, passing the Shubert. I hear a voice behind me. It is Moss Hart. "You've got the job," he says.

I am in a Broadway show.

I am in *Lady in the Dark*.

I am playing opposite Gertrude Lawrence!

Everything after this happens so fast that it is blurred.

And I had just met and proposed to the girl I was to marry. My meeting her happened, at least indirectly, through the other work I'd been doing—radio soaps.

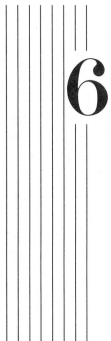

6

One of the attractive actresses who hangs out with the rest of us actors in the halls of NBC at Rockefeller Plaza, at Walgreen's drug store, at agents' offices, and at auditions is a woman who hates to see men floating around single. Though she has just shed a mate herself, she is actively in pursuit of mates for all her friends, and I unconsciously set myself up as a reluctant quarry for such pursuits. In fact, the idea of finding a mate is on my own mind because in my life game plan, at age twenty-eight I am supposed to be married already. I am a very programmed young man, bent on controlling my life. The world is in chaos and I want my life to be orderly. As I later find out, control is part of my alcoholism; all alcoholics are into control and they drink as a way of making them feel in control. In AA, control is the first thing you must renounce in the acceptance of a higher power.

At twenty-eight as a Catholic, I am rehearsing my Catholicism but not practicing it. I believe in a higher power but

I'm not surrendering to Him. I'm trying to control my religion, too. I use the confessional to control my absolution so I can sin at will.

Most of the girls I meet also seem to have marriage on their minds; I'm always being dragged home to make up a fourth for bridge but really to meet their parents. I also have a few—a very few—one-night stands where there are no parents to meet.

My friend the yenta and I see each other fairly often and soon she formulates a plan of action to get me married. "Have I got a girl for you!" She actually says that. "She's from the Main Line in Philadelphia. She's looking for a man. And she'll be going to Benno Schneider's with you. She's very attractive." Betty Heckscher *is* very attractive. She's tall, five-seven, slim, full-breasted, with a boy's hips. Her hair is chestnut, her eyes green. She's flirtatious, aggressive, and frank and wears her sexual attractiveness on her sleeve. Her friends and former boyfriends in Philadelphia call her "Sexy Hecksy." With her good looks, it's no wonder she wants to be an actress. From outward appearances, we are the ideal couple: I am tall, fairly attractive, with a commanding voice, and reasonably sure I am going somewhere in the theater.

Part of my friend's plan for me to meet Betty is that I get into Benno Schneider's class, which is the next best thing to the Group Theatre. (The Group, I find, is a pretty closed operation and tough to get into, even though I know Cheryl.) It is quite a coup to get into Benno's class, and I do. The next step is for me to do a scene with Betty Heckscher.

I am attracted to Betty from the moment I see her in class. She is my idea of beautiful. She emanates class and style. I learn that she is the only child of the marriage of Gwladys Crosby and Stevens Heckscher, who each have children by previous marriages. Heckscher, who died before Betty came to New York, had been an Assistant Attorney General of the United States, and when I meet Betty, her half brother,

Maurice, is Assistant Attorney General. Most of the Heckscher money is gone and Betty makes fun of the fact that she is known as an heiress. Jokingly, she says she already has her theatrical credentials: her late Uncle Gus (August Heckscher, a coal titan and patron of the arts) has a theater named after him.

Our teacher, Benno Schneider, is a master of the Stanislavski method. Stanislavski, who died in 1938, stressed the importance of inner identification with the character the actor is playing, eliminating artificial and mechanical acting techniques. This is what Benno teaches. Burgess Meredith, already a well-known star on Broadway from John Steinbeck's *Of Mice and Men* and Maxwell Anderson's *Winterset*, went to Benno's class the year before me. It's "in" with the right actors. Besides exercises and improvisations, pairs of actors are assigned scenes to prepare and bring to class.

Fate, or, I think, Benno Schneider himself, actually picks Betty Heckscher as the partner with whom I will do my first scene. Fittingly enough, it is a scene from Emlyn Williams's *Love From a Stranger*. I go to Betty's apartment for our first private rehearsal. We start talking, we start drinking, I fall in love with her, and then and there propose. The proposal is symptomatic of my hyper condition and of the hyper condition of the times. Everybody is going to war; the air is trembling with premonition. The unseemly haste of my proposal reflects my desire not to waste time with the expected routines of courtship.

Betty fulfills my fantasies and my requirements for a mate both socially and artistically. She is like the heroine of so many plays and movies I love: the typical Philip Barry wellbred, well-shaped aristocratic leading lady in *The Philadelphia Story* or *Holiday*. We do have common interests—the theater and a yearning for successful careers and building a family. But Betty and I hardly know each other. In fact, I don't know Betty at all, and Betty doesn't know me. The courtship scene we play our first night together when we're supposed to be rehearsing *Love From a Stranger* is, indeed, love from two strangers.

Betty didn't accept my proposal immediately; there was to be a not-exactly-protracted courtship of two or three months before I was accepted. In the meantime, we did get to know each other or, rather, to know what we wanted to know of each other. I took her everywhere in New York. I was working steadily in radio and had even bought a car. Since Cheryl Crawford had sort of adopted me as a friend from the Midwest, I was getting entrée to theater auditions. Betty took me to meet the family in Villanova, outside of Philadelphia on the Main Line, and, on another weekend, she had the nerve to get me to do what I never had before—go off to a country hotel in Connecticut and register as man and wife. I am so preoccupied with lying that I don't enjoy the clandestine quality of the weekend's laying. A roll in the hay in our respective apartments is easier for me to deal with.

As I got to know Betty, I also got to know her roommate Marian O'Brien, a charmer from a wealthy South Bend, Indiana, family. Marian was an inventor and an "idea girl." A few years later, she would work for the famous industrial designer, Raymond Loewy. When Loewy created the design for the classic 1959 Studebaker, Marian designed the leather interior. She also invented something called the "boater," a plastic diaper holder for babies. You simply snapped it on over the diaper, thereby keeping the sheets and the baby's other clothes dry.

Betty also has another friend, a blonde beauty named Carol DeHavenon, a two-time *Life* cover model. Betty keeps leaving me alone with Carol in her apartment to see what will happen. This is considered the acid test for fidelity, and since I never made a pass at Carol, I passed. With all these shenanigans, Betty and I never do do our scene from *Love From a Stranger*. We are too busy playing our own version of a courtship scene, she testing my fidelity to her with her beautiful friends and, a further twist, testing my friends' fidelity to me.

Betty, a wonderful and aggressive lady in everything she does, flirting included, inspires two of my friends to fall in love with her immediately. Unfortunately, the first is my old friend and recent roommate, Bill Kass. I point out to him that there is a conflict of interest and I ask him to move out. He does. I am so wrapped up in Betty and in my career that I don't have time to worry about friendships falling by the wayside. As for Betty's flirting, I feel ultimately it will fall by the wayside, too, and as long as I "end up with the girl" in this story, for the time being her flirting is all right with me.

Where Betty is aggressive, I tend to be more easygoing. In comparison to her, I am passive. While gregarious and open, I am also shy. Not only is my acting understated, I act that way in life; in the soap opera of my courtship, I play everything as low-key as possible, even with an overacting costar like Betty and would-be scene stealers like some of my friends.

One night, Betty and my friend Jake Klimo and I have drinks together and go to a cafeteria at the end of the evening. Jake is a writer who has boxed with Hemingway in Cuba and is very much into his own macho image. He looks past me across the table at Betty, locks eyes with her, and slowly breaks a glass in his hand, putting an effective end to the evening. I remember the sudden sight of blood and taking him to Bellevue myself to have his hand sewn up. I put him to bed in his basement flat and check him out the next morning to be sure he hasn't bled to death during the night. He hasn't.

"Are you all right?" I say.

"I'm fine," he says.

"Good," I say.

This is the last I see of him.

My own behavior is hardly exemplary. One of Betty's best

friends, Joan Tetzel, an actress and later the wife of character actor Oscar Homolka, is to be married at St. Patrick's. I have too much to drink the night before and sleep through the morning, missing the ceremony. My subconscious is going wild and looking for ways for me to revenge myself for Betty's flirtatiousness. I betrayed myself more than I betray Betty one night when, even after making the commitment to Betty, I found myself having a quick roll in the hay with someone I barely knew. But I was enough of a wrong kind of Catholic to confess that sin, forget it, and go on with Betty.

Just before we are really engaged, Betty and I go to a party at Sonny Whitney's apartment. Sonny is Cornelius Vanderbilt Whitney (sometimes also called C. V.). At the time of the party, he is married to Betty's sister, Gee. The Whitneys descended from Eli Whitney, who invented the cotton gin, while Cornelius Vanderbilt, to whom Sonny is related through his mother, once ran the transportation industry of America. Sonny is the best horseman and polo player in the country and heads the Whitney Museum, among other institutions. Betty says Sonny has a case on her, which is quite obvious from the attention he pays her the evening of the party.

Soon after, and not necessarily because of this, Gee divorced Sonny. For alimony, all she asked for was the Cézanne, the Picasso, and, I believe, the Gauguin. At the time she is commended for her generosity and later for her sagacity.

I don't know any of this, of course, when Betty and I arrive at Sonny and Gee's party in a penthouse on Sutton Place. The night turns out to be a high for me in every sense: endless glamor, art, booze, and a guest list studded with society and movie stars. It also turns out to present me with an enormous opportunity to advance my career. Hedy Lamarr is there. She is gorgeous. I have seen her in *Ecstasy* and I am flattered as any fan would be when she takes a shine to me and lets me sit at her feet throughout the evening. (Betty is well-occupied with Sonny, who is constantly flirting with her.) As Hedy and I sing *"Das Ist die Liebe der Matrosen,"* the only German song I know, Darryl Zanuck sees me and offers me a screen test the next day for Twentieth Century–Fox.

The following morning when I show up at the Fox offices, I have the shakes so bad from my hangover from the party that I don't get the test. I've blown it. I am devastated. There is no devastation like that of a habitual drinker who has been caught in the throes of a trembling hangover. The remorse is so all-consuming that it can only be dealt with by another drink. I go straight to a bar and drink away my shame. Another warning sign of my alcoholism that I don't heed.

Betty doesn't think I'm for real yet, I tell myself, so no details will be necessary about what happened to the Fox test. Promises are so profuse in show business that we never really believed the screen test would come through. When I see her later and sweep the whole thing under the rug by saying, "I didn't get it," Betty accepts this. I'm just another struggling actor to her, anyway, really.

But soon something happens that makes me pass muster as a serious suitor: I get the job in *Lady in the Dark*. I am young to be playing opposite Gertrude Lawrence but my voice gives me a maturity and Gertrude wants all the men around her to be young because it makes her seem younger. She also likes the fact that I'm tall. When she looks up at me, she has no double chin.

While I'm still rehearsing, and being a very earnest young man and practical enough to know there's a time when you should close a deal, I write Betty a very sincere note of proposal. I send it by mail. The letter is lost now, but Betty remembers a couple of lines from it. I send it on Easter and say, "Something has risen today besides Christ—it is our love." And later in the same letter: "We will make better children together." This is Walt Whitman's lifelong influence on me. In his poem, "A Woman Waits for Me" in *Leaves of Grass*, he writes:

> The babes I beget upon you are to beget babes in their
> turn,
> I shall demand perfect men and women out of my love-
> spendings,
> I shall expect them to interpenetrate with others,
> As I and you interpenetrate now. . . .
> I shall look for loving crops from the birth, life,
> death, immortality I plant so lovingly now.

What an impossibly cocky proposal in every sense! However, beneath the pretentiousness is my very real desire to
marry and start a family.

Having made my formal proposal to Betty on paper, the
next step was proposing to her marvelous but forbidding
mother, one of whose habits, I have learned from several
weekend visits at her home in Villanova, Pennsylvania, is
daily predinner martinis. Three; no more, no less. They are
kept frigid in an icebox in a safe in the den. Straight up
martinis, no ice. Mrs. Heckscher wears her hair in a Grecian
mode in tight gray curls on a patrician (matrician?) head over
a spine as straight as an arrow aimed at Olympus. On the
mezzanine of the Barbizon Hotel for Women on 61st Street
in New York City, we send Betty upstairs to her room while
her mother and I talk. When Betty is summoned to reappear,
her mother says, "I've turned him down." Then she laughs,
we have a couple of martinis, and start planning the wedding.

I'm on a roll.

I go with the rest of the cast to try out *Lady in the Dark* in
Boston. We are all excited; we think we have a hit but we
don't know yet.

It is opening night at the Colonial Theatre. Danny Kaye,
who costars with Gertrude Lawrence, Victor Mature, and

me, has a spectacular number. It starts with the orchestra playing a few bars. Danny asks the chorus, "Who wrote that music?" They answer, "Tchaikovsky." He says, "Tchaikovsky! I love Russian composers!" And then he rattles off the names of fifty-three Russian composers in about a minute flat—an incredible tour de force. He stops the show, no mean feat in a musical that is in itself a tour de force for Gertrude Lawrence.

Gertie has a number called "Jenny" that follows "Tchaikovsky." "Jenny" is a sort of "Minnie the Moocher"; it is good but not that good, but Gertie makes it that good. She makes it better than that. She adds bumps and grinds to the number on the spur of the moment and brings the house down, too. She tops Danny's ovation by a couple of minutes. And from that night on, even in New York, it is a contest between them—which Gertie usually wins.

Francis Lederer's tough apprenticeship in the theater was peaches and cream compared to Gertrude Lawrence's British beginnings in the theater. She had learned and practiced every trick in the book to climb to the top. I had seen her play in Samson Raphaelson's *Skylark* in Chicago, and she was like a dancing magician on stage. In case attention wandered away from her, she would pull handkerchiefs from secret recesses on her person. In the last scene of that play, she came on with bells on her toes.

Nobody topped Gertie.

Gertie was a wonder with the press, too, I learned. On successive days, I heard her tell completely conflicting stories to reporters about her background. One day, she tells them she had a convent upbringing. The next day, her past is shadier; she intimates she had been forced to work the streets for money to keep her mother alive.

She is just as variable on stage, and she makes every night in the theater an adventure. I play Charlie Johnson, the editor of the fashion magazine that Gertie's character, Lisa, is running. The play's conflict hangs on our relationship: Will she admit me into her life as a man? Will she come into mine as a woman? I keep calling her "boss lady," a phrase stolen afterward by countless movies. We have a couple of love scenes together. One night, she plays them for comedy, the next for tragedy. For me, a tyro on Broadway, working with Gertie is an exciting tour of duty. Life is different every night; life is wonderful.

Kitty Carlisle, later my leading lady and already married to Moss Hart, reminded me just how exciting it was doing a scene on the same stage with Gertie—indeed, how dangerous it was, particularly if Gertie had nothing to do in the scene. In *Lady in the Dark*, Vic Mature had to do a scene with Gertie sitting behind him; she mugged all during his scene. Moss catches this action one night and tells Gertie to stop it and sit perfectly still during Vic's scene. The next night, Moss comes by to see if Gertie is keeping her promise. She has, but she has also lit a match as Vic starts the scene and the audience watches, fascinated, as the match burns toward her fingers. Moss then tells Bernie Hart, the assistant stage manager (and Moss's brother), that Gertie is never to be allowed extra props. All goes well until one night Gertie tells Bernie a friend of hers, who was going to be out front that night, has sent her a bunch of violets and that it would please him if she could just have the violets in a vase on her desk. Bernie thought this a harmless enough request and let the flowers be placed where she wanted them. During Vic's big scene, Gertie very slowly ate every violet. One night, she took to doing dog barks during Danny's big number.

Gertie had a very low threshold for boredom.

She could be called on her tricks, too, I discovered, and would actually stop them. Natalie Schafer, who played Gertie's secretary in *Lady in the Dark*, notices on the second or third night that she isn't getting the same laugh on a certain line. Natalie isn't getting a laugh, period. The fourth night, she looks at Gertie and sees her breaking a pencil—which distracts the audience from Natalie's line—just when the laugh should come. When Natalie complains, Gertie apologizes and never does it again. So you had to forgive Gertie, though I found it was always wise when working with her to be very alert.

At this time, the theater is for Gertie what soap operas were later to become for me: a home away from home. It is where it's all right to let everything hang out. Ultimately, though, I think Gertie got bored with infinite variety and spice. At the time we did *Lady in the Dark*, she had just married Richard Aldrich, a conservative New England banker and producer. She had married him and was living happily ever after, throwing herself into her personal life— but not really, and not for long: Gertrude Lawrence died ten years later in the theatrical saddle, doing Rodgers and Hammerstein's *The King and I*.

The year *Lady in the Dark* opens, 1941, has to be the most dazzling year of my life. From living on subways and peanut butter, I find myself going to parties with Moss Hart and his friends. I eat at the Algonquin and Sardi's. I am, by everyone's declaration, a rising star—and I'm only on year five of my eight-year plan.

One party Moss invites me to because they need an extra man. They're playing charades, and to do *I Am a Camera*, Fredric March steps behind Edna Ferber, lifts her dress, and squeezes a breast as if it were the rubber ball on an old-fashioned camera. Everybody guessed it immediately. I am giddy with the excitement of it all. Just being at a party with members of the Algonquin crowd is its own bliss.

Danny Kaye and I are sharing a dressing room, but that is about all we share. The only thing we have in common is our respective successes in *Lady in the Dark*. I am an actor-actor and Danny is a nightclub entertainer who continues to do his enormously popular act at the Martinique, a club in the East 50s, even after *Lady in the Dark* starts playing. I am about to marry Betty and he is already married to Sylvia, who writes his act—the act that brought Danny to Moss Hart's attention for *Lady in the Dark*. Danny is from Brooklyn, and he's an inveterate Dodger fan. If you didn't know his father came from the old country (the Ukraine), you'd swear his fanaticism is genetic. Danny and I are both ambitious in our own ways. We are two isolated egos.

After *Lady in the Dark*, I didn't really see Danny until years later when we are both doing pictures. One day, I am recording a radio show at the old NBC studios at Sunset and Vine in Hollywood. I am in the midst of a recording session; the red light is turned off for a minute but everyone is still keyed up to performance level. Suddenly, two figures, caps pulled down over their faces, appear inside the studio door. One of them says, "What do you bums think you're doing?" Dear Lurene Tuttle, one of the best radio actors who ever lived, immediately swoops down on the interlopers, saying, "Right now, we're telling you to get out of here." It is Danny and Leo Durocher—Danny's idea of a practical joke. He is with Leo Durocher, still in a way close to his Dodgers. And he is still practicing the kind of pretension-puncturing humor that made him so funny: Danny's comedy often went for the ego jugular vein.

All we see is Danny's extrovert side, the broad strokes of his comedy; the man himself remains hidden, the cap pulled down over his face.

Vic Mature is in *Lady in the Dark*, too, and has the big dressing room next to Danny's and mine. Moss Hart has coined the term "big hunk of man" for Vic's character in the play and it sticks with Vic the rest of his career.

Carl Schroeder, his buddy, published a couple of movie magazines and he ran a centerfold of Vic under the headline WHAT HOLLYWOOD IS A MAN. A giant Victor Mature in a loincloth is in the center of the picture with each arm outstretched. Under one arm is a diminutive Tyrone Power; under the other, a diminutive Robert Taylor.

Opening night of *Lady in the Dark*, while we're in the interval between the first and second acts, Danny and I hear yelling in the big dressing room next door. It is Vic. He is a very emotional Italian and we find him jumping up and down on the tights he has to wear in the upcoming circus scene. The zipper on the back of his tights is broken. Danny and I get him back into them and safety-pin him together. The show goes on.

Vic's idea of getting ahead in "the business" is very different from Danny's and mine. For instance, his idea of getting in the business of television in its early days is to buy a store that sells television sets. This later becomes a successful chain of television stores—not show business but business business. Later, when he tried to join the Los Angeles Country Club and was told he couldn't get in because he's an actor, Vic says, "I am no actor and I've got thirty movies to prove it."

Even before we open *Lady in the Dark* in New York, I hear that Paramount sent a scout to the play in Boston and they want to give me a screen test. This time I go on the wagon—until the test is over, anyway. And quite a test it is. I take a cab out to the Astoria Studios on Long Island and walk onto my first real soundstage; Astoria has everything a soundstage in Hollywood does. Some of the first movies that were made were shot in Astoria, I dimly know this as I prepare for my test.

While this was a sort of acting out I'd dreamed of doing, everything was happening so fast for me that I felt I was doing it all under water, or in a dream. Things happened so fast, and then so slowly, and still all happening at once. One experiences a version of the relativity of time. It was happening to me and I seemed to be watching it at the same time. I was doing *Lady in the Dark* every night, so I always felt rushed. I was playing a man in the dark. There was a dreamlike quality to every one of my days in this period.

For the test, I do three full scenes in color, which is still comparatively new and very expensive in 1941: a scene from *Lady in the Dark*, a scene from Noel Coward's *Private Lives*, and a scene from Irwin Shaw's new play, *The Gentle People*. Other actors I've never met before work with me. The scenes from *The Gentle People* and *Private Lives* come out better on camera than does my scene from *Lady in the Dark*. It's as if I've overrehearsed my part from *Lady in the Dark* and can't get any freshness in it. The other two scenes have a spontaneity that distinguishes them. I feel it, and then I see it when they screen the test for me. Apparently, they think the expense they've gone to with my screen test is worth it: I am being offered the highest salary a beginner in movies has ever been offered—one thousand bucks a week (more than twice the $400 a week I am making in *Lady in the Dark*) for fifty-two weeks a year. Jack Wildberg, Cheryl Crawford's partner, gets me this fabulous contract.

All this fits in with my expectations for myself, even the fact that my eight-year plan didn't take eight years. The Paramount contract reinforces the rightness of my marrying Betty; it tells me I can support her in the style to which she has been accustomed and myself in the style to which I would like to be accustomed.

By the time I'm in *Lady in the Dark* and have my Paramount contract offer, I have spent two years trying to get the Louis Schurr Agency to represent me. They are the best in the business as far as musicals are concerned, and I know they have good contacts in Hollywood. I figure I'll just be lost in big agencies like William Morris. But up until *Lady in the Dark*, the only attention I ever received from the Schurr office was filling in at a poker game with two of Schurr's lesser male agents and the very grand, very big-eyed English star Estelle Winwood. It turned out to be a strip poker game, and the two Schurr agents were gay. I survived the strip poker game with most of my clothes on but with no contract to be represented.

Now here I am, an actor who has haunted agents' and producers' offices for months and suddenly I have the lead in a Broadway musical, I have gotten a screen test and an offer from Paramount, and what is the first thing I do? I went to the Schurr office and asked them to be my agent. What else could they say but yes?

Not much later there comes one day in my life when quite a few things happen. The reviews come in for *Lady in the Dark*; the show is a hit and my reviews are great. I actually put my signature on the movie contract with Paramount Pictures. My engagement to Betty Heckscher is announced in the *New York Times*—and I get my draft notice. A day to remember. The headline on the front page of the *New York Daily News* is CINDERFELLA TO WED HEIRESS. Being referred to as "Cinderfella" fazes me not at all. More people are talking about me, which means I'm hotter as an actor and that many more people will be aware of the show. The question is, how long will I be able to keep acting before I'm drafted?

Well, I was deferred from the draft because of a heart murmur. Although my medical condition made me uneasy, I could, at least, continue with the play. *Lady in the Dark* is packing them in. I'm definitely about to be married; in fact, the ceremony will be held twice. First, Betty and I have a Catholic ceremony one morning in Maplewood, New Jersey, performed by my friend Monsignor Kelley, whom I had met through Cheryl. Betty is in the confessional what seems like forever. The Monsignor finally stops her outpouring with the question, "Now you didn't commit murder, did you, my dear?"

Vic Mature is my best man and, since Betty has taken instruction in Catholicism from Monsignor, she is also baptized, has her First Communion, and is confirmed. Vic is not only best man but Betty's godfather. A nun who is in the chapel at the time runs up to Betty and hugs her. "Oh, my dear! Five sacraments in half an hour! Oh, my dear!" (In case you're counting, that's baptism, penance, communion, confirmation, and matrimony.) A week later, we have an Episcopal service in Bryn Mawr, Pennsylvania, near Betty's family home. It's a *Town and Country* wedding in every sense: the photographs appear in the July 1941 issue.

The two weddings are a perfect soap opera version of the Cinderella story as adapted for me as "Cinderfella." The good Monsignor himself, a former all-American and Golden Gloves boxer, a student of Freud and Jung, an English tutor of Pope Pius XII, a friend both of Thomas Edison and mafioso Frank Costello, is a character as theatrical as any soap opera fan could wish.

Gertie does her soap opera turn for me, too.

The night before Betty's and my Main Line ceremony, at first curtain call for *Lady in the Dark*, Gertie hushes the house, announces I will be married in Philadelphia the next day, and presents me with a queen's ransom in gifts. Broderick Crawford is in the audience. He is an old boyfriend of Gertie's. He was so jealous of her attention to me that night that he never really treated me civilly the rest of his life in Hollywood, though we had the same agent, Al Melnick, at the Schurr office. At one time, for a span of three years, we worked together on the ZIV television lot, where I did the television series "Dr. Christian" and "Lockup" and he did "Highway Patrol." I excuse him on the grounds that he's a heavy drinker.

There is no basis for Broderick Crawford's jealousy. Not only is Gertie married, she is literally like a mother to both Victor and me. We are babes on Broadway, after all. Once she supports me onstage when I have a hangover and have blown a succession of lines, and once she does it for Victor when he has flatted during a song: In each case, when someone in the audience tittered or made an audible remark about one of her boys, Gertie proceeded to walk downstage and play the rest of those scenes glaring at the offending member of the audience. Nobody was going to make fun of one of *her* boys.

Betty and I have rented a penthouse from Dorothy Patten (Cheryl Crawford's best friend, later famous for her Madwoman in Jean Giradoux's *The Madwoman of Chaillot*). Albert, Mrs. Heckscher's chauffeur, drives us to New York after the wedding reception. Betty and I get to bed well past midnight, but I'm up at 6:00 A.M. and rush off to work on my 7:00 A.M. soap, "Backstage Wife"—the soap Betty has just begun to play in real life.

As a just-married man, even with *Lady in the Dark* and my Hollywood contract, I continue with my soap operas. Not because I have to but just in case. There is always radio and there is always soap opera. But in real life, the next few days show me that Betty's version of "Backstage Wife" is very different from mine.

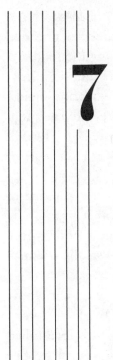

7

The scene is Dorothy Patten's penthouse in the upper fifties on the East Side of Manhattan. It is June 1941 and Betty and I are blissfully happy—all the perks of New York penthouse living and we're getting it practically free. It is romantic and Eden-like for the first week, and then Betty, my new bride, says: "I'm going out with Harry Geylin tonight. Isn't it wonderful he's graduating a ninety-day wonder from naval school?"

"But we just got married," I say.

"What's that got to do with it?" Betty says. "Harry's one of my oldest friends and I can't let him down. I've promised I'd go with him, and you'll be at the theater tonight anyway."

Dialogue fails me. Maybe this is the way it's done in Philadelphia society. There's not much time to think anything else because Harry Geylin arrives to have dinner with us before he takes Betty out. We are out on the terrace. I get some small comfort from the fact a lamb roast with a vegetable sauce of yellow carrots and red tomatoes is spilled on

Harry's white uniform before they set out, necessitating a temporary change to Navy blues. Maybe the fact I've had three manhattans makes me clumsy in serving the food.

I'm not alone, I discover, in thinking this date is a little bizarre. Actress Anne Francine, one of Betty's bridesmaids, who had grown up with her and who had a pretty racy reputation herself, also thinks Betty is out of line. Betty herself now admits it was bad timing, but flirting is a basic part of Betty. She is a genetic flirt, on her mother's side.

Other than this disquieting incident, the first rapture of marriage continues. We leave New York in a brand-new Buick. We are going west to introduce my new bride to my family. We are very aware of each other physically because we are very physically attracted to each other, but when we stop in Cedar Rapids at Uncle Ed Carey's so I can show Betty off to my relatives, she moves one of the local gentry to make a pass at her, the seriousness of which is forestalled by my alert cousins. Betty seems to be nourished by her flirtations whereas I am depleted by them.

I escape Cedar Rapids with my wife's "honor," if not my idea of married life, intact. I am dismayed by Betty's flirtatiousness but I don't discuss it. I want to be as sophisticated as she is, and I act as if I am, but I am not wise enough to handle her behavior: I am upset by it and yet I don't confront her. I keep thinking her flirtations are temporary clouds passing over the water; they turn out to be endemic squalls. I can't cope with what I'm feeling, so I just drink a little more. Drinking is becoming more and more the crutch I use for anything I can't handle.

There were no people to cope with in Yellowstone Park or the Mile High Hotel in Denver, so they became wonderful, pleasant landmarks on this westward trip—pleasanter for being unpeopled. I don't remember any serious talks. There was danger in serious talking: talking about our marriage, talking about the war. We just tried to keep it light. I mistakenly held onto the Victorian practice of sweeping things under the rug—my generation, and certainly my family swept anything that was awkward under the rug. It's the classic story of the alcoholic's family who are all dressed up in their living room, admiring their delicate china, and not saying a word about the two-ton elephant that's just stumbled into the room. They just keep on talking as if the elephant isn't there.

Betty and I arrived in Hollywood in July and rented a small California adobe house at 1518 Beverly Drive in Beverly Hills.

It's our first house, we have two servants, and we feel we have arrived. Betty has never cooked. I try to get her started by bringing home first editions of cookbooks and suggest that she make it a hobby, as collecting first editions always has been for me. Miraculously, she starts to cook. I discover this when she sends me to the market for spuds and I come back with the popular mentholated cigarettes by that name instead of the potatoes she wanted. I happily return for potatoes.

My father and mother are already living in Los Angeles. My father is semi-retired, managing two big trust funds for two wealthy former Sioux City families, the Martin families. My brothers, the twins Charles and Gordon, are already in the Navy and Army respectively. Gordon is getting married to a childhood sweetheart, Roberta Miller, in San Francisco. We all attend the wedding and we take the Owl, an overnight train that was then very popular, up to San Francisco and back. I drink my way up and I drink my way back. On our return to Los Angeles, I get down on my knees in the middle of Union Station to kiss the hem of my mother's skirt, symbolically atoning for my drunken behavior during Gordon's weekend wedding.

After the wedding, I had gone out on the town with one of my sister-in-law's bridesmaids, getting back to the hotel in San Francisco rather late. My behavior is my not-so-subtle revenge for Betty's flirtatiousness.

9 5

This is merely a highlight—or lowlight—of my first months in Hollywood. I'm not playing in a soap opera on radio, just in real life. Most of our time we spend doing serious ritual drinking and going to Ciro's and Mocambo's to be seen. I've simplified my drinking menu by now: scotch before, scotch during dinner, and scotch afterward, always doubles.

It was a real high for both of us in another sense, suddenly being thrust in the middle of the Hollywood scene, rubbing elbows with people we had both spent many afternoons watching in dark theaters. I was always on the lookout for Spencer Tracy, my idol, but I never got to see him. As I found out later, he was very reclusive, and you had to work with him to meet him. I never do.

Being in these nightclubs, there's a feeling of richness that's like what I felt the day my father let me loose in his friend's chocolate factory in Sioux City and said I could have anything I wanted. Still, the war is hanging over our heads, so we can't quite digest the feast that is around us.

Paramount Studio still doesn't have a picture for me, but between Betty's social and my theater contacts, we don't lack for people to drink with. The only work I do is posing endlessly for newspaper and magazine photos.

The whole process of publicity began for me with *Lady in the Dark* in New York. It gets more national and international in scope when I go to Hollywood and the product I am going to be in will reach more than the local New York scene. The New York effort is more concentrated and on a higher level than it is in Hollywood. In New York, the audience goes to the play; the publicity must be put out daily to alert its new daily audience. In Hollywood, the "play" goes to the audience.

Publicity is one of the things most actors relish. I am no exception. It is part of making a success of yourself in the business. I've always gone along with George M. Cohan's philosophy, "I don't care what you say about me as long as you spell my name right." Unfortunately, often that doesn't work out for me. One of the early press releases on *Take a Letter, Darling*, my second picture, says it is to be made "with Fred MacMurray and that newcomer, Frank Macdonald, late of *Lady in the Dark*." In fact, I almost never get my name spelled right. It is and continues to be a constant struggle. One famous Boston columnist wrote a full-page dissertation on the misspellings of my name; my name was misspelled in the headline. These things keep you humble, particularly since the first thing Paramount wanted to do when I reached Hollywood was to change my name. "Macdonald Carey is all wrong. It will never fit on a marquee." They never told me what they wanted to change it to because I flatly said no.

The publicity system at Paramount at that time was a major operation in itself. Rufus Blair was the number one head, as I remember, with Teat Carle as second in command. (Today Teat writes and talks about alcoholism among seniors in the United States.) Rufus is the man who said Hollywood is as hick a town as any. He called Hollywood "Double Dubuque." It is well known in Iowa that when you get old enough, you don't die and go to heaven, you move to Long Beach, California. Long Beach, like Hollywood, is just another suburb of Los Angeles, and Hollywood is really more of a hick town than Iowa could ever produce in reality. In the forties, when I arrived in Hollywood, to look at any starlet and her mother, who is usually out here with her daughter, is to see two typical Midwesterners. My father, a Midwest banker, had long preceded me here. Now that I think of it, Mother was actually from Dubuque.

At Paramount, there were numerous publicity agents on the staff. Each one was assigned a picture and one or more actors or actresses. There was a resident portrait artist in charge of all the photographs. Before the war, the studio took care of everyone's fan mail and supplied pictures for the fans. This stopped after the war was over, one of the first postwar economies.

There is a famous story about what happened when the bank took over the running of Paramount. They sent out efficiency experts from New York to pare down expenses and trim the number of workers on the set of a movie during its making. They'd seen some of the grips and light men idle on the set of the first picture they checked out. But when the efficiency experts returned to New York, there were eight more men working on each set than there had been before the efficiency experts' report.

I am the new boy under contract to Paramount. One memorable day I pose embracing and kissing each one of the eight starlets Paramount has under contract at the time (among them, Susan Hayward, Barbara Britton, who later stars with Richard Denning in the TV series "Mr. and Mrs. North," and Maggie Hayes, who later marries Herbert Bayard Swope Jr.) The gray double-breasted suit whose armpits I sweat through that day is the same one I later drench again in my first movie, *Dr. Broadway*. In that picture when I have a scene on the ledge of a skyscraper—actually at the studio on a stage twenty-four feet in the air with mattresses piled up on a parallel eight feet below me.

I am given *Dr. Broadway* a month after Paramount has decided not to waste me on a movie of the Graham Greene novel, *This Gun for Hire*. They are paying me too much money for that, so they give it to a short actor they've picked up for $75 a week. His name is Alan Ladd and the picture makes him.

Dr. Broadway is an F. Hugh Herbert script based on a Damon Runyon story. I am excited and suffering the usual stage fright at the prospect of doing this, my first movie. *Dr. Broadway* is about a real-life doctor in New York who took care of Broadway characters—gamblers, panhandlers, mobsters, and out-of-work actors—because they had all chipped in and paid for his medical education. I play the doctor, who is falsely accused of a murder. The plot has to do with my clearing myself and is mainly a comedy exploiting New York street language.

Paramount wants to be sure they've got a real leading man on their hands so they make me look like what they think a leading man should look like. I should have a widow's peak like Robert Taylor's. They dig out an extra Bing Crosby toupee and shape it into the aforementioned widow's peak and I have to get in for an early call with the women who are having their hair done so I can have my widow's peak glued and marcelled into my hair.

My training for acting in films was what I could pick up from other actors. It was assumed that I could act—I'd done the screen test—so they just kept me in a figurative holding pen until they had a movie for me. Now that I'm doing *Dr. Broadway*, I get to see what it's like to act on a daily basis in front of a camera.

The transition is not something I worry about too much. It's not just by chance that I have a lot of the best old hands in the business working with me on this, my first picture; they give me a lot of tips. One of them tells me you just turn that megaphone you use in the theater around the other way and talk into the big end. Everything in the movies has to be both smaller and more exact. You don't play as broadly as you do in the theater.

But acting is acting, whether radio acting, theater acting, or movie acting. All are the same in that you must pretend and at the same time play truthfully. Radio acting is just a little more suggestive in its pauses; during those pauses the actor lets the audience supply, in their own imaginations, a great deal of the emotion and action. The radio actor also has to suggest movement or physical effort in his voice (Is he lifting something? Is he kicking somebody? Is he being kicked?). A movie is more cerebral; the light in your eyes that the camera catches is the light of the actor's thought, "The eyes have it." Mitch Leisen, a director I worked with many times, once told me, "Watch Ray Milland's eyes. You can tell what he's thinking."

In many cases, the eye contact with your fellow actor is the thing that forges the link between characters in the scene. Even a beginner in pictures, if he has this eye contact, is already in the scene with the other actor. It doesn't matter if in real life he is in awe of the person he's playing with. With this eye contact, the framework of the scene—and the commitment to the character he's playing—involves the actor enough so that egocentric indulgences like awe or fear just don't happen. Stage fright, yes. I've always felt that before a scene, whether in radio, on stage, or before the camera. That's just part of acting. It gives the actor the extra adrenaline he needs.

When I was in Chicago, Walter Huston had seen his son John playing Lincoln in a WPA theater production of *Abe Lincoln in Illinois*. "What do you feel before you go on, John?" Walter asked. "Are you nervous? Do you have any stage fright?" "Of course not," John said. "I don't feel anything." "Then quit acting," Walter said. "Become a director. Anything but an actor." John, of course, became a director who occasionally acted.

With me in *Dr. Broadway* are some of the best character actors in Hollywood. These guys drink pretty good too and feel their working day should end before six o'clock. The production office says no. So the boys—J. Carroll Nash, Warren Hymer, and Joseph Calleia, the actor that critic George Gene Nathan said had "the aperient water moniker"—all start to drink at five o'clock. By five-thirty, as the rushes show us the next day, they are all swaying and toppling off their lifts.

1 0 0

That image is only a misleadingly fun-house, many-mirrored reflection of my own addiction to alcohol, which would have periods of intensity and then level off into periods of abstinence, even though I never drank before or during shooting myself. That I am a representative of my era doesn't help. There is a story told by Elaine de Kooning about New York in the 1950s that shows an almost deliberate, institutionalized drunkenness. This is from *Night Studio: A Memoir of Phillip Goston*:

> A waiter came over and Franz [Franz Kline] said "We'll have twelve scotch and sodas." The waiter said, "Are you expecting more people?" And Franz said, "No, for us. Six for her and six for me." Franz liked that sense of security. The whole art world became alcoholic. Everyone would have blackouts and repeat themselves and get so smashed they'd be staggering around. Everyone was a stand-up comic. It was like a ten-year party.

My first year in Hollywood at Paramount, 1941, is a sort of alcoholic blur. It is party time all the time, and Betty and I are both at the party.

Despite my own visceral reaction to seeing myself on screen in *Dr. Broadway*, the critics and the public like me. Public attention and adulation are not a coin I can spend, but if it means more jobs, I'll take anything they say about me. My wife, Betty, is part of it, too, and her glamour doesn't hurt.

Immediately after *Dr. Broadway*, I'm on to my next picture, *Take A Letter, Darling*, starring Betty's idol, Fred MacMurray. He's a man who is worth adoration. He is easy to work with and easy to get along with and does his best to make me feel at home. He is also a major part of one of the pools of "best people" in the movie business, what passed for movie society. Roz Russell, our leading lady in the movie, is a classy dame and it is a step in the right direction to be second man in the Mitchell Leisen comedy with her and Fred.

During the filming, Fred and I became friends and he became sort of a mentor to me. He helped me to feel a lot easier in front of the camera. Though I don't think Fred ever fell in love with acting as acting himself, just working with him, you felt comfortable. He's reassuring to be with. Betty and I see him socially, and she likes him in person as much as she thought she would when she had a crush on him on the screen.

There's little to tell about the plot of *Take a Letter, Darling*. Like most of the "screwball comedies" of the period that started with the 1936 *My Man Godfrey*, all the stuff with Carole Lombard and William Powell or MacMurray and Roz Russell has little or no plot. *Take a Letter, Darling* is *The Taming of the Shrew* plot—a woman bossing a man and, in the end, apparently succumbing to his masculinity. In this case, Rosalind Russell plays a lady ad executive who hires a man (Fred MacMurray) to be her escort and man Friday. Naturally, they fall in love. I play the other man who almost wins Roz, even though the audience knows I won't. I get good reviews again, particularly in *Time* magazine. Bosley Crowther in the *New York Times* is the one dissenting voice—and a harsh voice it is: "Macdonald Carey, a newcomer, makes one think of Mischa Auer trying to be serious."

During filming, I remember being admonished by Mitch Leisen to brush my teeth after lunch. Someone had got me into eating garlicky salads. Apparently Roz found the garlic breath hard to take in love scenes (although all I'd heard from her was an encouraging "He handled that scene like a pro"). Mitch advised toothpaste and Sen-Sen. To think I'd lived all my life with the memory of dear Elizabeth Passman's breath in the love scenes of *A Prince There Was* in Sioux City junior high school. The male ego—or mine, at least—is so great that after the war, I only remembered *Take a Letter,*

Darling as a triumph for me. But at my first Academy Awards banquet, I stopped Roz Russell as she was passing my table and asked if she'd forgotten me. She showed me I'd been enshrined forever in her memory by saying, "Oh, Mac, how could I ever forget you and your garlic breath!"

There are lots of ways of forgetting, of course, absent-mindedness and senility among them, but a drinking habit beats them all. I called Betty recently to check on her memory of the last prewar year in Hollywood and where we were living. She filled me in with a litany of times I was drunk—the more memorable ones being the weekend of my brother's wedding in San Francisco and the night I brought home an Army major and his wife, the two of whom I had picked up in a bar. I had then retired to the shower to sober up but passed out and spent the night in the shower stall.

Writing this book is uncovering much I had blacked out, so today I call Betty and do what I should have done as an AA member years ago. I confess that I realize how I had hurt her and I ask for forgiveness. I get it, but not the complete peace of mind I expect. That will only come, they say, when I consciously forgive both of us for drowning a supposedly indissoluble marriage, dissolving it in booze.

During the prewar years, everyone is very busy trying to have a good time. My main preoccupation is blocking out the thought of going overseas. I don't have any balanced perception of my marriage or of my relationship to my family or to society. People just aren't concerned too much with delving into these things. The main thing on everyone's mind is the war.

In early 1942, I am cast in a Marine movie called *Wake Island* with Brian Donlevy, Robert Preston, and William Bendix. We make most of it at the Salton Sea at the southern edge of California's Imperial Valley, near the Mexican border, and I try to keep sober. The following fragment of a longer poem is a chronicle of the Salton Sea location:

And wasn't I the good boy though
There I am on location at the Salton Sea
My wife, pregnant back in Los Angeles
And a group of us go into Juárez
To get loaded and visit a whorehouse
That is famous in the movie business

We're drinking Tequila and Bourbon and Southern
    Comfort
After turning down two wrong streets
We find it and instead of shaking hands
A young whore in the reception line
Avoids my outstretched hand
And shakes me between the legs
Everyone signs the house bible
Which has signatures of old stars
From Paramount and 20th for the last 40 years

And while my buddies have cosas sexuales
I sip my Southern Comfort on the piano bench
With the manager
And help him sweep out the living room
Until everyone is through

The next day I'm the only one with
A bad cold, a terrible hangover and a phone call
From a wife who doesn't believe this story

Wake Island, which was directed by John Farrow, who
was already married to Mauren O'Sullivan, is a fictionalized
account of the U.S. defense of Wake Island and its fall to the
Japanese. I play one of the last Marine pilots to be shot down
defending the island. There is one shot where a Grumman
plane taxis to a stop in front of the camp and I step out of

the cockpit. They get the shot by having me cling to the wing, which is away from the camera, while the real Marine pilot taxis in the Grumman F4F. There is a little cloud of dust and I step off the wing into the cockpit, landing right on the pilot's private parts, and then step out into the view of the camera as if I'd been piloting the plane. I know that Marine pilot never forgot me.

Wake Island was a sort of recruiting picture and it is considered one of the best of its kind ever made. The proof of that is that a good percentage of the cast enlists in the Marine Corps afterward. I am among them. But my enlistment is not quite as immediate as I wanted it to be. When we finished the picture, I went for my physical and although the heart murmur had disappeared, I was turned down for color blindness. I also had the shakes so badly the Marine Corps was not too enthused about accepting me.

Even though the neighborhood where Betty and I live, Franklin Canyon, has organized an Air Warden watch for marauding Japanese planes, I still have a dry-enough brain to think the Marine Corps is a better answer to the threat we are all feeling from Japan and I'm determined to get in. A house with two servants is no longer an affordable luxury, and we move to the Townhouse Hotel, where I start taking courses in the Bates method to correct my color blindness and farsightedness.

The irony of the fact that a Japanese eye test (the Yshihara charts) is keeping lots of good Army and Navy material out of the war effort escapes the military mind, but the Bates method, by reeducating the eye and the mind, wins the day for me and for many others. If, for example, as a child, you are not taught to say "chair" to yourself when you see a chair or "table" when you see a table, you will be blind to the recognition of that object's identity; similarly, if you are not taught to say "red" to yourself when you see red or "blue" when you see blue, you will be correspondingly color blind. For those of us who never learned color the first time, the Bates method taught us colors from the beginning. We worked with crayons and paint until we relearned the alphabet of color. In a month, I take the Yshihara color test again and pass.

My farsightedness was healed as well by easy exercises and by learning to relax the muscles around the eye that had stiffened and started to atrophy. Through these exercises, the eye is taught to heal itself and resume its normal shape. Four hundred candidates for the Marines, Air Force and Navy officer status have their eyes reeducated that year and successfully enter their respective services. Aldous Huxley wrote a book, *The Art of Seeing*, which describes and praises this Bates method. If I had been a Huxley fan before, by the end of my Bates course, I was a true follower.

When I finish the course, I am accepted into the Marine Corps on the same day Alfred Hitchcock asks for my services in a movie called *Shadow of a Doubt* (1943). I'm not to be inducted until sometime in November, so it's off to Santa Rosa, California, the location for the movie. Not only does location shooting lend a reality to the work you do, but your twenty-four-hour-a-day contact with the rest of the cast contributes to your relationships on the screen. The cast is put up in a hotel and a sort of camaraderie develops in the company, a little more closeness than occurs when you shoot the whole picture at the studio.

Shadow of a Doubt is not your usual movie. It is a "Who done it?" where the audience knows when the picture starts who done it, who the killer is. The question is, will he be caught before he kills again? It's about the killer, Joseph Cotten, and his psychic niece, Teresa Wright, her family, her small town, and a detective, me, who's after the killer. It would turn out to be one of the best pictures I was ever in and it happened to be Hitchcock's favorite of all his films.

Of all the directors I ever worked with, Hitchcock, or Hitch, as he was called, was the most human. Despite an

1 0 6

enduring reputation for being cold to actors and treating them like cattle, he was the most approachable and, consequently, the most memorable. I remember him, his wife, Alma, and his daughter Pat as an oasis of warmth in the cold world of moviemaking.

Of course, I most ardently recall the family of actors in that cast: Wallace Ford, Hume Cronyn, Patricia Collinge, Teresa Wright. The essence of *Shadow of a Doubt* is the ideal neighborliness of a small town and a small-town family. The subtle terror that the picture conveys depends so much on that nice normalcy being there to be threatened. Working for Hitch was a wonderful experience. Hume Cronyn and Jessica Tandy, his bride-to-be, became my friends, as did Teresa Wright, and Hitchcock himself, along with his wife Alma and his daughter Pat. Hitch and Alma are gone now, and in the true California way, I hardly ever see Pat Hitchcock (now Pat Hitchcock O'Connell) or Teresa, though we remain friends.

For me, I felt none of the standoffishness or putoffishness that others talk about in describing their work with Hitchcock. I always felt accepted as an actor and a person, though God knows one day I put his and Teresa's patience to the acid test. It was a final scene, shot in process on a mock-up of the steps of the family house of the picture, really a set at Universal. I have a terrible hangover and the shakes. Finally Hitch, a fellow drinker, though not of my caliber and intensity, says, "Get him a pint of bourbon."

This happened to another Carey on an MGM picture some years before. Harry Carey was said to have passed out on the set of *Grass* at MGM. "Call a doctor," somebody said. "Give him a pint of rum," his wife Olive Carey said. "That will bring him around." That they did and that it did. Harry Carey and I were not related, but somewhere, somehow, we must have had the same genes. Actually, when I opened in New York in *Lady in the Dark*, Harry and Olive were in the audience and they came backstage to congratulate me, though I didn't know them. "Welcome to the family," said Harry at the time. But I was already a family member, a bosom bottle buddy.

Hume and Jessica Tandy married while we were making *Shadow of a Doubt*. The day of the wedding Lon Chaney, Jr., and Broderick Crawford, who are in dressing rooms adjacent to mine at Universal, show up on every set of every movie at the studio holding jiggers of whiskey in their hamlike fists. They come up to Wally Ford and me on the *Shadow of a Doubt* set and try to make us drink what they have in their hands. Frank Lovejoy and Edmond O'Brien are on the lot shooting *D.O.A.*, and Lon and Brod try to feed them booze, too. After shooting, we're all in Crawford's dressing room drinking. Our party starts to break up. Some of us are going to Hume and Jessica's wedding. Eddie O'Brien never gets there. As I slip out, Brod is holding Eddie pinned to the floor while Lon is pouring a drink down his throat.

It is soon after that that we do the scene where Hitch felt I had to have bourbon to be able to play it. It's one of the last scenes in the picture, where Teresa Wright tells me, after the death of Uncle Charlie, "He thought the world was a horrible place. He couldn't have been very happy ever. He didn't trust people. He seemed to hate them. He hated the whole world. He said that people like us had no idea what the world was really like." Ironically, my line as Jack Graham, the detective in the picture, is "It's not quite as bad as that, but sometimes it needs a lot of watching. It seems to go crazy every now and then, like your Uncle Charlie."

My own craziness is so obvious you'd think this episode in front of Hitch and Teresa would make me wise up to where my drinking is leading me. But it is the only time in the movie business that I have been caught, my alcoholism exposed (at least, so I think). The incident preys on my mind during the war, and the first thing I tell Hitch when I come back is that I have my drinking under control. The next thing I do is start drinking again.

I wrote about Hitchcock in a poem, "How To Last in Show Business." It starts:

When Ingrid Bergman told Alfred Hitchcock
A scene was difficult for her to act naturally
He told her, "Fake it"
She said it was the best advice she ever got
He told me in *Shadow of a Doubt*
When I asked him how to play a scene
"Don't act
"Let the camera do the work"

I simplified the dialogue so it would scan. Actually, Hitch said, "When you see Uncle Charlie [Joe Cotten] enter the room, don't register surprise, don't register anything, just drain your face and your mind of any thought or emotion at all in that instant that the camera catches you." In Donald Spoto's book, *The Dark Side of Genius*, he says Hitch told Gregory Peck the same thing. The phrase he uses is, "Drain your face of expression." Spoto implies this is another instance of Hitchcock's backing away from involvement. On the contrary, I think it was part of Hitch's genius as a director in quickly communicating what he wanted to an actor.

Hitch loved wine, and while he tried to introduce us to some of the good Napa wines, my plebeian palate left me after the picture with cases of pink champagne made in the Simi Valley, which I don't think Hitch recommended.

All in all, I have wonderful memories of *Shadow of a Doubt*. Hume and Henry Travers were a delight to watch working. They played well together and obviously enjoyed working with each other. Henry was an old character actor and Hume

1 0 9

a rising *young* character actor who had just made his mark in the theater, most recently in George Abbott's *Three Men and a Horse.*

It was exciting to work with an old pro like Wally Ford, who had countless stories to tell about the business. He'd been an actor in stock and on the road with road companies until the point was reached when there were more closings than openings. *Shadow of a Doubt* was my fourth film; Wally had made countless films, most notably John Ford's *The Informer.* Mostly, I remember him swimming in the public swimming pool in Santa Rosa, still puffing his cigar. We swam when no one else was there, and while Wally didn't swim laps with the cigar, he did swim the width of the pool with it. Then he would carefully lay it aside, to pick it up again to go on puffing when he got out of the water.

Joe Cotten had a manservant he'd inherited from Orson Welles. He was a sort of dwarf called "Shorty". He acted, as he had for Orson, as a dresser, valet and houseboy. After the picture, Joe had us all to his house for a dinner party. It was after dinner and coffee was being served. The men were having brandy together in one room before they joined the ladies. Teresa Wright was in the lady's bathroom sitting on the John, the door of which had no lock. Shorty opened the door and, without batting an eye, said, "Do you want cream and sugar in your coffee?" It is not recorded what Teresa said.

When we finish *Shadow of a Doubt*, my enlistment date is postponed again. I have time to make *Star Spangled Rhythm* and a quick movie called *Salute for Three* both of which are Paramount's attempts to cash in on everyone's preoccupation with the war effort. *Star Spangled Rhythm*, which includes about forty people under contract to Paramount at the time as well as everyone working on the lot, is just a lot of songs, dances, and blackout sketches strung together. Although I could sing and dance, all I did was walk on as another representative of Paramount's stable of rising stars. (In fact, Paramount never did realize I could sing and dance.) *Star Spangled Rhythm* didn't run in movie theaters as long as it took to make—four weeks. *Salute for Three* is a potboiler, a romance between a GI—me—about to go overseas and a USO entertainer/singer, Betty Jane Rhodes.

The day I finish *Salute for Three*, I finally leave for boot camp in the Marine Corps. In one way, it is a relief to go. We have had at least six months of "good-bye parties" and the studio assures me it is not really good-bye, that the job will be waiting for me when the war is over. There is no trauma in going: I never permit myself maudlin tears over changes in my life; instilled in me by my father is a built-in faith in some kind of karma. Both Betty and I have expected this parting from the day we were married. Any moments of romance that we can steal, we do, but we are always literally under the gun, either for the shooting schedules of my pictures or my ultimate departure for the war.

When Betty's sister, Gee, suggests wangling a job for me stateside, I reject the offer because the whole point of joining the Marines is to go overseas and live the Marine experience I had acted in *Wake Island*. Betty supports me in this. We all feel a patriotic zeal to defeat Nazism and Fascism; a desk job anywhere in the States just wouldn't pull it off. Any fear I have is overcome by my innate optimism. It never occurs to me that I might die. I have faith that we will win the war and that I will be back to Betty and my career in no time.

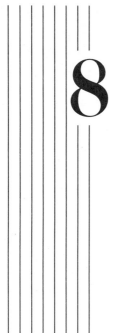

8

It is fall, almost winter, in South Carolina when I arrive at Parris Island for boot camp. I am two days earlier than my "platoon to be" had expected. One other guy from Texas hadn't got the word either, so for two days, three drill instructors count cadence and march-step this Texan in a ten-gallon Stetson and cowboy boots and me in my homburg and double-breasted gray suit (the same one I had sweated through at Paramount), marching us—sometimes double-time—to the mess hall and back three times a day.

The only thing that gets me through the eight weeks of boot camp that follow is what helps me get through anything: the utter ridiculousness of it all. An appreciation of travesty and farce do more to nullify pain than prayer or pills. I walked with bloodied feet for more than two weeks before the bureaucracy of the Marine Corps would admit they've given me shoes that were at least one size too small. This concession on the Marine Corps' part has nothing to do with the influence of my brother Charlie, who appears at Parris Island with his PT boat. He commands a squadron out of Washington, D.C., and has come down to visit me. Although he can't get me the right size shoes, he does get me off for an hour's visit aboard his boat, and I return to my Quonset hut with two oranges and my first knowledge of how much better the Navy lives than does the Marine Corps. Later I find out even the Army lives better than the Marine Corps, overseas at least. It is the Navy, the Army, and the Seabees who live high on the hog; the Marine Corps scrounged for what we got (at least we did).

But I'm off the point. Right here, right now, in boot camp, I'm being taught I'm the lowest of human beings. First the shoes. When I asked for shoes in my size, I was constantly being publicly told off, "What did you pay for your fancy-ass shoes in Hollywood? Fifty dollars?" Meanwhile, my heels had indentations, holes the size of quarters.

I write Betty in Philadelphia, where her mother keeps asking what they can send me, and request something to stop the bleeding and toughen up my feet. She keeps me supplied with quarts of Benzoine, which I need to keep using for weeks even after I get shoes that fit. To further convince me I am baser than most, I am given permanent charge of the latrine, which carries with it the title "Captain of the Head." I had to scrub the troughs with a small brush. As a result, I acquired a deposit of something unpleasant under my fingernails that took more time than I care to admit to expunge. To this day, I have a fetish about having clean hands.

Three of us have cots in a row: Cameron, Carey, and Caruso. We travel together through boot camp and officer's training in this juxtaposition. We remain in touch to this day.

After the second World War, Gary Cameron resigned his commission as a captain and reenlisted as a master sergeant, which put him at the top of that particular ladder and gave him more immediate rewards, such as running a publicity department and only having to take his orders from generals. He retired from the Marine Corps in 1988 and published a book about the Corps called *They Never Got the Word*. The title is a phrase first taught you in Marine Corps boot camp to warn you to pay attention. If you don't "get the word" when your drill instructor first tells you something, you're out of luck, you might be dead, because he won't repeat it; this goes for when you're to eat, when you're to get liberty, and when you're to duck when someone is shooting at you. (This is, in fact, the essence of boot camp: Listen and obey immediately.)

Paul Caruso is the athlete of our group. Before the war, he'd been a Golden Gloves boxer. The day we graduate from boot camp, everyone who has a grudge against anyone is given boxing gloves so all harbored resentments may be settled. For all of us, Caruso takes on Smitty, our tough and pugnacious DI, and to the cheers of every man in the platoon, dukes it out quite successfully with him.

After the war, I became godfather to Caruso's wife—a Catholic convert—and to four of his five kids. He became godfather to five of mine. He tried to give me pointers on boxing in boot camp and later back at Paramount after the war. What he really taught me is that I will never be a boxer. (Despite the jujitsu and judo and karate I got in the Marine Corps, and later with teachers Bruce Tegner and Ed Parker, the furthest I got was a brown belt in karate, but I've forgotten most of the moves.)

Officer training is not the vacation Cameron, Caruso, and I had planned. Now we have to learn a lot more complicated stuff as well as the basic Marine Corps twenty-four-hour drill: exercise, run, shoot, keep yourself, your locker, and your gun clean. At the end of our ten weeks of Office Training Candidate School, I am, with typical military reasoning, shipped off to Orlando, Florida, for training in radar (I'd had the word "radio" in my résumé) as a fighter-director or air controller. After Orlando, we are sent to Cherry Point, North Carolina. Betty is allowed to join me briefly in both places.

At Cherry Point, I was assigned to a specific Air Warning Squadron, AWS 3, and was made ordnance officer. My father had never allowed us boys guns; they weren't permitted in the house and I'd had no sudden epiphany in the expertise of weaponry since then, so finding out I am now supposed to be a weaponry expert is ironic. I have .50-caliber machine-gun school under one Captain Chinn, whose hair is completely white, the result of the constant percussion his brain cells endured at the Aberdeen Proving Grounds in Maryland, where guns are tested in cement-walled pits.

For a while, Betty and I have an apartment—one bedroom, over a dentist's office—in New Bern, North Carolina. It is hardly a second honeymoon, but we are happy to be together. We are also sparring with each other; this seems to be our pattern. Betty flirts and I react, usually by having another drink, and the drinks are very cheap at the Officers' Club. Vincent Sardi—owner of Sardi's Restaurant in the theater district in New York—is the captain of the mess, so the food is good, too. In Betty's and my apartment, there is a big double bed filling up a good part of the bedroom; the rest of the carpeted floor is covered with disassembled parts of a .38, a .45 Colt, a bizarre carbine, which has a bayonet attachment, an M1, a .30-caliber machine gun, and a .50-caliber machine gun. You have to walk a delicate maze to get to the bathroom. It isn't easy getting back, either.

While we are at Cherry Point, Betty suffers a miscarriage. We are both shaken up, but there's a war to be fought and we tell ourselves personal matters just don't matter right now. Other people allow themselves to be more honestly emotional: a major on the base whose wife is pregnant is so distraught when her water breaks that the ambulance that comes to pick her up is seen driving to the hospital with her in the

1 1 5

front seat and him prone in the back. (Incidentally, they never make it to the hospital; their baby is delivered on the hospital's front lawn.)

Both Betty and I are unwilling to seem vulnerable about things that are happening to us. The only thing that betrays our feelings is our excessive drinking.

Betty went back to Philadelphia while they got our Air Warning Squadron together and shipped us out to Miramar, the Naval Air Station near San Diego. When we learned my squadron will be kept hanging on a limb for several months before being shipped out, Betty joined me again. It was a bonus we hadn't expected. We moved into the Casa Manana, a beautiful old hotel on the beach in La Jolla.

When we get there, the Casa is really jumping. There are other Air Warning Squadron couples and lots of fly-boys with their wives. The fly-boys are mostly fighter pilots. They are flying Corsairs, a graceful bird of a plane, not the stubby Grummans we used in *Wake Island*. Some of the fly-boys who have already gone over have "bought it," and we are all apprehensive about shipping out to the Pacific. I, for one, am plain scared—not that I would show it to anyone, including Betty, but we do show it; we drink. My God, how we drink. Toward the last, the manager of the Casa is sending up martinis before breakfast to all of us.

One weekend, Betty and I go back to Hollywood to revisit the scene of my temporary triumphs. Nobody had ever really recognized me when we'd gone out to nightclubs before, but this time is quite different. Leaving Romanoff's one night in my uniform, I run into Dorothy Parker, who recognizes me from New York. She is quite drunk. She throws her arms around me and kisses me, the tears streaming down her face. "Thank God for you boys, Mac, and what you're doing for us!" The accolade is gratefully received, but "how un–Dorothy Parkerish," I think.

The next week, one of the other guys in the squadron

borrows my father's Buick, which Dad has loaned Betty and me. He gets drunk in San Diego and is picked up in the men's room for allegedly making a pass at somebody, a story none of us believes. Anyway, the Marines cashier him. It disturbs all of us.

One day, when we are to have a parade at Miramar, I have such a bad hangover I drink a half-pint of bourbon to settle my stomach and steady my nerves before the parade. After an hour standing on the parade grounds, that hot San Diego sun gets to me and during the parade I lurch and sway. I am put under house arrest and kept on the base. When they let me rejoin my group in La Jolla at the Casa, I stumble in the sand in a volleyball game and break my leg.

I am still not aware that I am drinking too much and neither is anyone else aware, because we're all drinking too much together.

Though I'm living at the Casa, technically I'm still under some kind of arrest, so when we finally get the word we are to ship out, I have to petition Captain Swope, my commanding officer, a wonderful guy, to intercede for me with the Marine Corps to let me go overseas with the squadron. While I'm waiting for an answer, Betty, along with the other wives, is indirectly encouraged to leave. She packs, and we say goodbye as if nothing is going to happen at all. It's not the kind of farewell you'd expect to have, but that's the way it was. Once she was on her way back to Philadelphia, I didn't ever think about the differences between us. I only thought of the things I loved about her.

I am alone in my room when I hear the Marine Corps' decision. Through Swope's intercession, they're letting me ship out with the squadron, but, as a result of what happened on the parade ground, I stay a second lieutenant through the next two advancements. (At the end of the war, I was only a first lieutenant, not a captain, like most of my buddies.) I still remember what the officer of the deck said when he

1 1 7

saw me hobbling aboard the transport in San Diego on crutches, one leg wrapped in bandages and plaster: "Boy, they're really scraping the bottom of the barrel."

It takes us almost a month to reach our first Pacific Island, Espíritu Santo, and by the time we arrive, I am able to walk off the ship without crutches. The leg has healed, the psychic wound never, but as an alcoholic, it is just another milepost in my lifetime pursuit of my alcoholic ghostly goal, just another self-destructive mishap that I ignore.

Joseph Campbell, in *The Hero of a Thousand Faces*, tells us to follow our bliss. As an alcoholic, I never let the fumes subside enough to see where my real bliss was. In my attempt to create a career and a family (which were my two real blisses), the blisses, the goals, were always blurred by alcohol. Whenever reality got too harsh with me, I'd usually take a drink. In a way, my two years in the Pacific were one long jag, with self-imposed periods of abstinence every now and then to kid myself that I am in control.

On the other hand, those two years away from everything familiar was a period that helped me collect myself to some extent. I became more focused as far as some of my principal values were concerned. Raising children was still my primary goal, but other, simpler goals became more important, one main one being contact with other people. Instead of becoming more insular, more American, through contact with armed forces from all over, we in the military overseas became citizens of the world. From starting to read again—I read a lot in the Marines; I had a copy of Shakespeare with me—and searching for standards that were universal, I learned it was important to reach out to other people and put selfish, parochial differences aside. My eagerness to improve myself increased, too. The deprivation I experienced in the Marine Corps added to my thirst for some kind of achievement when I got out.

Coincidence was operating: when we arrived at our first

station, Espíritu Santo, the first familiar face I saw was that of Ted Wojick, the Marine lieutenant I accidentally stepped on who was the actual pilot of the plane I was supposed to be flying in *Wake Island*. He is now a major. Through him, I meet lots of Marine pilots who are there. Espíritu is a sort of R & R place for Guadalcanal and anyone who is flying the slot up from the New Hebrides to Bougainville and then out to other island targets. The really classy Officer's Club belonged to the Navy; it is off limits for Marines and the Army.

It is more than eight months before our Air Warning Squadron is definitely attached to an operative Marine Air Wing and, until we are told to set up our own camp, we have nothing much to do. I decide to make my position as ordnance officer at least partly operative. If we are ever in the field, one of our duties is to set up a perimeter defense of the air strip we are defending with long-distance radar (long distance then being about one hundred and sixty miles). Since they took away our machine guns before sending us overseas, we have no weapons with which to set up a perimeter defense, so I organize a small group of two or three noncommissioned officers and we go to the junkyards behind the Seabees (a wordplay on CBs—construction battalions—glorified in *South Pacific*, the guys who build and maintain the camps and do construction work for the Navy). We climb over planes—F4Us, TBMs, and Corsairs—that have been shot down or scrapped. We arm ourselves with blowtorches and we scavenge half a dozen machine guns.

The torpedo bomber pilots become buddies of mine. They take me on practice dive-bombing runs (part of my stomach is still in the Pacific) and, with the help of some SNJs, naval training planes, I get my own logbook and am able to log about thirty hours of flying lessons. I never solo, but I get some sense of what flying means, something I think every air controller should have anyway. However, I never pursue the flying.

My friend from boot camp, Caruso, shows up on Espíritu Santo as athletic director for a Marine Air Wing. He also is the coach of the El Toro football team, whose members, former Rams and Redskins, have fallen into the Marine Corps hopper in the draft. *Wake Island* is a movie everybody has seen, and in Espíritu Santo and later, when I am shipping between islands, whenever I walk into the room where they are showing a movie, word of my coming has always been passed ahead and the whole audience of Marines and swabbies shout in chorus my line in the final scene of *Wake Island*: "Fellows, prepare to engage!" This immortal line follows me, or should I say precedes me, for two years in the Pacific. I am embarrassed but glad, too, that my name is being perpetuated.

Everywhere we go in the Pacific, we learn more about scavenging to survive. We get iceboxes from the Seabees. Our recreation officer gets a movie projector from the Army, silverware and linen from the Navy. By the time we get to our last post in Mindanao, we have a fully equipped photographic studio and a complete projection room. I hate to think how much of this stuff, as well as radar equipment, jeeps, and machine shops, was just shoved into the Pacific at the end of the war rather than having it take up space to ship back Stateside.

I spend many hours in our machine shop trailer making necklaces and bracelets out of seashells and airplane metal as gifts for Betty and the family. Everybody sends this junk home or collects it as trophies of war.

Spending hours in the machine shop is one way to kill time. For two years in the Pacific, that's what we had most of. It's why we played poker so much. There was nothing else to do. Cards are no more a part of my makeup than using my hands in the machine shop. My father was a cardplayer, though. Back in Sioux City, he had had regular bridge games and he'd also played poker regularly with some of the men who ran packing plants in the stockyards. Dad always took care of the money because he was the only one in the game they could all trust. I like poker and still play occasionally, but I can't call myself a cardplayer. Nevertheless, during the war, I played a hell of a lot of poker. In World War II and, I understand, in most wars, quite unlike in most war movies where every moment is action, most time is spent waiting.

There are also moments that are amusing, as I describe in this excerpt from an early poem:

In the Second World War I remember going
     ashore on a Pacific Island
To the south of Espíritu Santo in a boat
We had cadged from the Navy Pool for the day
It was early in the war—the Japanese still
     held Bougainville
But we had the day off. We walked ashore,
     two off duty Marine Officers
And introduced ourselves to the island
     residents—a Scot missionary couple
Who gave us tea and ginger ale and invited us to
Play tennis on their immaculately kept lawn
     tennis court
The net was taut, the lines were chalked
     clean white
On the clipped green grass court
"Why," we asked them, "Do you keep a court
     on this island
In the midst of the Pacific? Why do you keep it?
"Are you that rabid tennis enthusiasts?"
"No," they said, "We don't play. But someone
     might drop in."

After eight months on Espíritu, we were moved nearer action to Bougainville. There were still Japanese at one end of the island, but we were in a secured area. We spent four months there. The Army base had two tennis courts and we played regularly. The Army also set up a school they called the University of Bougainville, and I completed courses in refrigeration and auto mechanics. (The Careys don't have it in their genes to deal with anything mechanical, so this is really force-feeding.)

Our mess is the envy of the island. Like the Army and Navy, we even have vitamin pills in the middle of the dining table. It is the first I've ever seen of them. It is also the first I've seen Aussies. They are the remains of the Australian regiments who fought German Field Marshal Erwin Rommel so successfully in the desert. Now they find themselves here on Bougainville in the middle of the Pacific.

I make friends with the Aussies. Our squadron has been overseas for twelve months and we are all sick of each other. Camaraderie among the same group of men can be enjoyed for just so long; living together for two years, having no autonomy over ourselves, putting our lives in suspension, and not actually being in combat, our squadron experiences all the negative aspects of marriage without any of the rewards.

Being in the same company for so long under such sustained monastic conditions doesn't always bring out your best qualities on an individual level, either. One of my fellow officers is a racing fan and retires into a dream world of horses. He takes the *Racing Form*, which, for the two years we are overseas, is always delivered three months late. Despite this, he bets the races every day. Bets against himself. At the end of three months, he always pays himself off because he then gets the results in the copies of the *Racing Form* for the three months that have just passed.

On Bougainville, I opt for evenings with the Aussies for a while. Their beer is like dew on the lip and tongue. It is something called Cascade, made from the snows of the mountains in Tasmania. We trade a bottle of bourbon for a quart—or is it a large pint?—of this Cascade, and we play Australian poker every night. It is a mad game of seven-card stud, all cards showing. We play for a penny a chip because the Aussies are paid a pittance compared to us. Neil Munro, who was then an Australian major, remains a friend to this day. His son is now a teacher and comes yearly to the States for seminars. One of the other Aussies, Bill Henly, has gone back to Bougainville, where he runs a drug store.

The thing I remember most about Bougainville is the beautiful waterfall, where we'd go on a hot afternoon to sit on a rock and let the falling water pound and massage our shoulders and bodies. In the damp jungle, it was just wonderful. It fills this room in my mind, even as I'm writing this.

After four months, we leave for our first real invasion on one of the Philippine islands called Mindoro. It is a fairly picture-book landing. We go ashore in the dead of night, about three A.M., LSTs (Landing Ship Troops) and all. But no one is there, no enemy. The Japanese have left. I only remember two things about Mindoro: After Mass on Sundays, we'd go into the town and bet on the cock fights. The other is the first and only liberty any of us would have during our two years overseas. We get a ride, four at a time, in a DC-3 to Manila. Even though they are still fighting outside Manila, the town itself is relatively secure. I have a fascinating three or four days. It occasions this poem:

The Good Samaritan

Father Lopez admits
He steals when necessary.
His homily Sunday was the story
Of his Filipino Father
Who let a drunken marine
Who'd been in a fight
Sleep it off on his front parlor couch

1 2 3

And sent him off the next morning
With carfare to his base.
A homily on charity.

I told the good Father of my four days liberty
In Manila in World War II.
I am the youngest lieutenant in our group.
We have flown in from Mindoro.
Since I rank lowest I am sent off
To find a bottle of booze while others
Will wait for me at the apartment
Of a Miss Concepcion.

They are still fighting outside Manila
And there is a sudden blackout.
I head for the last light that went out
And knock on a door in the darkness.
I am admitted and asked my name and I say
I am from California, from Los Angeles,
From Hollywood, I had worked at Paramount
And yes I know their son,
Charlie Gomorra who is a makeup man
For Wally Westmore and plays the ape
In all the Dorothy Lamour movies.

We spend the night talking.
The next day and the next night.
Then it is Easter morning and I go to Mass
With the whole family and sit in the choir loft
Looking down on a sea of mantillas.
It is the Filipino women. All their men
Are off fighting the war and they
Fill the church with black lace and faith and hope.

I tell this to Father Lopez and ask him
Not to tell the story till I do.
He says he can't promise me anything
And reminds me that plagiarism is stealing
From one writer and research
Is stealing from several.

As someone recently noted, oddly enough, the cardinal for the see (a seat of a bishop's office) in the Philippines is one Cardinal Sin.

On returning to Mindoro, we prepare for what is supposed to be a big one—the invasion of Mindanao. We join a good portion of the fleet and start off. One of the four hundred members of our squadron is motivated enough to be the first man of us to flip, mentally and psychologically, that is. Just before we land, of all the officers, he chooses me to confide in. First, he asks me to hear his confession, then he says forget it, he's forgotten to tell me he is Jesus Christ and I am to let his mother and father know because they disapprove of his being where he is just then and doing what he is about to do. We take him off duty and a month later he is shipped back Stateside.

Perhaps he is the sanest of us all; he certainly beats us all home. We land on Mindanao, again at about three o'clock in the morning and again we are unopposed. The Japanese are there, but they have retreated inland. After we hit the beach, I am given a platoon and told to take them to the airstrip where we will rendezvous with the rest of the squadron, who have to take in all the radar equipment. My bad sense of direction comes into full play, and the first thing I do is get the platoon lost.

I try to keep my cool. It'll only make things worse if I get panicky. By some lucky accident, we stumble on a clearing and another platoon who aren't much more certain of our location than we are. Together we manage to find our way to the airstrip.

In my seven months on Mindanao, I improve my chess and my poker. We play almost every night. I meet Jack Wrather, who is, to be redundant, a Texan and a good poker player. His family sends him wonderful cans of delicacies, which he generously shares, but I don't like him just for his pâté and his caviar. I enjoy playing poker with him; Jack takes the place of my first Texan buddy in the Marine Corps, who was marched around in his Stetson while I was in my homburg and double-breasted gray suit.

Initially, I think Jack probably liked me because I was some sort of emblem or symbol of Hollywood, where he planned to move after the war. Indeed, when the conflict is over, he left Texas and what was apparently a bad marriage to come to Hollywood and marry Bonita Granville. Once there, he moved beyond his oil holdings to produce television—the show "Lassie" principally—and to own and operate the Disneyland Hotel, and the exhibitions of the Queen Mary, and Howard Hughes's plane, "The Spruce Goose."

Although our poker game at the Officers' Club on Mindanao really never gets out of hand—a big loss or a big win is around $200—the last two months on the island are really hard on the liver and kidneys. Instead of costing two bits or fifty cents, the club is giving all the drinks away free. The war is over and they have to get rid of their inventory. Unlike the jeeps and radar equipment, the booze is dumped into us instead of the sea.

All the men, enlisted and officers, collect souvenirs. Besides Japanese swords and guns, there are the native knives— machetes, bolos, and daggers. A lot of us have extensive collections, which we particularly replenish there on Mindanao. One day we go exploring east of our camp, about five miles, to find the source of what has become a steady column of smoke. The source turns out to be a factory for manufacturing these knives in almost assembly-line fashion. We then examine some of the rare knives we have so tirelessly collected and discover what we should have noticed before: American trademarks on the metal of both blades and handles. One prized knife has "Eveready" stamped in small print up the seam of the handle. They are far from the real thing; they have been manufactured for us, their tourist trade, from raw material they scavenged when we threw it out.

One segment of our squadron is sent to Malabang, where I visit for a couple of weeks. Until the second week, I feel isolated from civilization in the midst of the Philippine jungle with primitive natives around us. Then, in the midst of a chess game, an old wrinkled Moro edges up to the chess board and says, "No, no, no," as I try to checkmate with a bishop and a knight. "All right," I say. "Why?" He shows me how the move would cost me my bishop and the game. We soon learn these natives come from a culture much older than ours. Chess had been imported to the Moros in the Philippines from India in the seventeenth century.

Some of the squadron is sent to Davao, where the Japanese infiltrate the camp one night and steal food. That is as close as we come to the Japanese. An exception is my buddy Tom Rodd, who is sent to Leyte as an observer and who manages to survive the Battle of Leyte, the first place after Okinawa where the kamikaze pilots really operate all out. The ship Tom is on is hit by one of the suicide planes. Tom comes back to us with one side of his face frozen in temporary paralysis. After the war, he went back to his old job at J. P. Morgan. I had lunch with him on Wall Street ten years later and he was his old self.

Stuck in Mindanao, I am the lowest-ranking Marine officer in our squadron, having been passed over for a promotion because of the parade incident back in Miramar a year or so before. I am also the last officer in our squadron to leave Mindanao. The war is over in the Pacific, but it will be months

127

before I get home. When I finally get off the island, I get as far as Manus Island, where I again find myself the lowest-ranking Marine officer. My duties are to "break out" the live Marine bodies on the island who are waiting to go home—get them up every morning and have roll call. I am not the most loved Marine officer on the island—low in rank and low in esteem.

The month I spent on Manus was not too bad, though. I met a Navy officer named Bert Chance, whose father had been the Chance of the most famous double play in baseball, Tinker to Evers to Chance.

Bert and I regularly requisition a small Navy boat and go out with tackle and bait into the bay to fish. A friendly captain in an Army unit that handles the port in Manus has his chef cook our catch.

After a month, I get my name written in as the commander of a batch of Marines who are being shipped back to the States. I go with them. The first thing I want when I finally get ashore again in California is a carton of fresh milk. As the man says, "I'm proud to be the humblest of you all."

Then, too, the carton of milk is a symbol of my unspoken wish to be home again, "safe at last," in the arms of my loved ones, back with Betty, back starting a family and resuming my career. But even Ulysses had a problem when he came home. I soon find out I have one, too. In fact, I have several.

9

I arrived at the base at Miramar, near San Diego, and expected to be allowed to join Betty in Los Angeles immediately, or at least visit her.

But no, the Marines keep me at the base. Like a long-running character in a soap opera, I find myself stuck in a place I don't want to be. I'm back in the United States but I can't get back into civilian life. I've been out of the country for two celibate years, but I can't get out of the Marine Corps—or off the base—until I'm processed out.

Betty has spent most of the war as a secretary to the administrator of Shipley School, a girl's school in Philadelphia, but has quit and come to Los Angeles to meet me on my return. She and two friends are having a party and issue a blanket invitation to me and my friends. Whittaker and Wokowski—members of my old AWS 3 unit who are already discharged—take Betty up on her invitation for the party. She's hosting it with Janey Lawrence and Ginny Lee, and that makes me jealous and unhappy. Janey, who was a girlfriend of Spencer Tracy before her marriage, has something of a reputation, and I'm worried that it might be catching.

This is just the start of the reawakening of my jealousy.

When I'm finally discharged and go back to LA, we rent an apartment on the Sunset Strip. I expect our marriage to be better than it's ever been before. I not only missed Betty but I take it as a sign she has missed me when she presents me with a check covering all the overseas poker winnings I'd sent home to her: a small nest egg to begin making our new home. She soon also presents me with the information that she has a crush on her girlfriend Ginny Lee's husband, Leonard Lee, a screenwriter I had known at Universal before the war. During the war, Leonard had shown up as a captain in the Marine Corps, doing press and publicity, when I was at Quantico, and Betty met him there with me. Now Leonard and Ginny have split up, and Betty tells me she and Leonard are serious about each other.

Before I learned about Leonard's new role in Betty's life, she and I made our first purchase with my poker winnings —a Capehart-like RCA record-changing phonograph—a monstrous piece of furniture. When I find out about Leonard, I really feel it where it hurts. I'm angry and devastated. I tell Betty to get out and move in with him if she's so serious about him. She leaves to stay with Leonard, who, by this time, has left his wife. She takes the radio phonograph with her. That heaps insult onto injury. I tell her, "Live with him if you must, but give me back the record changer."

I got the phonograph back and wrote a letter to Betty's mother in Philadelphia saying I was brokenhearted but that I couldn't live with her daughter anymore. Before Betty's mother gets my letter, Betty changes her mind and decides to come back to me. Although I have misgivings, that's nothing new. I've always had misgivings about Betty's snap judgments and melodramatics. She is the type of person who thrives on crises. I'd bend over backward to avoid playing the heavy male and end up letting her dominate the field. In other words, I avoid confrontation; I won't recognize reality. When Betty tells me she wants to come back, my misgivings are overcome by my trying to be a good Catholic boy who doesn't believe in divorce. Besides, I've been planning, even fantasizing about, our reunion for the two years I was away. Once she wants to come back, I want her; I bury the hurt I feel and forget my compunctions about this reunion after a reunion.

We are together again—together in what a would-be conciliating priest tells us is "the mud at the feet of the cross." It seems we are at war with each other, Betty and I; from the moment we met and fell in love, we spend our lives hurting each other—lifetime enemies, lifetime lovers.

The sixteen months that passed after the war before I was given a picture to do were a true period of adjustment for us both. Before I joined the Marines, I was so preoccupied with working and playing so as not to have to think about the war that I never accepted my role as a marriage partner. Betty and I were like two children playacting at being a Hollywood couple. Now that I was back from overseas, we needed to make the marriage that we had never really begun to make before. We sensed this need, but our attempts to satisfy it were inept.

Since one of the reasons we got married was "to raise better children," now the first thing we have to find out is whether or not we can have them, given Betty's proclivity to miscarry. If we can't have children, we want to know why. This entails a thorough examination for Betty and fertility tests for me.

The tests go on for several weeks, but don't become a major trauma. However, masturbating at home or in doctors' offices and carrying semen around town in your pocket is not the happiest of occupations. We find out that I am fertile, but that Betty would have to spend at least the first six months of a pregnancy in bed. We decide to make another attempt.

In the meantime, Leonard Lee divorces Ginny Lee and moves to Portugal, where he later commits suicide. No one knows why. He was a strange, secretive man who had a fatal charisma as far as certain women were concerned. If Betty mourns his loss, she doesn't let me see it.

Life during the time right after the war is even more uncertain in one way than the days during the war: No one knows where they are now, what their position is in life. The most extreme act is taken in stride by everyone. Betty's quasi-affair with Leonard—Betty tells me it was never consummated even though she moved in with him—I soon accept as just another one of the deviations from the norm that everyone is going through at this time.

We bought and moved into a multilevel house at 1438 North King's Road above the Sunset Strip. The poker winnings Betty saved came to more than $2,000. This helped toward the down payment on our new house. We no sooner moved in than Betty was taken into the hospital to have her appendix removed.

There they discover she is pregnant and that the baby is due in October. We're excited, but the excitement is tempered by our knowledge that we must be very careful if Betty is to keep the baby.

Our house, with its six levels, is the worst kind for a pregnant woman prone to miscarry. You walk up to get to the entrance hall, then down into the living room, down again to the master bedroom, then up two flights to the next bedroom, up another to the third, and down again to the den. This means Betty is marooned in the master bedroom for most of the pregnancy. She decides it's only fair to let me go out some nights with the boys—not a wise decision because it's a privilege I sometimes abuse.

Paul Caruso, my friend from the Marine Corps, has settled in LA and is studying law at Loyola. While he's trying to pass the bar, he is doing some sort of work for Rudy Vallee.

Rudy has a bizarre house off Mulholland with a tennis court I occasionally play on and a two-car garage with space for only one car in front of it. A turntable had to be made in the pavement of his driveway so you can drive in or out, because the house is in a cul-de-sac.

Rudy's house is Old Hollywood in decor. He has a movie theater and projector in the basement, a bar, a pool, and a billiards room. In the attic, he has file after file of drawers and cabinets where he has stored and classified every radio show, every TV show, every engagement he has ever had, including every date he has ever played. He has every award and every prize he has ever won; he has wristwatches, clocks, hats, party favors, plaques, loving cups, programs, reviews, posters, a living history of everything Rudy Vallee has ever done. Rudy, a ladies man to be sure, is best remembered by some of us who knew his collections as a true hoarder. He even bridles at my talking to one of his secretaries in the corner at one of his parties. I am innocent of making a pass at her, but Rudy is possessive about everything he has around him.

About this time, Charlie, one of my brothers, got married and the reception was held in our new King's Road home. He left his wedding gifts with us while he took Mary Lou, his new bride, to Pebble Beach for their honeymoon.

Now, Charlie is an avid golfer, as is his twin, Gordy. They had been on the University of Iowa and UCLA golf teams in college. When I was sixteen and the boys were twelve, they were shooting in the sixties. They'd go to different state tournaments, one to Iowa, the other to the Minnesota Resorter Tournament, so that they wouldn't end up playing each other in the finals. They were so good *I* gave up golf and took up tennis.

When Charlie and Mary Lou come back from their ten-day honeymoon in Pebble Beach to pick up their wedding presents, I ask Charlie, "How was the honeymoon?" "Mac," he says, "it was wonderful. Pebble Beach has the most un-believable fourteenth hole!"

All of us actors at the movie studios who were away find that we have literally broken stride in our march to fame. Our main worry now is whether we're going to work again. It's hard for me to get back into the movie scene as an active participant even though I'm still under contract and pulling down a salary. The good news is my contract continues on the same terms, giving me a $250 per week raise every six months. The bad news is I'm not working, just posing for pictures and giving interviews for stories about what a prom-ising young actor I am. Promises, promises. I'm not acting except for the stories. However, the grapevine says the pub-licity stories are helpful; they're putting me back in the public eye. Even so, I'm concerned that maybe no one at Paramount is quite sure whether I can still hack it. I'm a little nervous about it myself, but I wish to God they'd give me a chance to show them I can.

While I am waiting for a picture, I try to keep myself busy. John Lund, Robert Preston, David Savage, and I get together for a concrete mixing party at our King's Road house, where we cement our basement, which has nothing but a dirt floor, thereby adding a new level to the house; yet another set of steps to climb. A screen magazine comes to photograph us. I take fencing lessons regularly at Ralph Faulkner's studio in Hollywood. Ralph choreographed and played the villain in most of the Douglas Fairbanks pictures and then in the Errol Flynn swashbucklers. He's been an Olympic fencer and, like Giorgio Santelli, with whom I'd studied fencing in New York and who was in his nineties when he married his fourth wife, Ralph lived a very long life. Fencers are legend-ary for their longevity.

At the same time as I study fencing with Ralph, I have judo lessons with Bruce Tegner, who has a little gym on

Sunset. I also take tap lessons with Johnny Mattson, who dances a wonderful low-to-the-ground tap, then more tap lessons with Louis Da Pron. I like to dance, it's great exercise, and I might be able to use it in a movie or a show. I play pickup tennis games everywhere I can, and there are regular poker games.

Betty, of course, is still confined to the house. Until our first child, Lynn, is born, most of my drinking was done at home. The drinking helps fill the hours. Fortunately, Paramount finally comes through with a movie for me while Betty is still pregnant.

Resuming my career at Paramount after more than a four-year absence from the screen is made easier by being cast in another Mitch Leisen directed movie with Fred MacMurray. Fred is one soul I know remembers me. About Paramount's memory of me, I have my doubts: Not only have they kept me waiting sixteen months for a movie, the first year I was overseas, Paramount sent me a carton of cigarettes, the accompanying note was signed "Your buddies at Paramount," and said, "Ed, we miss you—we're counting the days 'til you come home, Ed."

The movie, which we begin shooting February 1, 1946, is called *Suddenly It's Spring*. Fred and Paulette Goddard are the stars and I play the second lead, the other man. It is another screwball comedy, no plot to speak of. Fred and Paulette are in the middle of breaking up their marriage and I try to win Paulette. That's about it for the storyline. I'm disappointed that I'm playing the second lead, as I'm starting out on a lower rung of the ladder than when I left for the war. After *Suddenly It's Spring*, I go back to playing leads, and the picture is a good way to get my feet wet again; Fred is a good security blanket.

Fred has a funny relationship with the movie business. This poem sort of tells the story:

Parable

The first picture I made at Paramount
After the war was with Fred MacMurray
The first movie I'd made when I'd
Come out from New York four years before
Was with Fred MacMurray
I hero worshipped him
He was a star
But he'd remained unsnobbish
A human being
And one thing he said I'll never forget
"Never stay for the wrap party
After the picture"

Why not? I said and stayed
The first drink some big hulk of a grip
Comes over and tells me
What a great guy I am
To work with
The second drink
He begins hitting me on the
Shoulder—half joking—half serious
Third drink
He calls me a stuck up actor bastard

The exit is hard to find
The assistant wardrobe lady
Gets me out of there
Before I lose my skin

That's why you don't stay
For the wrap party.

With the exception of Westerns, when you are together
twenty-four hours a day in camps or on location, there is

1 3 6

always a sort of dividing line between the actors and the grips and electricians.

The poker game we'd had in Mindanao, Jack Wrather and I started again in Hollywood. We played every two weeks, rotating from one house to another. The players included Jack, Bob Preston, his agent, Lou Rance, Henry Rogers (whose public relations firm, Rogers and Cowan, handled most of Hollywood), one or both of my twin brothers, Charlie and Gordon, Bunty Lawrence, an agent, who, with his wife, Janey, were drinking buddies of mine and Betty's, and finally Bill Doheny, who really cooled the game for us because his bets were a little too high. (The Dohenys were big oil money—big even compared to Jack. Besides the family's notoriety during the Harding administration in the Teapot Dome scandal, they were one of the first California families of wealth to contribute heavily to the arts, to the Catholic church, and to the poor. A beautiful Los Angeles street that splits Beverly Hills from Hollywood is named after them.)

At the time, Henry Rogers is handling publicity for me. One night I arrive at the poker game with a postcard I've gotten with my fan mail at Paramount. It says: "We know who you are Macdonald Cohen. With your nose and the people you ran around with in New York, we know you for the Jew you are." All of us laugh, but we are really angry at the bigotry, and Henry asks to have the card so he can take it to the ACLU. Nothing ever comes of this, however, but it is a bizarre example of prejudice.

After another poker game, Bob Preston and I decide to try some marijuana. We get in his Lincoln Continental and drive to Central Avenue to a black after-hours jazz joint called Brothers. We have some drinks, listen to some jazz, and Press gets a couple of joints, which we take to the parking lot and smoke.

Press says, "We have to roll up the windows if we want to get the full effect."

After studiously finishing off one apiece, we start the drive home. It's a long drive back to Brentwood, where Bob lives and where I've left my car. We're driving through LA. We haven't even come to Hollywood when I watch how slowly the scenery is passing by.

"Boy, this must be strong stuff!" I say.

"We must really be loaded," says Press. "Feel how we're moving."

I say, "You're right. Everything seems like it's slow motion."

We are enjoying this sensation until we both hear at the same time the sound the car is making. The Lincoln is a gearshift and Press still has it in second. He gives a sheepish laugh, shifts into high, and our heads suddenly seem much clearer. After this initial try, pot holds no more charms for me. Besides, liquor is quicker.

"Funny," Robin Williams said about the sixties generation, "If you can remember Woodstock, then you weren't there." The same thing is true of much of my life: Much of the time, in the sense of really being with it, "I wasn't there"; drinking had become such a habit, it was now an addiction. There was a little buzz, of course, but it was the briefest of pleasures. Like the ad says: "A drink makes you feel like a new man —then the new man wants a drink."

About this time, Carl Schroeder, Vic Mature's old friend and publicist who now runs three fan magazines, publicly announces that I am out of the Marines and back in Hollywood. The columnists Harry Crocker and Hedda Hopper do the same. In the L.A. *Times*, Hedda says I have an offer to go to New York to star with Geraldine Fitzgerald in *Portrait in Black*, with Leland Hayward producing. In July, I have an offer to act with Helen Hayes in a new play by Anita Loos called *Happy Birthday*. These never materialize.

We finish *Suddenly It's Spring* and it's sneak previewed on August 30. My press is good. Betty's mother comes out from

Philadelphia to be with us when the baby, who is expected on October 5 is born. A girl, Lynn Carey, finally arrives on October 29, 1946. Mrs. Heckscher—I never call Betty's mother anything else—comes to Queen of Angels Hospital with us carrying a shaker full of martinis, which we consume in the waiting room during the night waiting for Betty to deliver. Drinking is not only sanctioned in our family, it is beatified. When Lynn arrives, we are ecstatic.

I hired Mrs. Moffet to help Betty when she brings the baby home. We also hired a new couple to do the cooking and housework. We soon found out that the new couple drinks. On Thanksgiving, we are waiting for our dinner to be served, but the only thing that comes out of the kitchen is noise. I run out to discover the couple we have hired at each other's throats. They are both loaded and the turkey is sitting un-cooked on top of the oven. I got them out of the house and picked up a cooked turkey from a deli on Santa Monica Boulevard.

These are wonderful times for us. My closest friend from my Marine days, Paul Caruso, lives nearby (on Doheny, of all places), and, of course, our poker game is going strong. Betty and I also have a group of people we see a lot of to-gether: Anne Baxter, John Hodiak, Anne's husband, Bunty and Janey Lawrence, and David Savage, who is a cutter (the movie business lingo for film editor) at Twentieth Century-Fox. We have regular Sunday tennis parties at Watson Webb's, another cutter at Fox. Watson lives next door to the MacMurrays and has a beautiful home and tennis court and a great chef. The garden and house are really attractive, early Americana all over the place. American eagles and cigar-store Indians abound. Watson now runs Shelbourne, Ver-mont, a complete New England village restored to its Rev-olutionary days' perfection—a Vermont Williamsburg.

Betty knew Anne Baxter from pre–New York days at the Provincetown Playhouse, where they were both apprentices.

For a time, Anne, John Hodiak, Betty, and I saw a lot of each other. Anne is always very chirrupy, running several speeds ahead of everyone else. One Thanksgiving, we all went to a party at the home of David Savage, whose wife, Carol, had a turkey in the oven. It was the first time she'd cooked one, so she asked Anne and Betty to take a look at it. They did and saw that it was a smoked turkey, which Carol had reduced to dwarflike proportions.

"Not to worry," Anne says. "Give me all your martinis." She takes the martinis, throws them on top of the turkey, and makes a stew. The rest of the party—Harry Morgan, John Arthur Kennedy (whom the movies called Arthur Kennedy in deference to John F. Kennedy, who was already making a name for himself in Congress), and Johnny's wife Mary—all agree it's delicious. Well, anyway, they eat it.

Everyone at Fox was usually at Watson Webb's at some time or other on the weekends: Gene Tierney and Oleg Cassini, Ray Milland, Fred MacMurray, Dan Dailey, Patricia Medina and her then-husband Richard Greene (the "gorgeous Greenes," as they were known), Ann Sothern, Howard Keel, Tyrone Power, and Walter Lang and his wife Fieldsie. Walter directed a lot of the Twentieth Century musicals, the most famous of which was *Can-Can* with Shirley MacLaine and Frank Sinatra, which Mr. and Mrs. Kruschev saw and disapproved of. Walter also lives in my memory because he said of Howard Keel, "He walks into a room as if to say, 'Penis, anyone?' "

Betty really fits into this group at Watson's better than I do. Betty and Watson are both part of the Eastern establishment. I never feel I've made it into this stratum of society, this particular, more chic group of movieland. I enjoy the company but I always feel a little out of it. It is reverse snobbery on my part, I suppose, but I feel with some of these people, like Fred MacMurray says he feels with the grips, that they are in a brotherhood that he is no part of. I should have been proud of my middle-class, Midwestern background, the fact that I am a common man, but it took me years to realize that the universality of this commonness is something to be proud of. In those days, I am childishly inhibited about it.

The area where I'm not inhibited is my acting, and finally it's going well again. *Suddenly It's Spring* opens in New York on February 26, 1947. The reviews are generally raves, both for the picture and for me. I know because I still have them.

I had started a scrapbook when I was a child and I continue even during my sixteen-month wait for a picture. I keep clippings to remind myself I'm alive and still in show business. I save reviews for the same reason. After three years of being a nonperson in the Marine Corps, this is a way of certifying I am an actor again.

It's hard enough to be sure of yourself when you're working everyday—self-doubt is the actor's occupational disease. Always we ask, "Do they like me?" Remember what Sally Field said when she accepted her Oscar for *Places in the Heart*? "You like me!" Even Laurence Olivier had continuing self-doubts to his dying day; when he was in his seventies, he suffered from terrible stage fright.

I don't believe actors when they say they don't pay attention to reviews. Not true. Even actors who don't read them are paying attention to them that way. I avidly collected reviews. Of course, I had a strong pack-rat instinct: as a child, I'd collected marbles, squirrel skins, one-reeler and two-reelers, stamps, and books. It is only natural that I would collect my reviews. Besides the pleasure of seeing my name in print—a pleasure I've never pretended to hide—I might learn something from a review, and it's a comment on a profession that I'm proud to be a part of. I enjoy acting, and having a steady job as an actor is its own reward because unlike other poor souls in business or other professions, it is a joy for an actor to go to work every day. Being a working actor is, for me and for all the actors I've ever known—even those who deny it—the ultimate transport, the ultimate happiness. Even when there's agony in it, there's fun. Even when you have to question whether you're doing it right or not, you're enjoying what you're doing.

The reviews for *Suddenly It's Spring* make me feel I'm home safe.

Kate Cameron in the *New York Daily News* says, "Macdonald Carey in the role of MacMurray's friend is making his first film appearance since his retirement from the screen five years ago, when he left to play a part in the war. We welcome him back with pleasure, as he is a smooth clever actor, who will be a great asset to Paramount Pictures." Howard Barnes in the *New York Herald Tribune* says, "Far better in giving antic twists to the proceedings is Macdonald Carey in the role of the husband's rich friend, who tries to move in on a broken marriage and gives subtle touches to a far from subtle show." Alton Cook in the *New York World Telegram* says, "Macdonald Carey is back from the war with his old droll slyness with a gag." In the *New York Sun*, Eileen Creelman says, "This is Carey's first picture after three years in the Marines. It should get him off to a fine start." I found this one I still can't believe: Ruth Waterbury in the *L.A. Examiner* says, "But oh that nice new shiny Mr. Carey. He's the one the girls are going to latch onto."

Bosley Crowther of the *New York Times* is the usual voice of dissent. He finds *Suddenly It's Spring* "a so-called comedy, a moth-eaten bundle of horse feathers—no more than a skit with pretentions—forced farce—exhaustively talkative." He continues, "even if Hollywood had not already run this husband-wife bit into the ground, this silly exhibit of wrangling would still be in a rut . . . except for one bit by Frank Faylan, there's not a glimmer of brightness in the whole thing." This is reassuring to me in a strange way. Bosley Crowther hadn't liked my work before the war either. I read this as his "Welcome home."

The *New Republic* is kinder. Shirley O'Hara says, *"Suddenly It's Spring* has its charming title and Macdonald Carey to recommend it. He steals the picture tongue in cheek and I'm grateful to him. Carey, a young actor, who if he doesn't go far, will prove once more that Hollywood is crazy, has the endearing qualities of a Spaniel, a deep voice, obvious intelligence and a knowledgeable talent. He played opposite Gertrude Lawrence in *Lady in the Dark* and since then has been in the Marines."

Variety says, "Macdonald Carey comes into his own with this picture. His Jack Lindsay is an insouciant combination of business man, playboy and lover that establishes him as a threat to leading men. He has an easy technique in concealing the depth of his artistry and a personal style unique on the screen." *Box Office Digest* and the *Hollywood Reporter* said, respectively, "Macdonald Carey, a solid sock as the other man . . ." and "His work here shows again that he is star material."

The columnists—Hedda, Louella, Harrison Carroll, and Jimmy Fiddler—are all kind. Louella, in *Cosmopolitan* magazine, ends her column with this typically Louella quote: "Will you, Mr. Carey, accept the *Cosmopolitan* citation for the best supporting performance of the month? Welcome home, Sir. It's mighty keen welcoming the likes of you back. Why don't you come over and see me sometime?"

The only thing that makes me realize I am not living in Eden and sleeping on a bed of roses is in a news note: the same week Betty went to one hospital for an appendectomy, I went to another for a hemorrhoidectomy. Waiting around for another picture must have been slightly stressful.

In April, I went on a junket to Salt Lake City for the premiere of a picture called *Ramrod* starring Joel McCrea.

Along for the ride are Preston Foster, Jane Withers, Henry Morgan, Martha Hyer, Van Heflin, Jackie Cooper, Richard Conte, Veronica Lake, Donald O'Connor, and Don DeFore. I remember that Richard Ney, who was married to Greer Garson at the time, brought his skis on the train with him. If he'd brought Greer, there wouldn't have been room for her; with all his ski equipment, he had to have a compartment to himself. I remember leaving the club car at one o'clock in the morning on the trip home and seeing Sonny Tufts sitting on the floor in the middle of one of the cars with a drink in his hand. I came back in the car at eight in the morning on my way to the diner for breakfast and Sonny was still there in the same position. However, he was now holding the glass upside down.

Sonny had made a big name for himself in several pictures during the war. Long before this, he'd been a legend even at Exeter, when I went there at age seventeen. He was in the class before me and had been kicked out for drinking and for placing an alarm clock in the chandelier of the assembly room set to go off when the dean addressed the graduation class. He was a big blond attractive guy who played ball at some Ivy League college and had so many broken bones the NFL wouldn't draft him.

Sonny was not the only one who was making a career out of drinking. A lot of us were doing the same thing waiting for the next picture. Just as a news note, the *L.A. Times* on May 26 mentioned these actors to watch: Peter Lawford, Burt Lancaster, Kirk Douglas, Dane Clark—and Macdonald Carey.

Two years after this, I'm in New York with Van Heflin judging a Miss Reingold contest. He leans over at lunch and says, "Are you getting blackouts the way I am? I keep forgetting what happened yesterday. Do you?" I told him I didn't remember.

I am doing more than just drinking, however. I am still

taking fencing, singing, tap, and judo lessons and still playing tennis every day and every weekend: not just for the
joy of it but to keep from going crazy waiting for my next
movie. When it comes, I am delighted. It's *Dream Girl* with
Betty Hutton. Mitch Leisen will again direct this one. It
is at this time that the studio begins confusing me with
another actor named Wendell Corey. Paramount even sends
out pictures of me to fans under Wendell Corey's name and
pictures of Wendell Corey with mine. The confusion persists
to this day. How long the confusion lasts, this poem will
indicate:

If It Ain't Broke Don't Fix It

A guy I know's publicity agent
Just gave a party
Celebrating the dedication of his star
On Hollywood Boulevard.
The fact no one came to the party was
    headlined by the Times.
Publicity is a doubtful Alladin's lamp to rely on.
I once did an awful movie with Shelley Winters called
"South Sea Sinner" where the Times reviewer
Panned me. Wendell Corey was
Awful he said. My publicity agent called the
Times and demanded a retraction. I got one—
The Times reviewer published a long piece apologizing
To Wendell Corey for having mistaken Macdonald
    Carey
For him.

Wendell Corey and I, though looking—and acting—nothing alike, had more in common than our similar names. We
both drank, we drank with the same people—not that there
were any people we wouldn't drink with—we ended up on

the Academy Board together, we ended up in a movie together—*The Great Missouri Raid* playing the James brothers, and at one time we even lived across the street from each other, but we are not the same person.

Wendell had starred in *Dream Girl* on the stage in New York and had been signed by Paramount because of it. I am put in the picture instead of Wendell. Despite my excitement about it, the movie is ill-fated from the start. The play *Dream Girl*, was by Elmer Rice, and was a hit in New York, but things happened to it in Hollywood. Originally it was the story of a normal, average girl, but one who never faces the reality of life around her and is dreaming her life away. My character, a hard-boiled reporter, is the one who brings her down to earth, brings her literally to life. I have to admit that, as much as I like him, Mitch Leisen was wrong as the director, because he made the girl's life in the real world as fabulous and opulent as anything she could possibly dream or imagine, thereby letting the fantasy out of the story like air from a balloon.

At this time, Betty Hutton was a hot Paramount property. She had made it in nightclubs and was in a Preston Sturges picture, *The Miracle of Morgan's Creek*. She'd married well, too: Ted Briskin, her husband, had just sold out his rights to Revere Camera, the first successful home movie camera, which was very popular.

Paramount is giving her its best in *Dream Girl*, and I am happy to work with her. But some odd things begin to happen during the filming. Betty Hutton starts to act like a star. She takes her voice coach, her hairdresser, and the cutter into the screening room with her for the screening of all the rushes. This entourage laughs only at Betty's close-ups. The other actors—Walter Abel, Peggy Wood, and I—get not a chuckle at the screenings in the master shots or in our close-ups. After a while, we simply stop going to the rushes.

The first cut of the picture is one long close-up of Betty. The first sneak preview was a disaster.

For the second sneak, they put me back in the picture a little—there are two-shots of Betty and me—but the audience still doesn't like it. In the third sneak, the cutter restores the rest of everybody's close-ups and the picture is accepted, but it is never really the smash it should have been because it was never made the way it should have been.

Typical of the weird way it was shot is one scene in which I call Betty from a phone booth and disguise my voice by talking through my nose. Whatever laugh there is in the scene comes from me disguising my voice. The sound man took care of that, however. At the end of the picture, he came up to me and said, "Don't worry about that phone booth scene. I know you had a cold that day. I fixed your voice up when I mixed the sound so you didn't sound so nasal."

The wrap party is also bizarre. Mitch gives extravagant gifts to everybody and Betty Hutton tops him. Each individual gets either a movie camera, an expensive radio, a gown, or a fur coat. Fred MacMurray was right. I leave early.

10

After *Dream Girl*, there is a summer of magazine layouts and tennis and drinking and radio shows and drinking. And promises from Paramount. Finally they get a picture for me—*Hazard*—in which I am starred opposite Paulette Goddard. It is a comedy directed by George Marshall, who is an old hand with that kind of picture. His experience in the business goes way back to silent films with Buster Keaton, Laurel and Hardy, and Harry Langdon. George tells me that in silent films there was an awful lot of drinking. As an example, he tells me about the morning Lloyd Hamilton, one of silent films' great unsung comics, came in loaded, holding a loaf of bread in his right hand. Lloyd rolled up the sleeve on his left arm and spread the length of it with mustard. When asked why, he said, "That's for making left-hand turns."

Only a drinking man would laugh at this story. All of us laughed.

Fred Clark was another drinking buddy in the cast. Fred, who is perhaps most famous for his role as the stuffy banker in *Auntie Mame* and as the original neighbor, Harry Morton, in "The Burns and Allen Show," is also an expert comedian. In the days we were making *Hazard*, we hung out a lot at the Cock and Bull at the end of the Sunset Strip. As I write this, a Jaguar agency just bought the property and closed it. But for years it was the hangout for newspapermen, sports figures, and actors. For almost thirty years, I spent many hours at its bar, and for twenty of those years, Fred was usually there, too. When he wasn't sitting with everyone else, he would be at the end of the bar by himself, signing checks to pay his bills. His bar stool was his office. On the other bar stools over the years, the tableau of drinkers looked like the Last Supper. They were fixtures. During sober periods, those of us who were of the sober persuasion would joke about going up to the Cock and Bull and checking out the frieze of habitués around the bar that for obvious reasons we called "the wallpaper."

The making of *Hazard* is a further instruction in the mores of the movies. It is a comedy about a girl (Paulette Goddard) who has an addiction to gambling. I play a detective who is accompanying her across the United States. The story tries to have an *It Happened One Night* flavor. One of the first days of the picture, we are on location near the Paramount Ranch around Agoura, at a lake. Paulette's character keeps trying to shake me, and in this particular scene, she pushes me into the water, gets in the car, and drives off. This is to be the last shot of the day because I'm going to rise from the lake completely mud-soaked. They've lost the sun, anyway. Before this last shot, however, the whole company has started to wrap, and as I climb out of the lake from the last take, I see almost everyone is on the bus. By the time I get into something dry, I have to hitch a ride on the prop truck, the last vehicle that is leaving. Most of the company has gone. Any early inflation of ego I had suffered quickly disappears.

Paulette is a kick in the pants. A tough little girl who grew up in show business, she was a Ziegfeld girl and a Goldwyn girl. Having been divorced from Charlie Chaplin, she is, at the time of this picture, married to Burgess Meredith. She tells me she doesn't like Burgess to drink because it "makes his face look like a potato" (could she have been referring to how *I* looked in the morning?). She is a complete realist, deservedly known for her business acumen—she is the one woman who got something out of Charlie Chaplin before they split up.

The first day of the picture, she volunteers to bring her own luggage for props. It's a matching set of about seven pieces. She has told the prop department not to bother to provide luggage for her. The bags are, of course, a major prop because they will be with her for the entire cross-country trip, but after they've been established in the first day's shooting, she takes them home. When they're asked for in the next scene, Paulette tells the company manager he'll have to pay $50 a bag for each day the bags are used in a shot. I don't know how many thousands Paulette made a week, but she was not above making a little carfare money on the side. She is a levelheaded woman with no pretensions whatsoever. Paulette made me feel more at home in front of the camera than any woman I ever worked with before. There are marvelous slapstick bits in the movie, thanks to our director's experience with all the great silent screen comedians.

It is during this picture—or, rather, during a day off from it—when something happens to me that the Paramount publicity office refuses to believe. My mouth begins picking up radio programs on Sunset Boulevard. Aline Mosby, the United Press correspondent in Hollywood, finally writes it up and the story greatly impresses a lot of the newspapers in the East. My dentist explains that my new fillings and the acid condition of my saliva make a perfect crystal set, a temporary radio receiver in my mouth.

After finishing *Hazard* the last month in 1947—the last of

only three films in two years—I suddenly get busy in 1948.
I do *Abigail, Dear Heart*, later called *Song of Surrender*, with
Wanda Hendrix and Claude Rains, *Streets of Laredo* with
William Holden, William Bendix, and Mona Freeman, *The
Great Gatsby* with Alan Ladd, and a film about the Borgias,
A Mask for Lucretia, with Paulette Goddard again and John
Lund.

Also in 1948, we move into a new home in Brentwood, at
1438 Mandeville Canyon. Soon after, the columnist Harrison
Carroll runs a story about the actors in Mandeville Canyon
forming a police reserve unit. He has strayed far from the
facts; though the famous character actor Jimmy Gleason
really has formed a mounted patrol to police the canyon, he
is the only active member of the whole unit.

While we're living in Mandeville, Pat O'Brien is an usher
for the twelve o'clock Mass at St. Martin of Tours at Sunset
near Barrington. When he passes the collection box, he stops
at Jimmy Gleason's pew and, if he thinks Jimmy hasn't put
in enough, stands in the aisle and holds the box under Jimmy's
nose until Jimmy coughs up a sizable amount.

Lots of other actors lived in Mandeville at that time, I
discovered. Robert Mitchum was across the street and Richard Widmark, Dick Powell, Don DeFore, Hume Cronyn,
and Tyrone Power all lived within a few blocks. I wrote a
poem about Tyrone Power and me:

Chauvinists Are Heir Born

I hate Hollywood kiss and tell books and stories
As much as anyone
But this brief tale is just
Bizarre enough to be told
It was just after World War II
And there was a photography fad

Involving a camera that took three dimensional
Pictures—stereoscopic
There was a large camera club with Harold Lloyd as
    president
That had monthly contests for best stereoscopic
Picture. I had never hoped to win until I met
One day with Tyrone Power
We had both been in the Marine Corps
He as a pilot and me as an
Air controller

Ty knows a man with
A collection of airplanes he uses
To develop air inventions to improve the quality of flying
Since we are all interested in aerial photography
We hire two models to pose in the nude while
We fly over Los Angeles in a DC-3
We take off (so to speak) at 10:00 A.M. and
Orbit the Los Angeles area for two hours
We take lots of shots—the best is of Ty and a naked girl
In the cockpit with the Los Angeles skyline in the
background
The girls of course are the only naked bodies aloft
And being professionals seem not a bit perturbed
Our amateurism is betrayed in the pictures we take

There are beads of perspiration standing out
In 3-D for all to see
Only on Ty and me of course
The shots turn out perfectly
But I don't think there are any extant
Our wives burnt them all
Strangely enough Ty's wife is the only one that is mad
My wife is happy that I spent the day
With Tyrone Power

1 5 2

We didn't win the contest
But to this day I watch the sky
Over Los Angeles and speculate
"What's in those airplanes?"

As for Bob Mitchum, he's as offbeat now as ever. Last year, when at the Cinema Awards Banquet rehearsal at the Beverly Wilshire, I am going out and he is going in. I say, "Hello, Bob." "Hello, Mac," he says. "You've moved." We both keep on walking.

Abigail, Dear Heart has lots of other titles before the studio settles on *Song of Surrender. Now and Forever* was among them, I remember, but none of them can match the melodrama of the plot. Claude Rains plays an older man who took a young bride, Wanda Hendrix. I play a wealthy, very upper class neighbor who, when he isn't fox hunting, is playing records of Caruso in a cave near Claude's house, thereby luring Wanda to his side. It is the first movie for Eva Gabor, who plays a Polish countess. Dear Eva, who has never ridden a horse before, makes her entrance in the picture riding side-saddle on one of my horses. I step up to lift her off the horse and as I gallantly make this gesture, Eva gets stuck on the saddle. She is almost impaled by the horn. She is stuck like a clothespin on the side of the horse and it takes two of us to disengage her.

A group of us used to meet in my dressing room for cocktails at the end of each shooting day. We called ourselves "the New York Players." Among those included are Nicholas Joy, an English character actor, and Dan Tobin, an Irish-American actor who tells wonderful stories and later is in our croquet group.

One great story of Dan's I will always remember. When he was young and poor in Ireland, the favorite dish was "prates and pint." When you asked what that was, Dan would tell you each child would sit around the dining room table with one lone prates (or potato) on his plate. There was a large empty dish in the middle of the table. Each child would point (or pint) at what he imagined was in the empty center plate on the table—prates and pint. This is my favorite story. We all go through our lives pointing at imaginary dishes before us, at least all of us do who are Irish and certainly all of us do who are actors.

Nicholas Joy was a fabulously good English character actor who had an unquenchable thirst for liquor and ladies. Later, when I made my first trip to France in the fifties, Nick, who was seventy-odd at the time, was on the *Liberte* with me. He'd been having an affair in New York with a woman thirty years younger than himself.

Just before we leave New York, Nick promises me any perk the ship has to offer because he has crossed the Atlantic twenty-six times with the same captain and crew, running the entertainment for them. We have farewell parties in our cabins. Nick's is the happiest and most crowded. I move my group to his cabin, but when we leave the dock, I don't see him again until we cross the Atlantic and hit Southampton. His New York lady had worn him out.

Ten years later, I saw him in London in a play I'd done in New York in the interim, *Anniversary Waltz*. He is in his eighties, still hail and hearty, still tippling, still tasting the grape, if not the ladies.

A Mask for Lucretia, later called *Bride of Vengeance*, was originally slated as a vehicle for Ray Milland. The story is about Lucrezia Borgia (Paulette Goddard) and her brother Cesare. The characters were, of course, going to wear Renaissance costumes—costumes designed by Mitch Leisen, the director, who was originally a costume designer for Cecil B. De Mille. Ray refuses to do the part because he has heard that Leisen is going to personally fit each of the men for his codpiece. Ray sees this as a possible encroachment on his masculinity. Thus, the part of Cesare falls into my lap. Having worked with Mitch on *Dream Girl* and *Suddenly It's Spring*, I am not worried.

Unfortunately, Mitch is more interested in the costumes than he is in the story. Phyllis Seaton is the dialogue coach and she does almost as much directing as Mitch. (She later became the mayor of Beverly Hills for a time.) John Lund says the picture is more than a little campy, especially with Paulette's little-girl voice saying lines like, "Whither shalt thou go, my liege?" and the suggestion of brother-sister incest between us. It is also notable for an early appearance of Raymond Burr on the screen in tights.

As anyone in the business will tell you, it's feast or famine when you're an actor. Richard Maibaum, who had been getting a doctorate at Iowa when I was there, is now a producer at Paramount. In fact, he's the producer who hired me to do *Song of Surrender*. Now he casts me as Nick Carraway (supposedly the F. Scott Fitzgerald character) in *The Great Gatsby*. It is a great role. As of this writing, there have been three film versions of *The Great Gatsby*. The first in 1926 starred Warner Baxter as Gatsby and the third in 1974 starred Robert Redford. The version Dick wrote and produced is the best. It has a hell of a cast: Alan Ladd as Gatsby, Betty Field, Ruth Hussey, Howard Da Silva, Shelley Winters, Barry Sullivan, and lucky me. Nick Joy is in this one, too; he plays a tippling, slightly boozy guest at a Gatsby party.

Alan was not very tall, and I remember one long dolly shot of a scene I had with him. We are talking and walking around Gatsby's pool in West Egg. We rehearsed this long dolly shot before lunch and in the rehearsal I am looking down at Alan. I am six feet tall; he is about five three or four. After lunch, when we shoot the scene, I am looking up at him. They'd put planks around the pool for Alan to walk on to build him up, and they'd dug a trench for me. I remember, too, all of us were drinkers—Nicholas Joy, Barry Sullivan, Alan, and me. We only drank at the end of the day, though, and we never drank with the director, Elliott Nugent. This is out of respect for his weakness, liquor. He had a reputation as an alcoholic. Supposedly, they had trouble finding him in order to start the picture. He had gotten on a train and stayed on it for a few days until he drank himself sober.

I didn't realize at the time that there's something that reflects the whole alcoholic syndrome here—buying tickets on a train that goes nowhere, just back and forth—and I didn't realize I was digging the same grave as Elliott.

The story is often told in AA of the alcoholic who goes to his first AA meeting and hears his own terrible experiences with alcohol repeated time after time. It takes a month, at least, of hearing these stories before he realizes the AA speakers are talking about their own individual experiences, not his. For an alcoholic to take a drink is to invite a trip that goes on and on through the same landscape. The addict takes on the role of Sisyphus, endlessly pushing a heavy rock that keeps rolling back on him. He drinks and repeats the same errors until he dies or goes mad.

A week after I finish *Gatsby* in April 1949 there's an article in the *L.A. Examiner* that says I'm taking riding lessons with Bill Holden at Myers and Wills Stables in Burbank in preparation for *Streets of Laredo*, which will start filming on location in Santa Fe. This is not quite true, as we go to Gallup, New Mexico, and I'm taking lessons *from* Bill. Talk about doing your own stunts, Bill could do anything. He was very athletic and a good gymnast. I was into riding, playing tennis, and taking fencing and judo lessons, but Bill was a natural athlete. Anything physical in a movie, no matter how difficult, Bill would do. I remember him teaching me flying dismounts. I never did learn the fast mount from the rear when you fly over the horse's rump with your legs apart. He could do that.

That June, it is the worst of times, it is the best of times: the worst of times because of my drink, the best of times because my career is going well and Betty and I are at our happiest. It is our eighth wedding anniversary. Betty decides to have a surprise party. She knows I'll forget, but just to be sure, she has Bill Holden and John Arthur Kennedy take me to a bar. We arrive back at the house at Mandeville at 6:30. I say to Bill and Arthur, "What the hell are all those people doing in my driveway?" We go into the house and it's a party. The Lunds, the Prestons, Mitch Leisen, Betty Hutton, the Hodiaks: Everywhere I look there are people. Mitch sees my face: "Don't worry, Mac," he says. "Ruser's Jewelry Store is open late. You can still call."

Before the filming of *Streets of Laredo*, I was doing a lot of horseback riding anyway as my house in Mandeville Canyon was half a mile from the stables where Beverly Hills polo is played. I can remember riding a horse right onto our front lawn and giving Lynn, our first child, a short ride. When the Argentine polo team came to Los Angeles and played on that field, they let me ride their favorite new polo pony. It's an unbelievable feeling, riding an animal so well trained it responds to the slightest pressure from your legs or hands—a step above the horses and ponies we get when we play in Westerns.

Lynn is now almost three years old. Betty and I are enjoying our roles as parents, our becoming a family. It's hard on Betty—she's pregnant again and has to stay in bed so as not to miscarry. We still have Mrs. Moffet, our nurse, from 1438 North King's Road, and Lynn is spoiled by all of us. I'm always taking her for drives, just the two of us. Mrs. Heckscher often comes out to visit, bringing Betty's former nanny (or governess, as the Heckschers call her), Anna Bilcsik. My mother is living nearby in the Park La Brea area of Hollywood, and Aunt Evelyn is soon to come out and join her. Mother is frequently at our home with my brothers, Charlie and Gordy, and their wives. The twins live in the valley, half an hour from where we are in Mandeville Canyon. It's wonderful that the Careys are all so near each other.

My father had died during the war, and we seem to be going on as if he'd never been there. For me, everything is still happening too fast to assess or even to react. It is years before I realize how much I miss my father—years before I face that fact.

Our house is on two and a half acres. I spend a fortune putting in a copper sprinkler system. We end up with a really beautiful and immense backyard. I am adopted into the movie croquet crowd because of it. It is the Hollywood branch of the "Swope and Zanuck Long Island croquet group." Howard Hawks, the famous director of *To Have and Have Not* and *Red River*, among other movies, is pretty much the head man. The core group, which includes Howard's brother Bill, Kent Smith, Jean Negulesco, Louis Jourdan, Phil Reed, and George Sanders, plays at our house, Howard's, and Sam Goldwyn's.

I remember a game one Saturday afternoon at Howard's home off Sepulveda Boulevard. The croquet game we play is an elaborate combination of old-fashioned croquet, billiards, and golf, with bunkers and sand traps. The concentration of the players, the seriousness of the game, is something to behold. The young lady who has been living with Howard is so incensed at his preoccupation with the game that she decides to move out. She chooses to do so in the middle of that Saturday afternoon game, carrying her wardrobe and toiletries across the croquet court to her car herself in about five trips. Howard is so engrossed in the game, he never looks up.

Another Saturday, Bill Hawks and Speed Post, who worked with a famous business manager called Bo Roos, and Kent Smith were playing at my house. The game had started at 3:00 P.M.; at 8:00 P.M., we were still playing the same game. It was so dark we held a white handkerchief in front of the wickets and shone a flashlight on them to guide the players' aim.

Speed, a bridegroom of six months, is informed at that moment that his new bride is leaving him if he doesn't come home with her. He stays and finishes the game at 9:00 P.M. She leaves him.

I have to leave our regular croquet game to go off to New Mexico to do *Streets of Laredo*. Alfonso Bedoya, the Mexican actor who'd made such a hit in *The Treasure of Sierra Madre* as a bandit, is with us in the cast. One day he comes up to Ray Lennahan, our marvelous Technicolor expert cameraman, and the director and says, "*Por favor*. Do the scene over. *Por favor*. This time be sure and get my smile." (He has marvelous white teeth.)

There were a lot of riotous nights on that location in Gallup, including the one when Alfonso's visiting blonde chased him down the hall and broke a bottle of booze on his behind. When we had the wrap party at the Paramount commissary, the director, who was at odds with Paramount, went over and peed on the cake.

I don't believe he worked at Paramount again.

Paul Clemens, a friend of Bill Holden's and a very good painter, famous for his Renoiresque nudes, came up to Gallup while we were on location. He painted several scenes of the shooting up there. Like a fool, I didn't try to buy any of them. Paul and Mona Freeman's husband, Pat Nerney, later wrote a book that was a bestseller in the movie colony. This was after they were both divorced. The book is called *The Little Black Book*. As I remember, it contained a list of all the most appetizing girls in town.

A month after we got back from Gallup, John Arthur Kennedy, Bill Holden, and I spent an afternoon together swimming up at Paradise Cove, past Malibu. Bill and I are full of ourselves, talking about *Streets of Laredo*. He doesn't think the picture is any good. I disagree. He hates his part because he's playing another white-hat hero. I have the best part, that of the villain—I get to shoot Bill Bendix under the table in a card game—and I play my character as the archetypal smiling villain. That's one sure way to successfully play the heavy, unflappable and smiling. Johnny Kennedy, who could act rings around both of us but who hadn't had a picture for a month or so and had none in sight, got tired of listening to Bill and me argue about the worth of the picture and said, "To hell with this town! Take me home. I'm going back to New York."

We take him home. He packs up and goes back to New York to be featured in Arthur Miller's prizewinning play, *Death of a Salesman*. He plays Biff, for which he receives a Tony.

The week before, we'd been at a party at Johnny Kennedy's house. I had left early and missed all the action. After I went home, Johnny said to Burl Ives, the famous folk singer, "I don't think Woody Guthrie is a better folk singer than you are." Burl, who was a very big man, gets up and tries to hit Johnny. It looks like some furniture is going to be broken. Bill Holden tells me he went to his car to get his gun just to be sure there's peace, but by the time he got back, someone has put Burl's guitar and several drinks between the two of them. It was a really Irish evening in every way. Sarah Allgood of the Abbey Players was there and so was Clancy Cooper.

Bill was a man's man as well as a lady's man, and there was no pretense there. I remember him asking me, "Do you fuck?" I wasn't used to such blunt honesty and I said, "Not particularly." The impression I gave was deliberately misleading; it was tantamount to saying I never was unfaithful to my wife—which was a lie—but in a way, I wasn't lying when I told him I didn't fuck particularly. I never really had any affairs; it was the rare one-night stand that I indulged in, and then I usually drank too much to perform properly. Even those episodes I blanked out of my mind. "Not particularly" is a funny answer to Bill's question in too many ways.

1 6 0

These are weasel words, indeed. It may be safer to sleep with the queen's maid than it is to sleep with the queen, but it's just as indiscreet and twice as damaging to your real-life partner's ego.

Bill might have slept around a lot, but he was at least honest about it. I wasn't even honest about it to myself. One thing that we did share was our alcoholic athleticism. A terrible part of male bonding is the toleration of excessive drinking: "Give me one for the road" or "Oh, well. He just had too much to drink" or "He didn't know what he was doing" or "Give him something for his hangover" or "He just can't hold his liquor." To this enlightened day, excessive drinking is still tolerated and swept under the rug.

Drinking buddies can express concern, however. While we were all at Paramount, each of us thought the other drank too much. Alan Ladd would pour a tumbler half full of whiskey and throw it down right after he finished work. I thought Bill Holden drank too much because he said he kept drinking as much as he could and staying up as late as he could so he'd stop looking like a juvenile. Bill told someone who told me that Bill thought I drank too much. If only one of us had listened to somebody.

It's amazing I can remember what Bill and I drank when we did *Streets of Laredo*, but I do: six martinis before dinner. But the weather in New Mexico was very dry and, remember, we didn't drink during the day. We always got up early and rode a lot to sweat it out. There comes a time, however, when you can't sweat it out. That time came for Bill. Drinking did him in, and even though we weren't close at the last, he was one of a kind and I miss him, as does everyone who ever knew him. His death scared me, and I hurt for him and for Ardis, his wife (actress Brenda Marshall). Even though they were no longer together, I knew how much she cared for him. As for my drinking, I slowed up for a while, but not for long: another powerful warning I managed to ignore.

Streets of Laredo, we hear, gets Paramount out of the red and we all get great reviews, especially my smiling villain. A month or two after the picture is released and is an obvious hit, I suddenly get a summons from Henry Ginsberg, the then-head of the studio. He calls me into his office at Paramount and tells me he just wants to be sure I know I have nothing to do with the success of the picture. I guess this is to forestall my asking for more money. It remains one of the most bizarre conversations I ever had in the picture business, but I'm told this was common practice at MGM, Columbia, and Warner Brothers as well, just to keep "the troops"—the actors—in line. I remember being on the Screen Actors Guild board years later when James Garner came in to enlist SAG's help in getting him out of his old contract. He was still getting $500 a week from Warner after starring in the biggest hit series for five years, "Maverick."

In August 1949, I went on loan-out to Universal Pictures to star in *Comanche Territory* (originally called *Bowie Story*) opposite Maureen O'Hara. *Comanche Territory* is about Jim Bowie and his creation of the Bowie knife. I protect Maureen from the bad guys and the Indians. That's about the whole plot. We shot the picture in Sedona, Arizona. I played Jim Bowie, the lead, and, the plot being what it was, his legendary knife played a costarring role in the picture.

One day, I go to the rectory of the local Catholic church, which is perched precariously on the ridge of a hill that had been strip-mined for copper. A Mexican priest answers the door. He sees nothing but my knife—I am in my character's costume—and he doesn't wait to hear my question about what time Sunday Masses are. He doesn't even bother to close the door. He just runs through the house and out the back.

Maureen O'Hara is a wonderful woman to work with. She's pretty much the tomboy type, very rough and tumble with her leading men, kind of a *Taming of the Shrew* Kate, like the women she plays in all her pictures. I liked her. In fact, I liked all my leading ladies, even those I didn't see eye to eye with (in other words, those who preferred not to share at least a two-shot with me). I long ago saw that it's a waste of time to dislike people, so why start with leading ladies? As Robert Bly tells us, the Indians used to invite even the coyotes to their ceremonies. They figured it was better to have your enemies in full view than out of sight. That way you can see what they're doing. This is a pretty good rule of thumb for living—and you haven't lived until you've had a leading lady.

On the other hand, you can't really live your own life if you have a leading lady (in the sexual sense, I mean). With the gossip and publicity, you might as well kiss any family life you have good-bye. It can also lead to problems while you're making a movie, especially if things go wrong between you. So however tempted I've been—and I have been tempted—I adhere to the dictum, "Never dip your pen in the company ink."

In the cast of *Comanche Territory* is one of the original flower people, the daddy of them all, Will Geer. Will, a former member of the Group Theatre, was one of America's best character actors. He is playing a plainsman, a man of the people, and he lives the part on location. He doesn't sleep with the rest of the cast of the movie company. When he isn't acting before the camera, he spends all his time down at the river with the hobos. Later, Will and his wife Ellen Geer start a sort of stock company in Topanga Canyon, a rustic canyon between Santa Monica and Malibu. Will has since passed away, but his theater is still running.

I no sooner get home from this location in Sedona than Paramount casts me in *Copper Canyon* as the villain vis-à-vis Hedy Lamarr and Ray Milland. The director is John Farrow, who directed me in *Wake Island*.

I remember the Farrows most for the times we spent together in later years when we were neighbors in Beverly Hills and our children all went to the Good Shepherd's Catholic school. One Christmas we were all at the Farrow house— the Careys, the Brinkmans (she is Jeanne Crain), and the Frawleys (Pat, the husband, owns the Schick Addiction Recovery system). The kids were putting on a Christmas play using the crèche in the inner courtyard of the Farrow's California Spanish-style home. It starts to rain. Little Mac—our fifth child—is playing Joseph, and when the rain stops, Joseph and the baby Jesus, which was a doll, are missing. Someone finds the two of them in the cloakroom. Mac says he didn't want the baby Jesus to get wet—one of the family legends that is retold often.

For location on *Copper Canyon*, we go right back to Sedona. Hedy Lamarr, I find, is still extraordinarily beautiful but she is also bizarre. She has an army cot on the set on which she lies resting until the assistant director calls the actors in for the shot. As soon as John Farrow says "Cut," she goes back to the cot and lies down.

There's a famous story they tell about Hedy. She was married to John Loder at the time. A Hollywood tour bus passes her house as John is out front mowing the lawn. One of the tourists says, "What the hell is he doing outside?" Hedy, by the way, doesn't remember that I sang German songs with her in New York years before at Sonny Whitney's house. She was always distant and cool, very much a European star.

Ray Milland is not as remote but is also somewhat reserved. The only time he ever speaks to me is years later when I am on the SAG board and he arrives one night to get the union's dispensation to pay the actors less in a film he is producing. Ray had become completely bald. He looks at me and remarks, "I see some of us still have their hair."

At the end of 1949, I make another picture for Paramount, *The Lawless*, directed by Joseph Losey, who, among other films, also directed *The Boy With Green Hair*, *The Servant*, *King and Country*, *The Go-Between*, *Don Giovanni*, and *Accident*. I'm happy to say I am the leading man in two of his pictures. Most of *The Lawless* is shot in Marysville, California. Gail Russell is the girl. She is a beautiful but tragic figure, destined to die alone not many years later, an empty bottle of vodka by her side. However, when we are making the picture, she is married to Guy Madison, who later is famous as TV's "Wild Bill Hickock."

During the filming, I have a room in the hotel on the same floor as Gail and I remember the martinis coming up there for her before breakfast. I know because the first day a tray is delivered to me by mistake. But in the evenings, I am doing my share of drinking, too. The Bartender's Ball, which not only I but most of the crew attended, is being held next to the hotel. It goes on twenty-four hours a day for three days. All drinks are a dime. Three days of continuous dancing, three days of continuous drinking. There are bands around the clock. Is it just coincidental that one of our producers is also an active alcoholic?

The Lawless is a picture I can identify with. It is about a newspaper editor—me—who comes to the defense of a Mexican boy's civil rights. The boy has been accused of killing someone and he's about to be railroaded into jail, if not lynched. Because I defend him, my presses are smashed and my offices at the paper trashed and burned, just like my Uncle John's were in Rock Rapids, Iowa, by the Ku Klux Klan. Soon after we finish filming, Joe Losey, an American, leaves for England, and he lives, directs, and produces in London for the rest of his life. He leaves because he's been blacklisted through the madness of the House Un-American Activities Committee—HUAC.

It is the McCarthy era. Many people lose their jobs during this insane, confused time. Many are falsely charged with being Communists, for that matter. Jane Wyatt, the actress who is most famous for her role in the picture *Lost Horizons* (1937) and on the television series "Father Knows Best," in which she played the mother, opposite Robert Young, tells me how she had been blacklisted as a Communist on charges that were never brought out into the open. When she and Monsignor Devlin, who was the licensed censor for the Legion of Decency (which censored films about that time), challenged the members of HUAC, Jane and the Monsignor were shown a thick book that supposedly contained evidence against them, but they weren't allowed to look in it. Nobody ever did see the evidence. Monsignor Devlin attested to the fact that Jane was a Catholic and a regular communicant, that she went to Mass daily. One of the congressmen said, "Oh, all these people [the Communists] lie all the time!"

This is the sort of witch-hunt many of us allowed to happen. During this period, Bill Holden helped me get on the board of the Screen Actors Guild, and I'm ashamed that I and the other board members did nothing to protect our fellow actors' civil and human rights. The whole United States was caught up in a sort of mass hysteria engineered by Senator Joseph McCarthy and J. Edgar Hoover, then head of the FBI. A lot of innocent people were so stigmatized that they could no longer work in the United States of America. Actors like Larry Parks, Lionel Stander, Sam Wanamaker, Alexander Knox and writers and directors—their careers were snuffed out. The only way I can explain my inaction is that I was living such a schizoid life—I was so fragmented and so self-involved—that I wasn't able to come to the defense of my colleagues and attack the perverters of truth. I wasn't even conscious that I'd made a choice, the choice of inaction. In view of the liberal background I came from, I was obviously not tending the store, I was out to lunch. I hope we've all learned never to let anything like this happen again.

While these very real events were happening, I was loaned out to Universal again to do *East of Java* (later released as *South Sea Sinner*), a movie that is about as far from reality as possible. There is not much of a story, just an updated *Rain*, the old Jeanne Eagles vehicle. Shelley Winters plays a hooker with a heart of gold. I play an American beachcomber somewhere in the tropics. A quote from Louella Parsons's radio show on Sunday, November 13, 1949, while we're making the picture, reveals something about the lies, paranoia, and false patriotism of the McCarthy era:

> Motion picture fans and Communists are trying to use your fan clubs to spread poison to the young people in the country. Macdonald Carey was the first to notice it and has written the President of his Italian fan club to refuse membership to any Communists. Good for you Mac!

This was totally false. I didn't have an Italian fan club and I never said any of this.

Here is a goofy quote I give about Shelley Winters that appears in the *Daily Compass* on April 4, 1950: "In addition to all her other attributes, Shelley has 'primal appeal,' says Carey. 'Before we finished the movie, we took some torchy stills,' Mac recalls. 'Shelley was wonderful about it. After four hours of posing, she said, "Now let's take some with me in your position." ' "

Shelley not only said this, but in two-shots during the filming she started to upstage me by maneuvering to have her face more fully in the camera than mine. The simplest response to that was to get as far downstage from her as possible, with my back almost to the camera so that they'd have to come around to the other side to cover the scene completely. We ended up with two over-the-shoulder shots so that both of us were featured equally anyway. I'm one of the few names missing from Shelley's list of beaux in her amusing best-selling autobiographies.

When we're shooting *South Sea Sinner*, Shelley has no time for me or anyone in the cast. She is always on the phone with her agent or with Bill Goetz, the then-head of Universal. By this time, she has already made a big hit in *A Double Life* with Ronald Colman and she's been up for an Oscar, so she's hot. I start the picture on the basis of getting first star billing. A month after we finish, Paramount asks me to give the top billing to Shelley. She and Universal are pressing Paramount to do this. I say okay, it's all right with me; I don't think much of the picture.

I also think Paramount wants it that way because Shelley is coming to work for them and director George Stevens in a really important picture. Theodore Dreiser's novel, *An American Tragedy*, will be a film, *A Place in the Sun*, with Elizabeth Taylor and Montgomery Clift. Shelley will play the other key role.

When she appears on the Paramount lot for *A Place in the Sun*, Paramount gives her a dressing room next to mine. It is just a month or so since we'd made *South Sea Sinner* together and it is the end of the day. Shelley passes me and doesn't even nod. I go after her and physically stop her. She looks blankly at me. "It's me," I say, "Mac Carey. We just worked together." "Sorry," she says, "this is an engrossing part. I was preparing."

She prepared well. She won an Oscar.

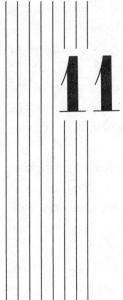

11

During the shooting of *South Sea Sinner*, Lisa, our second child, was born on July 12, 1949. Betty had lost a child after Lynn through a miscarriage. Because we knew she had trouble carrying a baby to full term, this was not unexpected but it saddened us nonetheless. As is characteristic for us, we do not dwell on it. We just move on.

For Lisa, as she had for Lynn, Betty stays in bed almost the whole nine months. I promise her a mink coat this time as a small reward for her sacrifice. Some of the fan magazine stories come up with lines that must have irritated, if not angered, Betty as well as the reader. Here is a quote from *Movieland* for January 1950: "And she wanted that mink coat now—while she was young and gay and full of love and life. She quavered a few of these thoughts to Mac and he smiled at her. 'You mean I can still have it?' With the mink coat in the making, Betty thriftily suppresses a wistful desire to have more than two in help. Always pleased when she finds a special on pork chops, or a good buy in the market, she knows she'll manage with the help she has."

The truth is, a mink coat is the last thing on my mind or Betty's. We are elated with Lisa's birth, as we are with the birth of all our children. For me, it is the realization of the scenario I had dreamed and is more fulfilling than any of the movies I do. But the movies, thank God, continue; with our growing family, I need them.

Work is good in and of itself. I'd always felt too much of my time at the University of Iowa had been involved in studying the arts of stage design and stage lighting along with classes in the theory of drama and directing. They were not completely wasted, but the hours would have been better spent just acting. After being denied the chance to act in high school and while a freshman at Wisconsin, I was thirsty even then for more actual work on the stage in front of an audience. I am now, of course, in front of a camera.

When I am home, I am a loving father. I read to the children, I play with them, I take them to church. But often I'm away on location—as I will be for the next sixteen years. I don't spend as much time working out my role as a father as I do working on a part, simply because I'm not there enough to do so. I think I spend more time posing for magazine and newspaper layouts on my splendid family life than I do having a splendid family life.

For the most part, Betty and I never live beyond our income. I have a business manager and my twin brothers take care of any cash I invest. Gordon is a stockbroker and Charles an insurance agent. He is to soon inherit the Northwestern Mutual Agency for Los Angeles. Quite a plum. Charlie particularly snares most of my investment money, which goes into insurance policies. He, I believe, insured almost everyone in our poker group. I remember that Frank Lovejoy, who was in *South Sea Sinner* with me and who had bought insurance from Charlie, was approached by my brother a month before Frank died and was reminded again that he had let his policy lapse. He kept forgetting to pay it; $200,000 went out the window.

In 1950, I did another picture for Universal called *Mystery Submarine* and it was a hokey melodrama. I played an FBI agent disguised as a doctor. The girl in the picture was a Swedish actress named Marta Toren, who had dark brown hair and the most beautiful eyes I have ever seen with the possible exception of Elizabeth Taylor's. We made the entire movie in a real submarine in San Diego, a claustrophobic four weeks.

I then do a picture back out in the open in Sonora, California, *The Great Missouri Raid*. This time my costar is Wendell Corey, the actor some people always confuse me with, people who don't know us. Appropriately enough, Wendell and I will play brothers, the James brothers.

Wendell plays Frank and I play Jesse. The whole company drinks together every night, and at the end of the first week, the producer says, "I made a big mistake. Wendell should be playing Jesse and you should be playing Frank." Since the picture is about Jesse in the main, this is not the highest of compliments. Just another example of the Corey/Carey confusion. A couple of years later, when I am at Columbia for some charity bash, Harry Cohn comes over to my table while someone is performing, kneels down beside me, and says, "I want to apologize to you. I meant to cast you, not Wendell Corey, in my new picture, *No Sad Songs for Me*. The part he's talking about is the lead opposite Margaret Sullavan. Disappointed, I figure now that Cohn knows who I am, he will soon offer me another lead. But that was not only the first, it was also the last contact I ever had with Harry Cohn.

Anne Revere is also in *The Great Missouri Raid*. She is one of the unfortunate actors who is to be blacklisted without cause. Ward Bond, who plays the representative of the establishment who is always pursuing the James brothers in the picture, in real life is such a rabid anti-Communist that he almost froths at the mouth when he sees red.

At the end of April 1950, a bunch of us, including Tony Curtis, Jan Clayton, and Scott Brady, are sent to Salt Lake City on a publicity junket for the opening there of *Comanche Territory*. There is a parade downtown. The Harlem Globetrotters are also in the city, and who do I see in the crowd but an old friend from Sioux City, Iowa—Lester Wilkinson, who is now playing with the Globetrotters. He was the black guy I helped get into the Civic Society in Central High, my high school fraternity—which up to then had been lily white. We have time only for a brief hello.

Later in the 1950s I go to MGM to do a musical comedy called *Excuse My Dust* with Red Skelton and Sally Forrest. I get to do a lot of barbershop singing and to drive some antique cars. It's fun, but that's about it. I also do a Western with Alexis Smith called *Cave of Outlaws*. We shoot it inside the beautiful Carlsbad Caverns of New Mexico. In the picture with us are Victor Jory, Edgar Buchanan, and, in his first important screen role, Hugh O'Brien, who later becomes famous on television as Wyatt Earp.

I'm not just doing movies anymore, however. Television is taking off, and I'm beginning to do television shows (or video shows, as they are called) as well. Live television is for me, as for most actors, the nearest thing to theater outside of theater. It is literally *live*—not taped, not filmed; we just have one shot at a performance. This makes it incredibly exciting. The pay is phenomenally good, as well, usually five grand a crack and usually including a free trip to New York with expenses paid and time to catch up on the New York theater. The following is an excerpt from an interview in the *Brooklyn Eagle* on April 12, 1950:

> Carey thinks that a tie-up between Hollywood and television (note the small "t") will be coming along soon. As

a board member of the Screen Actors Guild, he is watching developments closely. As a family man, he hopes that the day when everybody will have their own television set is coming soon. The Careys have one set in their bedroom for the benefit of Mrs. Carey.

At the time, some people are thinking television is just a fad and has no future, but it turns out to be the future—and though I don't know it yet, it is certainly my future.

In 1951, we moved from Mandeville Canyon to Beverly Hills to a bigger house. Our third child, Steve Carey, was born on March 30 of that year, the first son in what was predominantly a female household. (Betty's mother is often there; there's the nurse, Mrs. Moffet; and Anna Bilcsik, Betty's former governess, is spending more and more time with us.) When we move, we don't have a bassinet for Steve as he is that recent an arrival, so we move in with Steve in a dresser drawer. Our new address is 620 North Cañon, and it is to be the happiest house we have. There's a swimming pool this time and room for a playground for the kids. There is an awful lot of action there. It is also the first home for our next three arrivals: Theresa, born July 12, 1952; Mac, who arrives on April 22, 1954; and Paul, who comes into our lives on February 7, 1956.

The Edgar Bergens live next door. Wendell Corey, Rita Hayworth, and Richard Whorf (a well-known theater actor with the Lunts) live across the street, as does Dr. Jessie Marmorston, a famous endocrinologist, and her producer-husband, Larry Weingarten, a nephew of Louis B. Mayer. During Betty's long sieges with her pregnancies, Jesse is very helpful with medical and moral support.

Also across the street are other friends, the Bob Andersons. Bob is a Beverly Hills real estate type. His family had owned and run the Beverly Hills Hotel, as well as the first three blocks at the western end of Beverly Hills, south of

Santa Monica Boulevard. In that area was the Encore Room, a nightclub and bar within easy walking and drinking distance from our new house.

The bartender at the Encore Room was Bill Howard, who had previously been an agent in the Louis Shurr Agency, which represents me. Bill was the son of Dorothy Lamour. The Encore Room was my favorite bar in Beverly Hills. There were nightclub acts in the back room, including, for her first West Coast appearances, Joan Rivers. Lots of singers and comedians broke in their acts there. Lots of people in the industry hung out there. For me, as I said, it was a short ride home. Miraculously, I always made it home, although Bill Howard told me one Sunday, "Boy, were you lucky last night! You made an illegal U-turn in front of the store [the Encore] and turned up Santa Monica and went up Beverly. They'd been waiting for you and they screamed forth in pursuit on Cañon, their lights flashing."

At the time, I am oblivious to all this as well as to the implicit warning in it. Ten years later, I will not be so lucky.

In July 1951, after Steve is born, Betty and I took our first vacation, our first real honeymoon. I had vowed that if I ever got the chance to keep acting, I'd never stop for a vacation. My attitude about taking time off is perhaps explained by this comment I made on July 10 of that year in the New Orleans *Port-of-Spain Gazette*:

> The first sixteen months after the war I wasn't placed in a single movie. . . . Oh, it happened to a bunch of us who'd been in Hollywood before. We were all kept on the payroll and it was okay money and all that. But the inactivity, the just waiting around for something to happen to your career, does something to a guy. Perhaps that's why there's an occasional alcoholic and neurotic among actors.

It strikes me as strange that I never realized I was just another of those alcoholic and neurotic actors. My self-absorption was complete, however. A lot of it must have been transferred to Betty. It's no wonder she went her own way in a sense. Despite all our babies, we kept estranging ourselves from each other. When I wasn't working or drinking, I was immersed in lessons from the day I came back to Hollywood after the war—fencing, singing, tap, ballet, judo, karate, tennis. The lessons never stopped. It wasn't until I stopped drinking, though, that the learning really began.

Looking back over scrapbooks can be very painful. The hypocritical state I'd been living in is transparent from the feature stories about me, where I'm named "Father of the Year," "Big Brother of the Year," "Head of National Bible Week," "Head of National Sunday School," and all the while I'm in a constant state of denial. The life I'm living is really that of "Drunk of the Year."

I think the thing that helped me keep myself deluded about my drinking was how busy I constantly was. How could I do all these things and have a drinking problem? I reasoned. It never occurred to me that perhaps keeping busy was, like my drinking, a way of avoiding having the time to look at myself and get to know myself. It was also a way of avoiding confronting the problems I had with Betty. This insight only came to me with time and sobriety. At thirty-eight, I wasn't stopping to analyze anything. My work was my obsession and took most of my attention. In my scenario of being a working actor, a husband, and a father, I never stopped to think that there was more of myself that Betty wanted me to share and more of my career that she, as an actress, might have expected me to share with her.

Betty had been an actress when I met her, but when I married her, I began to think of her as my wife and as the future mother of our children. Now that we had three children, I never questioned whether there was anything more she wanted. I assumed, I suppose, that being the outspoken and aggressive young woman I married, she would tell me if there were. But it's hard to hit a moving target, and perhaps I never slowed down enough for her to tell me what was on her mind.

In October 1951, I was off again. I led a contingent of Hollywood stars and producers, and a representative to Iowa as part of a national campaign to resuscitate the movie industry, whose gate had fallen, partly because of the popularity of television and partly from increased competition from foreign films. The campaign, called "Movietime USA," has been launched by the Motion Picture Association. Groups like ours are sent from Hollywood to our home states to drum up business. My first speech at the Des Moines Country Club is pretty much the same as my message throughout the state of Iowa, in LeMars, Ida Grove, Newton, and other towns and cities: "You are the people who make the movies. It's up to you to tell us in the movie industry what you want. We will give it to you." Of course, this is the same message the TV industry is trying to send to people right now; the medium changes slightly, but never the message. It is quite an exhausting week. We do it all by car—I was with a reporter and a driver—about six towns a day.

Also in 1951, I do the first of three pictures at Twentieth Century–Fox for producer Dick Sale, who always works with his wife, Mary Anita Loos, the daughter of Anita Loos of *Gentlemen Prefer Blondes* fame. The first picture I do for Dick is a comedy called *Let's Make It Legal*, by F. Hugh Herbert and I. A. L. Diamond. Claudette Colbert plays my wife and Robert Wagner (called R. J.), in his first picture, plays my son. It's a pretty fair comedy and they still play it for TV reruns. (Don Rickles used to say he uses my reruns for a night-light.)

Zachary Scott is the other man in the picture, and Marilyn

Monroe is in it, too. She has just a few lines and she's late being made up on this particular day. I remember because we're shooting at Hillcrest Country Club across the street from Twentieth Century–Fox and I go back to my dressing room at ten o'clock to get something and stop by makeup for a touch-up. A beat-up Jeep is driving me over and back. Well, there is Marilyn being made up and a uniformed chauffeur comes in and says, "Your car is waiting, Miss Monroe." He walks out with her and takes her in the limo across the street to Hillcrest; I get in my beat-up Jeep and go back.

She has one speaking scene, and that's with me. I am Hugh; Marilyn is Joyce. Victor MacFarland played by Zachary, is courting Claudette, my divorced wife, whom I'm trying to win back. This is the scene in its entirety:

JOYCE

Huey!

HUGH

Hello, baby. How's it going?

JOYCE

Doll, you said you were going to do something about it.

HUGH

About what?

JOYCE

That Victor MacFarland! My motor's been racing since I first laid eyes on him.

HUGH

I think I can arrange for you to meet him—through a mutual friend.

1 7 7

JOYCE

Who is that woman with him? She doesn't give anybody else
a chance.

HUGH

I'll see that you meet her, too.

(DISSOLVE AS THEY WALK AWAY)

Marilyn, even then, was always late getting on the set,
usually by an hour and a half. Her final hour-and-a-half-late
arrival on this picture comes when there is a ballroom scene
in which I'm supposed to be dancing with her. She keeps the
director, Dick Sale, and Claudette, Zachary, R. J., and me
and a ballroom full of extras waiting the customary hour and
a half. Dick bawls her out. Marilyn says she'll have Dick
fired, that she's going to get on the telephone and call a higher-
up at Fox. Dick says, "Go ahead and call, but first apologize
to the company." She does—apologize, that is. She never
makes the call.

Marilyn did work again for Dick Sale, though. Only two
years later, the fabulous part of her career began. In one
year, she was in *Gentleman Prefer Blondes*, which Dick directed, and *How to Marry a Millionaire*. None of us realized
how quickly she would go to the top and how just as quickly
meet her death. Even though we worked together, her career
is something I was never a part of. To most of us in the cast,
she was a complete stranger, a pretty young woman who had
a few lines and who knew the right people.

When *Let's Make It Legal* is released, I do another junket,
this one in New England. There are four of us in the tour:
R. J. Wagner, Joyce Mackenzie (an actress who was in the
picture), Larry Carr (a jazz pianist), and me. We do a thirty-
minute skit with singing and dancing. How wonderful it was
when we did it, I don't know, but one of the numbers we

used was "The Three Bs," the three Bs being Bach, barrel-house, and boogie-woogie. When we appeared in Boston, we stayed, of course, at the Ritz, where all the theater people stay with pre-Broadway tryouts, and Cheryl Crawford was there trying out *Paint Your Wagon*. Seeing her starts the old itch in me to get back in the theater again.

Before I go back to Hollywood, I stop in New York and do one of the first big live TV shows for charity, "Lifeline." Produced for NBC by Herbert Swope, Jr. (who is married to Maggie Hayes, one of the eight girls I kissed for publicity my first week at Paramount), it is about blood banks. I emcee and narrate, reading the whole thing off one long sheet of paper—the first time I ever used something like a cue card, but not the last.

Nineteen fifty-two is a busy year for me. I begin it by doing a movie at Twentieth again for Dick Sale, wherein I play opposite Anne Baxter. It's called *My Wife's Best Friend* which the French, who have a fondness for the picture, call *Seules Les Femmes Savent Mentir*, the literal translation of which is "only women know how to lie," a reflection of male chauvinism at its worst. Like *Let's Make It Legal*, *My Wife's Best Friend* and the next movie I do almost immediately for Dick, *Meet Me After the Show*, in which I star opposite Betty Grable and in which Marilyn Monroe has another brief part, are screwball comedies with the slightest of plots: *Legal* is about a wife divorcing her husband because of misunderstanding; *Meet Me After the Show* is about a wife threatening to divorce her husband for his inattention; and *My Wife's Best Friend* is pretty much the same.

Anne Baxter, who was Frank Lloyd Wright's granddaughter, was a bright and precocious actress who started working professionally when she was sixteen. Our friendship, through Betty, gave us an easy familiarity that helped us assume the roles of man and wife. Working with Anne was very comfortable. Betty Grable was easy to work with, too. Although

I had never met her before we started shooting, it's as though we've done many films together. She is a typical trouper and has a lively sense of fun.

Betty has the reputation of being very amorous. I never see signs of her fooling around, but Dan Dailey, who purportedly had an affair with her, used to say whenever Betty's name came up, "See this bump on my head? That's from Harry James's trumpet." We never know, of course, whether these things really happen or not.

Because I sing in *Meet Me After the Show*, I'm quickly signed for another musical, *Excuse My Dust*, at MGM with Red Skelton. I play the comic villain to Red's comic hero. The highlight of the picture for me is a barbershop quartet number I do, and outside of a race with vintage automobiles, the picture's best moment is a smashing dance number by Sally Forrest. I'm doing the picture because it's work.

Still in 1952, I did a melodramatic suspense picture, *Count the Hours*, opposite Teresa Wright. Jack Elam was also in it and it started his prosperous career in movies as a heavy. It was one of the first pictures directed by Don Siegel, who later married actress Viveca Lindfors and directed, among other films, the classic *Invasion of the Body Snatchers* and *Dirty Harry*.

We do *Count the Hours*—Teresa and I, at least—sort of on spec. I sign on for $10,000 down and a hefty percentage of the profits. I think Teresa had the same deal. Making the picture is bizarre. The first day of shooting in the Van Nuys courthouse, the producer, Ben Bogeaus, keeps coming up to people and asking, "Don't you think the coffee is good?" It's too bad more attention wasn't being paid to the script.

When the picture wraps, Ben has obviously run out of the shoestrings it has been made on, and the party is held on an empty stage at General Service Studios. Ignoring what I had learned from Fred MacMurray and from my own experience, I am the only actor who shows up. The food and drink consist of a card table holding a bottle of gin, a bottle of bourbon, a bottle of scotch, half a dozen bottles of soda, and a package of potato chips. There is also a stack of paper cups. Ben, who's been walking around on location asking everybody if they didn't think the coffee was good, stands up on two apple boxes and addresses all the grips and electricians. They haven't been paid for two weeks. He says, "I'm going to have to ask you to give me fifteen days to get your salaries." That is the start of his speech. There is so much shuffling and mumbling going on, I don't wait to hear the rest. There is danger in the air, and I am, in a sense, a part-producer because of my percentage.

I leave the party sure of two things, that I'll never get the balance of my salary and that my percentage will never be paid off. But two weeks later, my agent with the Shurr office, Al Melnick, calls me in to ask me what I'd take for my percentage; Siegel, it seems, has a deal to sell the picture and pay everybody off. I sell him my percentage for $30,000. I think Teresa does the same. Well, Ben gets $4 or $5 million for the picture and finances at least fourteen movies out of that. In the movie business, though, it's sometimes better to take the money and run. You never know.

Although I have lived in Hollywood almost ten years by this time—excluding the three years I spent in the Marines —and there are many people I'm friendly with, my closest friendships are with Paul Caruso and Dick Sale. The friendship between Paul and me was forged in the Marine Corps, a bonding that was, in a sense, a return to childhood. When I was a boy, my best friend, Bill Kass, and I had the experience of seeing things that were new to us at the same time; we shared the same reflexes and responses. Being in the Marine Corps with Paul was the next best thing. After three years together in the corps, we continued this friendship in civilian life. He keeps me on level ground. Just looking at Paul reminds me that I was once "Captain of the Head."

1 8 1

Outside of Dick Sale, most of the people in the movies I work in fade in and out of my life as I fade in and out of theirs. Nobody stays in one place long enough, particularly me. After the children are born, whatever time I have, I spend with the family. This encompasses the part that is fun, and which my children all remember with joy—the times when I'm not away on location and we take our Saturday or Sunday trips to the beach or go fishing on the pier at Paradise Cove, and the not-so-fun part, when I read to them after dinner or supervise their nightly prayers.

Another reason it's hard to stay in touch with people is the place we're living—Hollywood. Hollywood is actually a state of mind that covers Los Angeles, Beverly Hills, the Hollywoods proper (north and west), Brentwood, Bel Air, West Los Angeles, Santa Monica, Pacific Palisades, Malibu, and the San Fernando Valley. It's a big area. Most people who live in Beverly Hills or Brentwood don't drive out on the spur of the moment to the valley to visit someone. There are casual friends I see when I play poker, croquet, or tennis, but when I work (and I'm working all the time), there's no room for a frantic social life—especially when I'm in a movie or a series and I have to be there at six or seven in the morning and get home at seven or later at night.

Although I worked with Alan Ladd, Roz Russell, Paulette Goddard, Maureen O'Hara, Red Skelton, Alexis Smith, Claudette Colbert, and Betty Grable, I never connected with any of them except professionally. You play scenes with actors for one movie or even two or three and rarely touch their lives personally, nor, most times, do they touch yours. Bill Holden was a friend, as was Bob Preston, and Lloyd Bridges and Howard Duff were tennis friends—but only for short spurts. The business does that to you. Hugh O'Brien bought a Chevy convertible from me and we had the same business manager, but that's all. Anne Baxter and Teresa Wright I saw socially for a while, Anne mostly because Betty

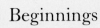

Mother and Dad

Mother and me

Me, one year old

Me at three

Growing Up

At the lake, 1927

At home, 2711 Jones, 1928

Quartet from Sioux City
Central High Glee Club—Mac
at right

With twin brothers Charles
(left) and Gordon, 1929

Aunt Evelyn

As Charles the
Wrestler, *As You Like
It*, Globe Theatre,
Dallas, 1936

University of Iowa,
me as George
Washington in
Maxwell Anderson's
Valley Forge (1935)

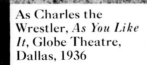

Don Gallagher,
me, Jane Wernli,
Bill Kass

Macdonald Carey, the genial First Nighter himself

"Pick of the Air"—Everywhere

Behind "First Nighter" is a prestige that only seven years of successful performances could have created. Newspaper and magazine radio editors rate it "Pick of the Air"—everywhere!

"The First Nighter," 1937

SATURDAY MORNING HEAR
ETHEL MERMAN
and
MacDONALD
CAREY
starring in
"LINCOLN HIGHWAY"
11 A.M.—WEAF
presented by
SHINOLA
SHOE POLISH

Starring in *Young Hickey*, my first soap opera, Chicago, 1938. Me, Templeton Fox (my leading lady), Betty Caine, unidentified child actor

Anniversary Waltz, 1954—with Kitty Carlisle

The young Macdonald Carey

Carey Soars To Fame

By HELEN EAGER

Overnight success is more or less an accepted thing in Hollywood. It's more unusual on the stage. Yet there's a shining example of such a thing in Gertrude Lawrence's "Lady in the Dark" at the Colonial.

One of the star's numerous lovers in the musical play is Macdonald Carey, a young man making his debut on the big time. Even before the play opened movie scouts were journeying to Boston, trying to lure him from the footlights to the Klieg lights. Three different companies are offering him fancy contracts. He was showered with lavish Christmas presents from these companies. And the funny part of it is that not one of these companies would have any part of him last summer and early fall!

Carey has been in New York for a couple of years, appearing in such radio "soap-operas" as "Linda Dale," "Stella Dallas," "John's Other Wife" and "Ellen Randolph." It was on one of these programs that Cheryl Crawford and John Wildberg heard him and tracked him down for their theater last summer in Maplewood, N. J. He had appeared in stock in the mid-west, barnstormed in tabloid Shakespeare and had appeared on the "First Nighter" radio program, out of Chicago, for two years. His appearances in Maplewood were his first in the East.

Encouraged, he made the rounds of the film companies. One of those now trying to sign him gave him a test, but nothing came of it. He tried several legitimate producers with absolute zero in success.

Then Wildberg brought him to the attention of Moss Hart, author of "Lady in the Dark." Carey went over to the Music Box. Hart looked him over, shook his head and murmured: "too young." Sam H. Harris, the producer said the same thing. Kurt Weill, who composed the music, looked dubious. "Well, won't you let me read something?" begged Carey. Yes, they'd let him read. So he read a side or two from the part. No one said anything "for what seemed like five minutes." Then they said they'd let him know in two weeks. He went over to Sardi's to regain his confidence with a few drinks and then thought he'd call his house to see if there were any messages. There was one. But what a one! It was from Moss Hart telling him to pick up an entire script at Harris' office and report for a complete reading the next day.

After the complete reading he again got "We'll let you know in a few days." He gave up all hope of getting the part, for dozens of actors were trying for it. That evening he was walking past the Music Box on the way to a date when he heard his name called and an arm stuck out of the theatre. Moss Hart was at the other end of the arm and the voice and he told Carey that he'd been decided upon for the part and that contracts had been drawn up.

Carey still can't believe his good fortune, for his role of business manager of the magazine is one of the richest in the play, outside Miss Lawrence's of course. And he has confirmed the judgment of Harris, Hart and Weill by giving a superb performance.

The intensive rehearsals for "Lady in the Dark" have necessitated his curtailing his singing lessons, but he hopes to continue them when the play moves to New York, although he has no opportunity in the play to exhibit his baritone voice.

One of the biggest kicks he's getting in Boston is going to the Copley Plaza, where he used to tea dance when he was a student at Exeter.

He's naturally amused and pleased at the attention suddenly showered on him by movie scouts. But he has a run-of-play contract with "Lady in the Dark" and he wouldn't want to go to Hollywood unless he could have a contract which would permit him to return to the stage.

Macdonald Carey is his real name —a heritage from his Scotch-descent mother and Irish-descent father. He thinks he ought to change it because people are forever calling him Donald MacCarey. Carey Macdonald or half a dozen other things. Personally, we think Macdonald Carey is a swell name.

BOSS-LADY AND BOSS-GENTLEMAN—Gertrude Lawrence and Macdonald Carey in one of the less dreamy scenes from "Lady in the Dark" at the Alvin. They're busy editing a fashion magazine.

With Gertrude Lawrence in *Lady in the Dark* on Broadway, 1941

Marriage

THE PHILADELPHIA INQUIREK '. TH

Mac' Carey
Year's Boy
'Cinderella'

NEW YORK, April 19 (INS)—
Several summers from Sioux C...
college freshman first gained...
he told himself college fre...
The professors were right up...
shipped on a ship and the rou...
head lines, and the som...
Like many tourists he...
the Hollywood stunne...
it was. It was in H...
up Hollywood Boule...
had continued with g...
actor was going to f...
street with a pa...
absolutely no...
Boston, how...
Macdonald...
returning...
ship to...
here w...
York...

M'DONALD CAREY
WEDDING JUNE 6

Bride Is Half Sister of
Mrs. C. Vanderbilt
Whitney

Villanova, Pa.—Special. Miss
Elizabeth C. Heckscher, daughter
of Mrs. Stevens Heckscher, a...
sister of Villanova, and E. Mac...
donald Carey of New York, an...
Los Angeles, formerly of Sioux
City, will be married Jun...
6, at Bryn Mawr, it...
1938. Miss Heckscher...
tended the Acade...
was gradu...
In 1934 ...
Her ...
Sh...

BETROTHAL TO ACTOR DENIED
Miss Elizabeth C. Heckscher, daughter of Mrs. Stevens Heckscher of Villanova, whose mother yesterday denied reports of her engagement to Macdonald Carey, of
Sioux City, Ia., an actor. The two met in the theatre.

"Cinderfella" marries his Betty

Newlyweds
(PHOTO, JAMES HOPKINS
FOR MADEMOISELLE)

This Is
No Movie—
This Is
a Real War!

In the service:
Gordon (Army),
Charles (Navy),
me (Marine
Corps)

Mess: Bob Preston, Betty, me, John Lund,
Dave Savage

Jungle duty

Settling
Down

War's end, 1946. "...before his return to the cameras in *Suddenly It's Spring.* The Careys took a personal hand in furnishing, wiring and adjusting the heating, installing the radio phonograph..."
© 1946 PARAMOUNT PICTURES, INC.

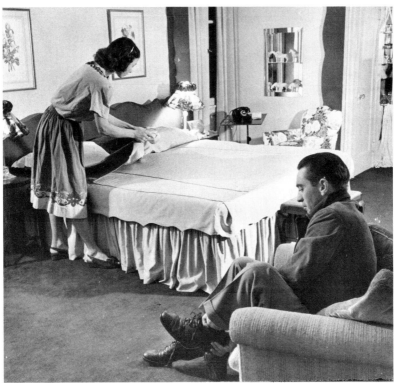

Domesticity

Careys: Lisa, Steve, me, Lynn (back row); Mac Jr., Theresa, Betty, Paul

From the Carey Photo Album

Paul, Betty, Steve, Mac Jr., me, Lynn

Lynn and me

Macdonald Carey
Jr., Paul Gordon
Carey, Anna
Theresa Carey,
Macdonald Carey,
Lynn Carey

Lisa

Paul, Lisa and me

With Shelly Winters in
South Sea Sinner
(© 1949 UNIVERSAL PICTURES CO.)

With Ruth Hussey in *The Great Gatsby*
(© 1948 PARAMOUNT PICTURES.
PHOTO: KAUFMAN)

(© 1949 PARAMOUNT PICTURES)

With Ray Milland in *Copper Canyon*

With Turkhana
chieftain during
filming of *Odongo*.

With Phyllis Thaxter
in *The Seedling Doubt.*
ABC-TV, The Frank
Sinatra Hour

Schlitz Playhouse

On the road
with *The
Music Man*

Macdonald Carey—
Actor,
Catholic,
Poet,
and Friend

Meeting Pope
John Paul,
Columbia,
South
Carolina, 1987
(L'OSSERVATORE
ROMANO; PHOTO:
ARTURO MARI)

Giney Milner, me, Ronnie at
the ranch

Book signing: Peggy
Lee, me, Dr. John
King

Theresa with her
children, Vytas
(back) and Aras,
1990

Lois Kraines and me,
1980

With Marilyn Monroe
in *Let's Make It Legal*

Son Steve, his
wife Indy and
their children

Norma Dauphin

Early scenes (1970) from *The Days of Our Lives*

Macdonald Carey

and I went to parties with her and John Hodiak. Both Anne and John are long gone.

I think, in one way or another, all of us in this business are loners or we become loners. "I don't know him," and "I don't know her," are common phrases in Hollywood. In a way, this is true, and in a way, it's not. If you work in this business long enough, you meet everybody—though you may know nobody well. Competition is a fact of this life, of course, but it's not important to me. I took note only peripherally when I saw Ardis Holden—who is the actress Brenda Marshall, but still Mrs. Holden—coming onto the set to watch me work when I got back from the war. She had heard about me from Bill and was checking me out as possible competition for him. It never occurred to me to let this interfere with my friendship with Bill. But every friendship is secondary to my work and my family.

Of course as James Whitcomb Riley says, there's a time when a feller needs a friend, and in the spring of 1952, this is it: Paramount decided to end my contract.

12

The way I find out I'm no longer with Paramount is strange. I go down to the studio and find my refrigerator turned off and a bill lying there for washing six pairs of socks.

I had known it was coming. My agent told me he was looking for some outside pictures for me, and Paramount was letting everyone go in a wave of economy. But what a way to go. It is so impersonal.

I spent enough years of my life there to have warm memories of the old Paramount as it used to be. During the time I was working there, the actors, the directors, the writers, the producers, and the costume people were all part of a family atmosphere within the confines of the Paramount lot. Actors, public relations people, costume and set designers, we would all sit together. The directors, the producers, and the writers had their own tables. It was a coup when an actor was asked to sit with any of the latter and there might be a job in it. We all knew each other, and when we weren't on the studio lot, we were at Oblatt's across the street, having a drink or maybe lunch, or a block away at Lucy's restaurant where you met your agent or other people in the business, or you had publicity interviews. There was a genuine sense of family. This was also true at the time at Universal, at Fox, even at MGM, the behemoth of all the studios. Despite the jolting reminders, such as the sudden termination of my contract, that you were working for a corporation, there was a warmth and a community feeling that no longer exists in the industry. Today, everything is independently produced, for the most part. There's no longer a stable of stars or a school at the studios for actors and actresses starting out, a sense of belonging somewhere in the business.

There are always two families you belong to and you work for in the picture business: one is your own, of course, the other is the company you're working for. When Paramount terminates me, I have a sense of loss, of being without an anchor. While my agent looks for work for me, I throw myself even more into my numerous lessons. I'm just not the type to lose myself in social life; even my drinking is done with people in the business—it could lead to a job. Stress is never far from the door. A new picture is not on the horizon and everything is not all it could be at home, even though a new little Carey has been born, Theresa.

Betty is always subtly—or not so subtly—reminding me that I'm not living up to her ideal as a husband or as a star. Even when I was at Paramount, she wasn't happy. One night at Ciro's, when we're sitting with some of the Paramount brass, she makes some derogatory remark about my acting. Bill Meiklejohn, the then-casting director for Paramount, turns to her and says, "Stop knocking him. Mac's a great actor and a lot bigger star than you realize." Now that I'm not at the studio, this undercurrent of displeasure at my status in the business is even more apparent in Betty's attitude toward me.

1 8 5

I feel this and it makes me miserable. I tell Betty how I feel. She tries to be more supportive, but it doesn't kill her dissatisfaction. The only thing I can do, I feel, is to get more work. In the meantime, I can take my lessons and drink to dull the pain.

In our household, we never miss the cocktail hour, of course, but our cocktail hour is never limited to three martinis, like Mrs. Heckscher's. If we eat out, I never order a single drink, it's always a double. Several doubles. After dinner, there's always room for a few scotches before bed, either at home or on a visit to a local bar, with or without Betty.

In spite of my fears, or perhaps because of them, I'm never really out of work long. Ten days at the most. There's always something. Bill Meiklejohn is right: I'm more of a star than Betty realizes. Jobs keep coming in in TV, theater, and, of all things, radio. While I'm doing what turns out to be the last live radio series for NBC, "Jason and the Golden Fleece," with William Conrad as my sidekick, I get a play offered me back East. My costar will be Maureen Stapleton, who is just becoming famous. The prospect of getting back to the theater and working with Maureen is very tempting.

In September 1952, I try out *Tin Wedding* for the Theatre Guild at the Westport Playhouse in Connecticut. They had had success with William Inge's *Come Back, Little Sheba* and thought they had another sleeper in this "kitchen play" by Hagar Wilde. It concerns a downtrodden midwestern lawyer and his wife on their tenth wedding anniversary. Meddling relatives tell his wife of his fling with a beautician, and she kicks him out until the beautician intercedes on his behalf and the wife takes him back. Working with Maureen was wonderful but challenging. The play is a comedy, and it's hard to set your timing on laugh lines with Maureen because she changes her movements from night to night. Working with the changeable Gertrude Lawrence was nothing compared to this; at least you knew where Gertie would be when you said a line. Maureen would suddenly be stage left Tuesday night when Monday night she'd been stage right. She is brilliant, however, and there was a chemistry between us. We were both hopeful about *Tin Wedding*. The critics liked us, but the play just didn't make it, and the Theatre Guild doesn't bring us in to New York.

Disappointment goes with the territory, however; you just accept it and go on to something else. Hopefully.

John Ireland, an actor who, at this time, is also out of work, is a neighbor of mine. He is married to the actress Joanne Dru. They live on Beverly Drive, a block away. We all belong to the West Side Tennis Club, which is partly owned and run by one Jack Broder. Jack has a Western he wants to produce based on a story by Mackinlay Kantor, a respected Western novelist. Since John and I have starred in Westerns, this seems a natural for us. We decide we'll all do the movie with everyone on a participating basis. Joanne will play the girl; John, who specializes in villains, will play the hero; and I will play the heavy—a part I always enjoy because it's always richer to play than the hero, who's straight and simple as ABC.

The script is just not right, however, so each night John and I write a scene and the next day we shoot it. John also directs. We shoot it in color and in 3-D. It's final title is *Outlaw Territory*. Lee Garmes, who has a great reputation for his camera work, is our cameraman.

It turns out Lee's expertise does not include the new optic technology or the knowledge thereof that is involved in three-dimensional pictures. Betty and I are vacationing in Hawaii at the end of the filming on our imagined profits: 3-D has cleaned up at the box office with two pictures, *House of Wax* with Vincent Price and Arch Oboler's jungle picture, *Bwana Devil*. I get a wire in Honolulu to come to Philadelphia for the opening. I leave hurriedly, fly to Philadelphia, stand in the lobby of the theater, and hand out 3-D glasses to the customers as they go in. The glasses were necessary for the three-dimensional effect. Half an hour into the picture, the audience starts to come out, first one by one, then in groups. They are all rubbing their eyes and complaining of headaches and asking for their money back. The optics are all off: when you look at the picture, whether with glasses or without, the image is blurred.

The picture was ultimately released in two-dimension and in black and white. The color was bad too. A *House of Wax* it isn't; it doesn't recoup its cost until it sells to television.

Dick Sale comes to my rescue with a movie that is to be made in Spain. Released as *Malaga* and finally called *Fire Over Africa*, this mild melodrama is the first of several movies I made overseas, mostly for English companies and mostly for Columbia Pictures. Most of the overseas pictures I do—and that everyone does in the post–World War II years—are done because it's the only way American and English companies can get their dollars and pounds out of Spain, Italy, and France. These countries' economies have frozen the money. In Spain, it is often oil money that has been invested. The film stock, the sets, the locations, the workers, and the technicians are financed in *pesetas*, then the film company takes the product—the movie itself—out of Spain.

My life was pretty stressful as I headed to Spain. Betty's and my incompatibility was becoming more pronounced as I spend more time away on location. It was obvious that she was restless about not having a career; she felt left out. Although she didn't say so directly, Betty acted as though it's my fault.

I find myself feeling guilty, whether she says anything or not, about her unhappiness. I add to my guilt further. When I am in New York for a live TV show, I see a woman Betty and I know and she and I go to bed together. She's married, too. She wants to break off her marriage and continue with me. I don't share that feeling. Whether she tells

Betty or I tell Betty, I don't know, but Betty finds out. The affair never goes any further. The woman divorces her husband and I go on living with Betty in a further state of siege.

When I was on my way to Spain for *Malaga*, I stopped off in Paris for a week and had lunch with Betty's aunt, the Marquesa de Polignac, whose family manufactured the famous Pommery Champagne. In her dining room at each place setting were permanent faucets that, when turned on, run Brut Champagne. I only eat one meal with her, lunch, and we have dry white wine.

My leading lady in *Malaga* is Maureen O'Hara, with whom I worked in *Comanche Territory*. Dick and his wife, Mary, Maureen, and I are put up in a sort of pension in Malaga. Jim Lillburn, Maureen's brother, goes there two weeks before we do. He is very Irish in his culinary taste and has assured the kitchen we all prefer a diet of steak and potatoes exclusively. That's what we get for the first two weeks there, until we eat up everything they've stocked up for us. Mike Frankovich is the producer; it is his first movie. His delightful wife, Binnie Barnes, comes along and plays in the picture. She also provides some of the costumes.

I read the following piece at a Variety Club tribute to Mike Frankovich at the Beverly Hilton in July 1990:

If You Goof, Don't Bleed

World War II has just ended
But lots of big corporations in America
    and England
Can't get their money out of other countries,
Shell Oil alone must have a billion tied up
    in Spain
Which needs every dollar and pound to stay
even pretend solvent.

So I'm in Spain and Malaga with
    Maureen O'Hara
Doing a movie for a British company
And an American producer and director
To get somebody's money out of the country
In the form of film.

The producer's wife has brought in trunks of
Her old clothes for wardrobe for the extras
Most of whom are prostitutes.
A regiment of Franco's army is being used
    tomorrow as extras
They are being paid in wine
A bottle per man per day.

The first scene is in a brothel
I'm tied to a pillar
And hit by the heavy.

The heavy is an Englishman
who's been brought along
From England as a stunt man.
This is no American stunt man who knows his business.
I try to tell him how to throw a roundhouse
Right hook aiming just short of my face—but to
follow through and that I will take it
And above all not to be afraid of hitting me
Not to pull his punch.
Of course
He is afraid. He pulls his punch.
He hits me right in the nose.
"Cut," says the director, "It's no good
You look as though you're afraid to hit him."
"I am," says the stunt man.
"Well," the director says, "We'll try it again."

190

We do another take and he hits me again
Now my nose won't stop bleeding—
So the director puts a bulletproof vest on me
And shoots me
With blanks of course. I can actually feel
The blanks because I'm sensitive by now and
They are full load blanks at close
     Range—which I have a
Healthy respect for since I've just finished a
Western where the villain shot himself in his
Private parts when his gun got caught in
     His holster
As he tried to fast draw.

At the end of the day I drive back to the
Hotel from the bordello with the whores
They precede me off the bus
The Spanish assistant who is their pimp
Gives the last girl a kick in the behind
To hurry her on her way.
I'm following him so I take one giant step to
     the rear and
Kick him in the ass
It's the end of an imperfect day.

Before I leave Spain to go back to England for last-minute
interiors and post-production dubbing, a process by which
lines that were inarticulate or blurred on location are rere-
corded. This is usually called "looping." A line or parts of a
line are put on a loop of film and run over and over while
the actor, watching his mouth on the screen, tries to duplicate
the line the way he originally said it. In most movies, even
those done in Hollywood, there is post-production dubbing.
While there I get a call from New York. It is Moss Hart
asking if I'd be interested in doing a Broadway comedy he'll

be directing. The offer couldn't have come at a better time. Betty is pregnant again and the show is a certain job. I would be making less money than I could making a picture, but the salary is a large one for Broadway, and I have no movie coming up. I go back to LA, unpack, pack again, and go to New York alone to do Jerome Chodorov and Joseph Fields's *Anniversary Waltz* with Kitty Carlisle, Mrs. Moss Hart. Betty and I decide not to move the family back East until I am sure I have a hit and Betty and the new baby are well enough to travel.

Anniversary Waltz is about a couple—Kitty and me—who, in an unguarded moment, reveal to their teenage children that they had premarital sex. The most talked-about scene is when the children literally broadcast this news on television and I, their father, kick in the television set (thus figuratively biting the hand that was to feed me the rest of my theatrical life). The story is just salacious enough—for those days—for Ed Sullivan to decide not to put us on his show after we open.

While we were rehearsing, I stayed in an apartment on Sutton Place. I was glad to be back in New York and working on a play, which cuts the pangs of loneliness. I was glad to get away from the stress of my marriage but hopeful that when Betty and the kids come to join me things will be better.

When *Anniversary Waltz* arrived in New Haven for our first out-of-town tryout, I was standing with Moss in the railroad station as the rest of the actors and our baggage were coming off the train. "Here come the gypsies," Moss said. "That's what we all are, Mac. This part of the theater never changes, nor does our status. Always remember that. We're gypsies."

What he says is strangely comforting. In a sense, it is the same thing my aunt Evelyn told me in Chicago many years before. "Remember, Mac," she said, "if you don't have humility, if you aren't really humble in whatever work you do as an artist, whatever you're doing won't have any truth in it." Both quotations can justify an actor's insecurity and keep his ego in place at the same time.

We open at the Broadhurst in New York on April 7, 1954. Despite a bad notice from Brooks Atkinson, the play is enough of a hit to run, as it ultimately does, for 615 performances. I sublet Gene Tierney's apartment on 85th and Park and wait until the end of the school year for Betty to bring in our new baby, Mac, and the rest of the family. I actually sublet the apartment from Gene's mother; Gene is in a sanatorium at the time suffering from a nervous breakdown. Although I know her casually through Watson Webb, the connection to her mother is made through Moss and Kitty. There is an eerie feeling staying in Gene's apartment. I keep seeing her there in my mind's eye, knowing that she's isolated someplace, away from everyone who loves her.

I haven't worked with Moss since *Lady in the Dark*; he is as creative and charming as ever. For us actors, he is particularly good. He has a way of making every moment seem full and wonderful. Just to watch him take out his gold cigarette case and tap his cigarette on it (even though I don't ever remember him smoking), just to be with him, makes the moment richer.

During rehearsals, Joe Fields and Jerry Chodorov, who wrote *Anniversary Waltz*, trust him completely. If the actor wants to change the line or a bit of business, Moss will say, "Okay, try it tonight—if it works, if it gets a laugh, keep it in." Nothing is holy writ until you get to New York and open. Then you change nothing. Once we have opened, we never know when Moss will be in the audience. He checks the play and the performances constantly. After the first three months in New York, he comes backstage after a performance and says, "Okay, tomorrow we have a complete rehearsal. Some very sloppy things are going on here." And hit or not, we rehearse until we get the play back to what Moss thinks is its proper shape. The actors love him. He has an incredible zest for life, as does Kitty—a quality that must have brought them both together.

Kitty is a dear to work with. She treats everyone equally and has an ear for everyone's troubles. She is certainly there for me in my hour of need. In *Anniversary Waltz*, I play a volatile, terrible-tempered Mr. Bang, who yells a lot. After six months of the show, I come down with laryngitis. I can hardly croak. First Kitty finds an eye, ear, nose, and throat man for me, a doctor who is already treating the entire cast of *South Pacific*, which is playing a block away. (It seems that to avoid makeup, the bare-chested CBs in *South Pacific* were using an ultraviolet lamp to keep up their tans, the worst thing they could be doing. The ultraviolet rays are drying up the mucous membranes in their throat and lungs, resulting in hoarseness. The doctor makes them start using makeup. As he points out, people who lie in the sun in Palm Springs or in Florida usually have husky voices.) Unfortunately, the doctor's treatments and a week's vacation in Bermuda aren't enough for me. Kitty gets me started with singing lessons under Maestro Fabri, who was her teacher and Dorothy Kirsten's. I go to his studio in the old Metropolitan Opera building on 39th and Seventh, just below the theater district, and he helps me start using my voice correctly again.

One Sunday, I fly back to Beverly Hills for little Mac's christening. After the christening, when everyone has left, a reporter comes to interview Betty and me as part of a magazine layout. I have to get up the next morning at the crack of dawn to go back to New York for the show. It gets later and later. Betty and this guy are still talking and drinking and I have to go to bed. I try to kick the guy out and get Betty to come upstairs with me, but it's impossible. Betty is encouraging him to stay. Finally, it's practically morning. I have to get ready to leave and I haven't spent any time alone with Betty. Worse, she's been paying more attention to him than to me.

I should've been used to it by then, but I wasn't. Tennis

partners would be brought home and their laps would be sat on during cocktails, at least while I was in the room. I felt jealous every time, and I had another drink.

Finally, Betty brings the children east and we move to a house in Greenwich, Connecticut, where we stay for the last year of my eighteen-month run with the show. Betty is back in her milieu and we are getting along. Her best friend, Marian O'Brien Donovan, lives in nearby Westport, and she is happy with my success on Broadway.

One night, we have a party for some theater people and, of course, Marian and her husband Jim. Linda Christian, divorced from Ty Power, came up from New York. Betty and Marian considered Linda an outrageous flirt (a lot of pot-and-kettle calling here), so they decided to play a trick on her. Linda brought with her the dress she planned to wear in New York the next night to stun the boys. When she was not looking, Betty and Marian took the stitches out so it would fall off her when she put it on.

Linda never tells us what happened. She just calls me at the theater and suggests I take out a pretty Filipino friend of hers who is visiting New York. It's a retaliation I don't help her with, though I'm tempted. The visitor is a stunning young woman, and wealthy besides, but Betty and I are enjoying each other; I don't want to tempt fate.

While we were in Greenwich, an odd thing happened with Lisa, our second oldest, who was seven. Some little boys, not much older than Lisa, got her to take off her clothes and they whipped her with twigs. We had a scene with the neighbors about it. It is a bizarre happening and nobody knew who to blame for what. Looking back, it may be a small foreshadowing of Lisa's later mental illness.

Things are happening around me that should be clueing me in to the perils of alcohol, but I remain oblivious. The actor who portrays the TV repairman in the first and last acts of *Anniversary Waltz* always goes for a drink during the second act. One night he doesn't come back for the third act. He has died at the bar. Howard Smith, a marvelous character actor who plays my father-in-law in the play, faints one day during rehearsal and we think *he* has died. He doesn't seem to be breathing there on the floor and his mouth and tongue are green. When the paramedics come, they take one look and one of them says, "Don't worry. Just let him sleep it off. He's just chewed too many Clorets." ("How reeks the goat on yonder hill—who ate his fill of chlorophyll.")

Doing a play on Broadway again is exhilarating at first, but after six months, it becomes shackling, a daily job I have to do. I see very little of the family. I take the commuter train from Greenwich to New York late every afternoon and return on it late at night, getting to my home at twelve-thirty or one in the morning, when everyone is asleep. I am keyed up from the show, so I have a couple of drinks by myself and go to bed. By the time I am up in the morning, the kids are gone. This is my schedule six days a week; twice a week I have to leave home in the middle of the morning, since they are matinee days. So there is Sunday and a few hours four other days a week to be with the family.

Having a job in the theater is good, though. After a year, Kitty leaves and is replaced by Marjorie Lord. Majorie is sweet and very easy to work with. Phyllis Povah, the character woman, takes a dislike to her, however—she dislikes anyone who makes her change her timing (as any actress would when replacing another actress)—and this makes for some odd scenes backstage. The Booth Theatre is a small house, and there are only three dressing rooms stage right by the backstage entrance. I have top billing and the first dressing room. Marjorie has the second and Phyllis the third. When Phyllis wants to convey a message of any kind to Marjorie, she shouts past Marjorie's door—sometimes over Marjorie's head—for me to tell Marjorie. This way she avoids speaking to her.

I don't know what finally resolved this situation, but it went on for several weeks. That Phyllis could be temperamental was not a surprise. When Moss, who is a big fan of Phyllis's comedy talent, first announced he was casting her, Joe Fields and Jerry Chodorov objected. Moss said, "Forget your objections. Hire her, give her her salary, and all the trouble she can make."

I leave *Anniversary Waltz* in 1955 after eighteen months in the role—quite enough—because of an offer to do a nighttime TV series, "Dr. Christian," which is, of course, more financially rewarding. Jean Hersholt played Dr. Christian in a series of movies at MGM and the character is still fresh in the public's memory. I am to play the original Dr. Christian's nephew—Dr. Mark Christian—who carries on his practice. Jean fell ill as we started the series and after two weeks he died. The only evidence of the original is his picture on my desk and, I hope, some of his bedside manner.

It is a grueling schedule, two half-hour shows a week. ZIV, who produces it, allows two days to shoot each half-hour show. They're using teleprompters, but you can't rely on them. You have to learn the lines or you can't play with any reality. Every spare minute, I am learning my lines. Since I am the star, it's expected (and I've always found this to be the case) that I won't work Screen Actors Guild hours. There is no "turnaround time" for me—a certain number of hours off between the end of one day's shooting and the beginning of the next, and no "golden hours" pay for overtime. I start with the crew at six and work until midnight, if necessary. The series, which we shoot for the first part of 1956, runs for only one season. I believe we do thirty-six episodes and the show gives their first jobs to Stuart Whitman and Angie Dickinson, among others.

Around this time, Sheldon Leonard, whom I'd first met at Cheryl Crawford's theater in Maplewood, New Jersey, called me to say they are recasting the wife's role on Danny Thomas's half-hour comedy, "Make Room for Daddy." Sheldon asked me how Marjorie Lord is to work with, and I was glad to tell him how ideal a leading lady she can be. Sheldon went on to produce and direct the show for years, with Marjorie playing opposite Danny.

In 1956, I am offered a movie by Republic Pictures called *Stranger at My Door* with Patricia Medina and Skip Homeier (who made his name on stage in Lillian Hellman's *Another Part of the Forest*). Republic Pictures is not known for doing quality stuff, but this offbeat Western turns out to be just that. It is one of the best pictures I've been in since *Shadow of a Doubt*, and it's thought to be the best movie Republic ever made. It is the story of a minister, a man of God (me), who harbors a fugitive from the law to save him from a lynch mob and who hopes to convert the man from his criminal ways. The fugitive threatens to alienate the minister's wife and son, wooing them to his way of life. The minister performs heroically in taming a wild stallion and, in the process, regains his control of the household.

The action shots—the shots with the horse—are incredible. They are among the most exciting horse chases and horse acrobatics seen on film. The story and dialogue are good too. It is directed by William Whitney and written by Barry Shipman, who writes scenes that are a delight to play, dialogue that is a delight to say. I'll never forget Pat Medina running into the gale stirred up by the wind machines, dirt and grit blowing into her face and her tremendous black eyes. It's amazing she wasn't blinded.

My next job takes me all the way to Kenya to do *Odongo* (a Swahili word meaning "of the earth") for Columbia. I learned some Swahili for that picture. It was at the end of the Mau Mau uprising and I left my home in Beverly Hills at 620 North Cañon Drive with a warning from our black cook to watch my back in Kenya. There had been endless terrorist raids by the Kikuyu, the Bantu-speaking people of Kenya, on the white settlers.

On the plane to London, I read *Something of Value* by Robert Ruark, the first book to personalize the murders and rapes that the Mau Mau committed. I stayed in England just long enough to get malaria shots, cholera shots, and several other kinds of shots. With a queasy stomach, I went on from London to Nairobi; I finished reading *Something of Value*, and the rest of the way to Kenya I read the British *White Paper*, another record of the murders and rapes and massacres by the Mau Mau.

Flying over Africa for the first time is an experience of green that will not leave my memory. It was a deeper green, though a different green, than I would see in Ireland. Given the state of my stomach and apprehensiveness of my mind, that green held connotations of wild fertility and casual death that were infinite.

My first night in my tent in our camp was the most disturbed and disturbing night I have ever had. At dinner in the main tent, a British bounty officer sat next to me and regaled me with the fact he has just turned in a severed hand to the district office in Nairobi, government-required proof that he's killed a Mau Mau.

My tent is lined with mosquito netting, which is also lined with mosquito netting, and there is mosquito netting around my bed. There is also a canvas floor.

In Africa, the sun doesn't linger when it's going down; it is light then suddenly it is dark. You hear a noise getting closer and closer. You turn your flashlight out the front of the tent and see a veritable carpet of insects moving toward you. The carpet stops at the entrance, thank God.

But now you hear the animals. Carr Hartley's animal farm, where we are to film most of our scenes, is a mile away. The farm has representatives of all of the animals in Africa.

1 9 9

Carr furnishes animals for all the zoos of the world: zoos in Berlin, London, Los Angeles, the Bronx. The whistling, the trumpeting, the grunting—the babel of noise from all his animals—are sounds that are soul-shaking. And with my mind full of blood and machetes and weird religious rites, "disturbed" is a mild description of that night.

Rhonda Fleming is the female lead in the movie. She plays a veterinarian, I play a white hunter. Rhonda has made quite a name for herself in Hitchcock's *Spellbound*, in *Gunfight at the O.K. Corral* with Burt Lancaster and Kirk Douglas, and in *Home Before Dark*. Her husband at the time, Dr. Lou Morrill, visits her for a while and luckily for me, is on the scene when I am called to make a forty-foot dive off a cliff into what seems a very small piece of water. The English stuntman (the same one who had hit me when we shot *Malaga* in Spain) is going to do the dive, but he would have broken his neck. Lou, who'd been an Olympic diver, offers to do the dive for him and for me and saves our lives in more ways than one.

Rhonda has a great sense of humor, which we see on the night Lou goes back to the States. She is every bit as much of a practical joker as our English crew, which is famous for its jokes. I wake up that night to find my tent pulled down around me. Rhonda is the culprit. The rest of the cast of *Odongo* are more staid English or native African actors.

A veteran of Westerns, I knew what hams the horses could be. When a director in a movie Western calls "Action," the horses automatically, unfalteringly move to their marks. It's hard to get them to move otherwise in a scene. In Africa, doing *Odongo*, I have animals who've never seen a camera before but somehow they've all picked up on this movie technique. I have a scene with a baby elephant. When the director says "Action," the elephant relentlessly moves to my mark, really upstaging me. Of course, I can't get to my marks—he is on them. I try hitting the elephant but with little success.

The assistant director finally resorts to carrots and cabbage to lure the elephant away from the center of my scene. The apes and chimpanzees—they are the real competition. One chimpanzee is a fixture, almost a character, in lots of the early scenes. It is a Technicolor picture and the film has to be processed and developed back in London, so it's two weeks before we get a report from London as to how our work is going. The first wire from the London-based producer read like this: "First two weeks fine. Carey and Fleming and chimp great. Get more shots of chimp."

In *Odongo*, we work with several tribes of Africans. This excerpt from a poem of mine explains:

The one movie I made in Africa the majority
    of my scenes involved
Different tribes in Kenya—The Turkhana,
    Bantu, Masai and
Kikuyu so
I ad libbed most of the picture in what is the
    lingua franca
Of all Africa—Swahili. The picture never quite
    came off
Because when I had to dub a major part of
    the movie back in England
I hadn't taken notes and had to guess at the
    words to match my mouth.

I have some wonderful shots of the Samburu and myself dancing, also a wonderful one of me and the Turkhana chief who worked on the picture. His umbrella is the insignia of his rank. You are wise to have the wind at your back when you deal with the Turkhana. Their hair, done up in a bun, is plated and puffed up with cow dung. Holes are punched in this mess to hold an occasional ostrich feather. But I found all of the different tribes to be warm and loving, and since

2 0 1

I'd done my homework and learned Swahili, I felt I was accepted by them. Fraternization of a sort was tolerated with a man, but *Mogambo*, an MGM picture with Clark Gable and Ava Gardner, had just been shot in Kenya and the members of the tribes I talked to looked down on Miss Gardner. She had tried to join the men in their dances. This is something that is just not done in Africa.

In 1956, our sixth child, Paul, is born. From a very early age, he is a special little boy—at least, the girls think he is. When he is four and five, being driven to pre-kindergarten and kindergarten, by Aggie, a marvelous Scot who is the official chauffeur for an awful lot of Beverly Hills Catholic children, including ours, he is escorted to the front door by a different little girl every day. Aggie is almost a dwarf of a woman who can barely see over the steering wheel when she drives. Every Beverly Hills Catholic child of that period knows her.

One of the other movies I did in 1956 was a really terrible one called *Man or Gun*. Its premise suggested that it's the gun the character I play carries that does the killing, not me. The producer, Albert Gannaway, tried to save and use every bit of film he had paid for. For instance, in all panning shots, the strip of film used includes a head, before the part used in the take, and a tail, after the take. Gannaway prints the whole thing. If the scene is supposed to show the posse riding out of town, he prints the first part where the riders mount their horses and enter the frame as well as the posse riding out of the frame and dismounting.

When I came into the studio to see the final cut of the film, he stopped me before I got into the projection room. "You won't recognize your performance," he says, and I don't. There's a scene where I come into a saloon, lean against the bar, and languidly close my eyes for a second before I shoot someone. He apparently felt it was too short, so he's reprinted four times the moment when I close my eyes; in the movie it looks as if I'm winking.

Audrey Totter is the female lead in this picture. There is a parallel romance between the heavy, James Craig, and an Indian maiden, played by Jill Jarmyn. Craig's career is the living example of a screwy side of the motion picture business. He'd been hired by MGM because he looked and sounded like Clark Gable. MGM put him under contract and kept him in small pictures so Gable would have no competition. It was said MGM pulled the same stunt with James Whitmore because he looked and sounded like Spencer Tracy.

In 1959, I made a picture for Phillip Dunne and Charles Brackett at Twentieth called *Blue Denim*. Marsha Hunt, who was and is a dear friend, played my wife, but the story, which had been a play by James O'Herlihy, was really about Brandon de Wilde and Carol Lynley, two up-and-coming teenage actors. It was considered daring for those days. When Carol Lynley, who plays my daughter, is taken to an abortionist, I race to the rescue, flatten the dirty doctor, and bring her home to have the baby. A real right-to-life picture, but pro-choice versus right to life wasn't the issue it is today. *Blue Denim* startled people because it was the first time teenage sexuality, pregnancy, and abortion were discussed openly in a movie. The play made something of a stir and the picture did, too. Like *Rebel Without a Cause*, it dealt with teenage alienation as well as sexual issues, and we were just about to enter a new era, the sixties, where suddenly the old ideas about morality are thrown out the window.

During all this, I am playing in celebrity tennis tournaments with Lloyd Bridges, Howard Duff, and James Franciscus. We play in Las Vegas, all over California (including Pebble Beach, in Clint Eastwood's tournament), in Toronto, Canada, and Mexico City. In between, I keep up with my dancing lessons, my judo, my karate, and my fencing. Any day I'm not working, I'm doing at least one of these. I never think my drinking will affect my physical condition because I'm working out so much.

In the spring of 1959, John Farrow, through the intercession of Maureen O'Sullivan, signs me to play Patrick Henry in *John Paul Jones* starring Robert Stack. It is Stack's first big movie break. Three weeks before I am to leave with the company for Spain, where the picture is to be done, I play in a tennis tournament at the Beverly Wilshire Hotel (they had tennis courts then) and I pull a tendon. This grounds me, but Betty and I get a teacher from Berlitz to come to the house three hours every day to give us Spanish lessons while I'm laid up in bed. I go overseas on crutches, just as I did in World War II. A London paper mentions me passing through town as the "old crock" who's been hired for the movie. It's unflattering, but at least they noticed me and I'm looking forward to using my Spanish.

Betty comes with me and we continue our Spanish lessons in Madrid. They were about $20 an hour in Beverly Hills; in Madrid, they're 60 *pesetas*, about $3 an hour. I take them a couple of hours every day in the morning since we don't really start shooting until noon. Part of the fun of learning Spanish is understanding the Spanish slang the grips use. They call *John Paul Jones* "Juan Pablo Cajones."

This is also a great time for Betty and me in other ways. We take side trips with the little Citroën we've bought. We go to Seville, Toledo, Avila, and one long trip to Granada, where we run into Dorothy Maguire and John Swope, two refugees from Los Angeles, who are also having a second honeymoon at the hotel near the Alhambra. It is a renaissance time for us as far as our marriage is concerned. The children aren't there to be worried over and we're exploring a country new to us. We're drinking only wine now. I feel more relaxed than I have in years.

When my part is over, my Spanish is good enough for me

to be drafted by a Spanish producer to star in and help write a picture on Father Damien, the Belgian priest who worked with lepers on the island of Molokai and who got leprosy himself. My doing this so infuriates John Farrow, who had written a book on Father Damien, that he never speaks to me again. John had been a naval person with the Australian Navy. He was a friend of Mountbatten's and was quite a character. He was quite a drinker, too. I remember one evening at his house when Monsignor Donovan, no stranger to the grape, came into John's study in Beverly Hills. John had had a few, and the Monsignor said, "All right, John. What is your exact latitude and longitude?"

I never get to do *Father Damien*. The money disappears for the financing, but I have a new job to come home to, a new nighttime series called "Lock-Up," another ZIV production. I play Herbert Maris, a real-life lawyer who devotes his life to defending and springing people from prison who have been wrongfully convicted and jailed. Lots of actors get their start in "Lock-Up" episodes, Burt Reynolds among many others. ZIV is still a hard taskmaster; from early 1960 to the end of 1961, we do two half-hour shows a week, sometimes filming from dawn to midnight, seventy-eight episodes in all. A wonderful character actor, John Doucette, is my sidekick. Jack Herzberg is our producer. I first met Jack when he started out in the mail room at Paramount. I was to meet Jack again later—as one of the first producers on "Days of Our Lives."

After "Lock-Up," I work again for Joseph Losey in London in *These Are the Damned*, wherein I play an American in England who comes to the rescue of a young girl who is running from a gang of motorcycle toughs. In the chase, we stumble on the government's hiding place for children who are the offspring of people who've been exposed to radiation. The actress is Shirley Anne Field, who's just done *Saturday Night and Sunday Morning* and Olivier's *The Entertainer*. It is Oliver Reed's first picture. Alexander Knox and Viveca Lindfors are also in the cast. It is a "ban the bomb" picture and never gets shown in the United States because at the time Joe Losey is considered a Communist. Columbia produces it and Columbia buries it.

The same year, 1962, there is another picture in which I think I've done good work that Columbia also buries. It's called *Stranglehold*. I play an actor who is falsely accused of murder on a night he was drunk. He has to retrace his steps to see what he did during the missing hours—hours that he had blocked out. *Stranglehold* is shown in the United States one night on TV and then is forgotten. I'm still trying to find it. Strangely enough, when I did the picture, I made no connection between the alcoholism of the actor I played and my own alcoholic nature.

Soon after *Stranglehold*, I do a spy picture in Ireland called *The Devil's Agent*. It is an independent picture financed by three companies—British, German, and Irish. The cast, too, is international. Besides me, there's Christopher Lee and Curt Jurgens and a few members of Ireland's Abbey Players. It is my first and only trip to Ireland and it leaves me with many fond memories.

We shot the picture in Bray, about thirty kilometers out of Dublin. The Careys are from Limerick, Galway, and Roscommon, but I had no time to try to locate any of them.

Some of us in the cast are put up at the Old Conna Inn, owned and run by Cyril McCormick, the son of the famous tenor John McCormick. The Old Conna is a former Irish manor that has been converted into a hotel. There is a dining room and a bar, two large lobbies and suites named for famous Irish literary figures. There is the Yeats Suite, the Synge Suite, the O'Casey Suite, the Gogarty Suite. I get the Yeats Suite. A maid comes into each bedroom every evening and puts a hot brick in at the foot of the bed to make our sleeping more cozy. And the walks in the misty Irish nights are eerie and mystically wonderful. As I've written else-where, "I swear I saw the faeries."

I never see the picture, though. If it plays in the United States, the run is so brief I never catch it. And they never tell me what it's about. Nobody is ever given a complete script. We're just given several pages at a time.

The first weekend we are there, they drive me into Dublin so I can go to confession. I walk into an old cathedral. I am early—the first one in the confessional. The priest, hearing my accent, asks, "Where are you from in America?" I say, "California." He says, "Where in California?" I say, "Hollywood." "Oh, no," he says. "I spent two years there. Is so-and-so still there? Do they still have the red cars?" On and on the questions go. After fifteen minutes, we get down to confession and I emerge from the confessional to be greeted by the disapproving stares of a long line of Dubliners, a line that has formed to wait for this dirty sinner to get through. I go to the other side of the church to spend enough time saying a penance to measure up to the length of my stay in the box. I come out of the church with more guilt than I came in with.

My affair with the church in Dublin is not over yet. I go there to Mass the next day with the staff, a staff headed by two very pretty colleens. It is a ten o'clock Mass, and as I start to go up for communion, no one else is going. One of the Irish lassies stops me. She says the Bishop of Dublin has decreed there is to be no communion after the 8:30 Mass. This, she says, is to discourage the drink—people coming to communion with hangovers or with liquor on their breath. I go back to the sacristy and say I want communion. The priest says no, it's the Bishop's rule. I say, "Are you refusing me communion?" The priest says, no, it's the Bishop's rule. I say, "Are you refusing me communion?" He says, "No, kneel down." I get my communion then and there. I'd been elbowed aside by old ladies in Spain going up to the communion rail, but never before had I been told I couldn't take communion—and in Ireland, no less, where the Catholics are supposed to be more Catholic than the Pope.

I'm asked to go to Belfast to do a TV show. Here I am, a good Irish Catholic boy, going into the Orangeman's Ireland. We drive up in a Volkswagen, me and this Irish type who reminds me of Wally Ford in *The Informer*. He has sort of attached himself to me. The weather is clear as anything until we reach the border where Protestant Ireland begins. Immediately it rains. The rain continues the whole day and night that we are in the Orange country until on the way back when we cross the border again. The downpour stops and the weather is clear as could be until we get back at the Old Conna.

When the picture is over, I fly home and as I am coming into Los Angeles, you can see the flames from what I learn is a fire in Bel Air. I have a message from the film's producer, Emmett Dalton, for his daughter, who lives on Chalon Road there; it's a street that has been hit by the fire. The day I go up to deliver it, I find her house to be one of the few houses that has been spared. The house on either side of her has been burnt to the ground.

Throughout the 1950s and early 1960s, I'm also doing some of my best nighttime live TV shows, including several segments of "Climax." The first, "The Chinese Game," is directed by a young John Frankenheimer and features Rita Moreno in her first big part. I fall for Rita completely, but she's much too young for me, just a teenager, as a matter of fact. She's as attractive and sexy and talented today as she was then. For the "U.S. Steel Hour," I do "Moment of Courage" with Kim Hunter, who's a joy to work with, a comedy with Joan Caulfield, the first live TV show at NBC Burbank, where most NBC shows (including "Days of Our Lives") are taped today, and a drama with Jan Sterling, a friend who shares my agent. I also do a "Playhouse Ninety" and several

"Hitchcock" shows and Rod Serling's "Outer Limits." I love the action; I'm working all the time, and the work is very varied, just the way radio work used to be.

Fred MacMurray came up to me one night at a party at Walter Lang's and said, "How do you feel doing television shows?"

"It's no different," I told him. "It's acting. If you're on a series, the hours are just a little worse."

"I just don't think I could hack it," Fred said.

Of course, he goes on to do "My Three Sons"—and on and on.

I do the last live color TV drama for NBC in New York at the Brooklyn Studios. Nina Foch plays my wife and Robert Redford plays my son. Nina Foch is already a respected actress. This is the first I've heard of Robert Redford. Movies haven't discovered him yet. We ride back to New York together from the Brooklyn Studio a couple of times, and he talks about being just married—having his first apartment—sleeping on a mattress on the floor and having crate boxes for chairs. When we're doing the show and we're on the air, one of the cameras bursts into flames. Bob Stevens, who is producing, immediately takes over from the show's director and runs the show off the top of his head. Oddly enough, I do this same story later on film as one of the "Hitchcock" series.

The episode in Brooklyn with the burning camera is typical of the difference between live TV and filmed TV, and, with the possible exceptions of an occasional "Hitchcock" or "Outer Limits," filmed TV is not as good. Filmed TV is uniform, while live TV—whether the script and cast are outstanding or not—always grips you with its spontaneity; it is live in every sense. As a member of the audience, you know you are seeing it as it happens.

The show with Redford and Nina Foch is a case in point. It isn't just the chance fact that one camera breaks down and the director has to improvise, it's that everything that happens in the show seems to be happening to you, the audience. When the villain is seemingly dead in his grave and you see—from the corpse's point of view—the dirt being shoveled in on top of you, the empathic response is more acute. People and events seem more real because the audience knows it's happening at that moment. The simplest of words spoken by the actors has a sharper ring of immediacy and truth. The audience experiences the nearest to what the audience in the theater experiences: the complete suspension of disbelief.

Even "Flight into Danger," the "Alcoa" show I do with Patricia Barry and Liam Redmond, has this quality despite the fact that it's set on an airplane that's supposed to be in the air. It is the story of a planeload of people whose pilots come down with food poisoning from the airline food—the story of the moment—and an aging ex-fighter pilot aboard is asked to take over the controls and land the plane with directions from the ground controller. We do it live, and until the last moment when the pilot lands the plane and says, "Damn it. I did a lousy ground loop!" the audience is held taut and apprehensive. This story has been remade a couple of times, and it was parodied in the 1980 picture *Airplane!* with Robert Stack playing the ground controller and Lloyd Bridges as the aging pilot.

There are many dangers with live TV, of course. If the action is on an airplane, the actor just can't walk out of the scene. But he can—and often has to—improvise. If his gun doesn't fire, he can choke his victim to death. Of course, then the detective investigating the murder also has to improvise.

Although the audience loves live shows, live TV broadcasts suddenly stopped, just as radio soap operas suddenly stopped. In both cases, it wasn't that they weren't popular and that they didn't continue to be popular but rather that the advertisers and advertising agencies found they could get cheaper advertising and more of it if they had TV programs canned.

In the case of radio, a spot on a deejay program anywhere in the United States was one hundred percent cheaper than a radio soap. It was all a matter of economics.

For the actor, live TV shows, such as "Climax," "Studio One," and "U.S. Steel," made *you* feel alive. They could sometimes make you feel on the edge of death, too. I remember one episode I did for "Matinee Theatre," a series Albert McCleary produced for NBC at NBC Burbank. It was a daily one-hour show that you rehearsed for seven days. On the seventh day, you arrived at three o'clock in the morning for your final dress rehearsal. The show was broadcast live at 11:00 A.M. for the East Coast and was taped to be rebroadcast for the West Coast.

One actor, who, on the show I'm doing, has lengthy speeches and whose lines carry all the exposition for the plot, goes absolutely mute when we go on the air and answers every question with this line: "You may be right, you may be wrong, but I don't know." I have to fill in the exposition myself.

George Raft apparently never bothered to learn lines, but he was a star and could get away with it. The screenwriter had to show George responding in some way to other characters, so there was always a sidekick; when another character would approach George and ask him something, George would say, "Tell him, Bill," and the sidekick would give the answer. Playing the sidekick was no way to break into the business because the camera would stay on George while the sidekick spoke. George would nod and flip a coin to show he was alive.

The actress Lili Darvas used to tell this story of her experience with Steve McQueen and his first live TV show, which to her misfortune happened to be with her. In the opening shot, Lili's character meets Steve's character. They are supposed to have a long scene together establishing their relationship. Well, the assistant director gives the countdown, five, four, three, two, and points his finger at Steve, who has the opening line. Steve goes absolutely blank and says, "Hello, Mom. What do you say?" and doesn't say another word. Lili has to fill it all in for him—who they all are, the terrible predicament they are in, what happened yesterday, what is happening now, and what might happen next. McQueen never speaks another line.

After the show, Lili, who had a car waiting for her, saw McQueen standing forlornly alone outside the studio. She says, "Can I give you a ride home?" "Thanks," says Steve, who gets in the car. After a few minutes, he says, "Gee, I sure learned a lot working with you today." "What's that?" asks Lili. "Well," says Steve, "that you've got to learn your lines." If you think back and remember Steve's pictures, he never did talk very much in them.

I can't resist telling of my own encounter with Steve. It was at one of the many bars at a then-new popular nightspot called the Warehouse, which really was a warehouse in West Hollywood. Steve came up beside me and I heard him say to the bartender, "Give me a glass of champagne but put it in a beer glass so it looks butch."

That "Matinee Theatre" I do also boasts a juvenile who is hot. He is playing my son. In the scene, he's come home late, has missed school, and I'm supposed to give him a long lecture. Again, the show is live. If you're in every scene, you sometimes have to run from set to set to get there when the next scene starts. While we're on the air, I run to the set of my boy's bedroom and no one is there. He's forgotten he has that scene. I have to address an empty bed, which you never see. The camera just stays on me as I fill in his responses, "Oh, you think that, do you? Well. . . ." Apparently what I do works; no one ever comments.

Doing live TV is hazardous sometimes for me in other ways. Twice when I'm in New York, and I've been catching up on theater and staying out late, I have a dreadful hangover, so I go to a doctor and get a shot of B-complex and calcium, then I take a Miltown to calm and harness the extra energy I get from the B. I never stop working, but in between times, I never stop drinking.

I don't realize it, but I'm practicing typical alcoholic behavior: running away from my emotional and marital problems by obsessing about work and about drinking. Once Betty and I got back from Spain to Los Angeles, we were there with all our old problems. Again, I don't confront them. Even when I tell Betty, "We can't go on like this"—a perfect soap opera line if I've ever heard one—and she agrees, we still don't do anything about it. I go on drinking.

No wonder I keep running in circles.

13

In 1962 I'm still running, and I am running in all directions. Betty wants to move, and though I'm not crazy about the idea, I feel she's due something to make up for her frustration at not having an acting career. As a matter of fact, she is studying for a new career as a real estate broker when we move into a new house at 812 Foothill. Betty finds the house, and it is a good buy. It is larger than our previous house and gives our six children a little more privacy. It has a spectacular lawn in the back that stretches on forever to the pool. A lot of the bushes and flowers were supposedly planted by the famous horticulturist Luther Burbank.

Once again, we have moved up, and, although the property is well-priced, it is an extra burden financially, particularly considering the money we put into the house for improvements. The new kitchen alone cost twenty-five grand. We also built an apartment over the garage for Anna Bilcsik, who has now become our kids' nanny. While all this was going on, I did occasional theatrical movies and movies made for television—*Tammy and the Doctor*, "Playhouse Ninety," *Miracle on 34th Street* with Teresa Wright—and I'm trying to keep up with my work on the boards of the Screen Actors Guild and the Motion Picture Academy.

When Bill Holden helped me get on the SAG board in 1949, one of his closest friends was Ronald Reagan, who was then the Guild's president. Ronnie I knew only casually. I met him through Bill at Ardis and Bill's house in Toluca Lake right after the war, in 1946 or 1947. The only topic of conversation I remember from that evening is wine vintages. We were all amateur wine connoisseurs. Thereafter, I saw him when we both served on the board.

After Ronnie resigned in 1960, he started working for General Electric as a spokesman, first on "Death Valley Days" and then on what he called "The Mashed Potato Circuit." Soon thereafter, after so much exposure to corporate philosophy, he, a lifelong Democrat, became a Republican and adopted the Republican corporate philosophy. He was making "the speech" up and down the land, an apologia for that corporate philosophy. I remember running into him at a black-tie dinner party. We had a moment together over coffee and brandy after dinner and Ronnie said to me (I wasn't getting any pictures to do either), "Get yourself a speech. It's a business in itself. It can be a new career for you." The next I heard of him, he was governor of California. He later parlayed that "speech" into the presidency. I saw him at his birthday party in 1986 at the White House. I never asked him if he remembered that conversation.

When I was in Milwaukee, Wisconsin, doing a play, my brother Charlie, who was one of the hot Northwestern Mutual Insurance agents and who had sold me many dollars' worth of policies, introduced me to the director and chairman of the board of Northwestern, who invited me to sit in on a board meeting. He opened the meeting with the following remark: "This meeting is only concerned with our enemy, the federal government." That, of course, was prime Republican corporate philosophy. Get the government off our backs and out of meddling with business. Enough of these regulations.

The experience shook me but confirmed me as a liberal Democrat.

I worked on the SAG board up to and including 1965, when I was on the committee with the producers negotiating a new contract. Most of the nitty-gritty negotiating was done by national executive secretary John Dales, his assistant Chester Migden, legal counselor William Burger, and the offices of George Chandler, the committee chairman.

Negotiations begin in May and end in August. We win the right, for the first time, of pay-for-play in TV for reruns of movies and also pay for overtime. This is a ground-breaking decision for actors.

Before this, during the sixteen years from 1949 to 1965, the most visible work I do is during my vice presidency, when I go to Mexico City to represent our American entertainment unions at an international meeting of show business unions. I give my speech in Spanish, I follow the Cuban speaker, and then, warmly received, we get the promise and support from the international unions in the event of any future strikes. This is, as I say, the most visible work I did for the Guild. Usually I just served on the board every month at meetings for discussions and voting.

But I am always a union man, even if we had faltered in helping individual performers who were blacklisted during the House Un-American Activities Committee hearings— and had been so blind in 1958 as to go along with the committee headed by Ronald Reagan to sign a contract limiting residuals from television reruns to only those pictures made after 1958. This cuts out residuals for most of my movies, at least forty of them. Television is so new in 1958, we don't see the implications of this and the rank and file is clamoring for a settlement of the strike: they're out of work and they want to go back; this issue doesn't affect them as much as it affects the leading players. In fact, those of us who are leading players are appealed to to be "unselfish."

I was a board member of the Academy of Motion Picture Arts and Science for nine years. In 1964, I was assistant treasurer and in 1965 I received a scroll from the Academy for helping stave off the last-minute AFTRA (American Federation of Television and Radio Artists) attempt to stop the Academy Awards from going on. The attempt began with an edict from AFTRA the night of our final dress rehearsal. AFTRA was striking and wanted to keep all entertainers from appearing on the awards show. Union man or not, shutting off the Academy Awards would have been cutting off your nose to spite your face. The Academy makes the major portion of its income from the Academy Awards show. It finances the Academy building, the Academy library, and the Academy scholarships for directors, cameramen, and designers. The Academy Awards show is also the greatest advertisement that exists for the movie industry and is a showcase for movie industry people, especially actors. Though I am in the position of damned if I do, damned if I don't (would I be called a strikebreaker?), I call AFTRA and help mediate an exception for the Academy. The Academy Awards go on.

This is also the year we get a bylaw passed limiting to actors the selection and voting in the actor category of the awards. We also determine for that year that outside of "Best Picture," only members of a particular branch of the industry are eligible to vote the award-winners for that branch.

Soon after SAG gets its new contract (not related to the threatened AFTRA strike), I get myself off the board of the Academy because I'm doing so much television I feel I'm more a television actor than a screen actor. I'm not getting jobs in movies—the studio contract system is virtually finished, fewer pictures are being made, and, like most of my contemporaries, other leading men from the studio system days, I'm not being asked to be in them.

Besides television, I have also been doing stage work—musicals and plays on the road and in stock. I play Jackie Gleason's part in *Take Me Along*, which is based on Eugene O'Neill's *Ah, Wilderness!*. In the New York production, Jackie demanded as salary $1 more than anyone else had ever received on Broadway. He got it. I get paid $2,000 per week, and I have a wonderful soft-shoe routine Louis Da Pron has taught me and that Dolores Blacker, a wonderful dancer and choreographer who choreographed for Donald O'Connor, has perfected. (She is teaching tap rather than performing because she's come down with the worst disease a dancer can get, multiple sclerosis.) Later, I use the routine and variations thereof in productions of *The Music Man* and *Guys and Dolls*.

Doing a musical again is exciting and fulfilling and is, in a way, a repetition of my circumstances in high school when my English teacher wouldn't allow me to be in the plays but I was able to perform in Gilbert and Sullivan operettas. In musicals I can sing and dance. In fact, I get to sing and dance even more than I did in *Lady in the Dark*. In *Take Me Along*, I play drunken Uncle Syd, a lovable reprobate who falls in love with a spinster who tries to reform him. Come to think of it, reprobates are the roles I play in *The Music Man* and *Guys and Dolls*—Harold Hill and Sky Masterson—both of whom fall for proper types who try to convert them. I seem made for these parts.

We perform *Take Me Along* in Sacramento in a tent theater-in-the-round. It is 105 degrees outside and 110 degrees in the tent. I earn my money. We all do. *The Music Man*, which I do in Long Beach, and later in Iowa, is immediately rewarding in that the *New York Times* reviews it and there's talk of taking it to Las Vegas. Most important, Allan Scott, who, with George Haight, wrote *Good-bye Again*, a hit Broadway comedy of the thirties, sees me when we are held over in Long Beach and asks me to do his new play, *Memo*.

Memo we hope to take to New York. The play is produced by Shepherd Traube, and fifty percent of the money comes from my friends, at $2,000 a share. To show you how cheap it is to produce a play in 1963, the nut is $100,000. The leading character in *Memo* is patterned on Sylvester ("Pat") Weaver, the former genius head of NBC TV—and Sigourney's father—who had revolutionized the TV industry with "The Today Show" with Dave Garroway and "The Tonight Show" with Jack Paar and then Steve Allen. He uses the television camera as no one has used it before: cameras on skis, cameras in the hands of parachutists, and on-the-spot TV picture reporting of news events. Things we take for granted now were done under Pat's tutelage for the first time. (Long after this, I am drafted by Mr. Weaver to explore the idea of one of the first cable networks for Los Angeles. This slips out of his hands—and mine.) The play is called *Memo* because of the constant flow of memos Pat Weaver sends out to the desks of his subordinates.

When I leave on September 25, 1962, Hedda Hopper headlines CAREY RETURNING TO BROADWAY ALONE and then:

> Macdonald Carey is going to be on his own when he goes to Broadway in a couple of weeks to do *Memo*, a play that kids TV. Betty won't take their six kids out of school and move east, as she did when Mac did *Anniversary Waltz*.
> "It won't be the first time he's been away," she says.

In the cast with me were my old friend, the brilliant comic actor, Fred Clark, and Alan Alda, in what I think was his first Broadway play. I never got to know Alan very well. I was too preoccupied with the play and he, in addition to the play, was preoccupied with a script he was writing. (Later,

I briefly got to know his father, Robert Alda—the original Sky Masterson on Broadway—when he played on "Days of Our Lives.")

We rehearse *Memo* in New York and take it first to New Haven and then to Boston for its tryout. I am still drinking at night and not in the greatest physical condition; in New Haven, I come down with the flu. I get through the week there, but when we hit Boston, I can barely stand on my feet and I have laryngitis. We rehearse in Boston for a day and night on Wednesday. I feel I can't go on for our opening night Thursday. I tell Allan Scott and Shepherd to postpone our opening night, and this is the biggest mistake I could have made: Eliot Norton, the chief Boston critic, is outraged. If the play has any merit, he is so angered he can't see it and the next night, when we do open, Mr. Norton kills the play with a terrible notice.

Walter Matthau and the company of a Lillian Hellman play are also in Boston and also at the Ritz, where we are staying. People in both companies are having birthdays and they are celebrated in my suite as well as the other company's. We have several birthday cakes. I wake up the next morning with a hangover and the sight of icing all over the chairs and the carpet, a dirty white scene whose motif is repeated in the view through the windows of the Boston Common, which is covered with dirty white streaks of melting snow.

We close in Boston. My friends lost their money and my reputation is certainly damaged. I dread going home and facing my friends with the obvious explanation of this flop. The trip back to New York is exceeded in grimness only by the flight home to LA and a Betty who didn't want me to do the play in the first place.

After *Memo* flops, I do a succession of plays on the road: *Calculated Risk* in La Jolla; *Oh Men, Oh Women* in Cherry Point, Michigan, Topeka, Kansas, and Ohio; *A Thousand Clowns* in Ann Arbor, Michigan, and Wichita, Kansas; and

Take Her, She's Mine in Milwaukee—a run I will never forget because it is the first dinner theater I play and it is disconcerting to hear champagne corks popping on your laugh lines. I also remember the run because it is in Milwaukee that we hear the news that President Kennedy had been shot.

I went on to do *Guys and Dolls* in Charleston, North Carolina, and in St. Louis, where I played at the St. Louis Municipal Opera House in the park. It has two tremendous trees on either side functioning as wings on a stage that is as wide as a football field is long. Watching the rehearsal of *Meet Me in St. Louis*, the next musical that was to follow us, I saw Anita Gillette, who had to enter saying, "Psst." She had to suspend the "psst" from one tree to the center of the stage. Only a singer like Anita had the breath to do it.

In *Guys and Dolls*, Jack Harrold, who plays Nicely Nicely, is a trained singer from the New York Civic Opera and he helps me a lot with my singing. We vocalize together every night before we go on. Jack had a Mrs. McClellan as a singing teacher in New York and one of his fellow pupils—Alice Mack Rowe—is teaching in LA. I have taken lessons with Alice ever since.

After *Guys and Dolls*, I heard from Ruth Goetz, who wrote *Gaslight* among other hit shows. Ruth has written a new comedy, *Madly in Love*, for Celeste Holm and she wants me and Jean-Pierre Aumont to play the men. Celeste, of course, has been a star ever since she played Ado Annie in *Oklahoma* and Jean-Pierre Aumont is an international star, first in Paris for a work of Cocteau, in New York for *Amphitryon*, and in London and New York opposite Vivien Leigh in *Tovarich*. The three of us meet only onstage. We are in three camps: Celeste and her husband Wesley Addy; Jean-Pierre and friends from Europe and New York; and me and the rest of the cast, which includes my old friend Martin Huston, who played my son in *Anniversary Waltz*. Marty and I are amused by this separatism, but it's not the kind of thing you allow to interfere with your work on stage. Celeste does a marvelous job; it's a tour de force for her. Jean-Pierre and I are mostly her straight men.

Celeste, Jean-Pierre, and I are staying in the same apartment hotel, but they make Celeste move because she has her dog with her and they don't want dogs. She and Wes get an apartment over the theater where the dog can be happy. But now Celeste has a problem with another animal. Warren tells me that Celeste went to Sea World to visit the dolphins, who were enclosed in a big tank; the sight of her excited them so that one of them splashed water on her and bit her. Very undolphinlike behavior.

The first week of our two-week run in Miami, the producers of *Madly in Love* realize the play is in trouble. They fly in George Abbott and Abe Burrows, who take one look and say "Forget it." Nothing can save it. Unfortunately, we are already booked in Palm Beach for two weeks. We go there knowing we'll close when we are through with the run.

Our Palm Beach opening is something. It is the winter season and everyone comes. Lid Morrison, an old friend of Betty's and mine, gives me a party on opening night. Her yacht is parked there and though the opening night party is on shore, the next morning she calls me and says, "Mac, you were wonderful. The play was very nice. We want you to come to dinner tomorrow night on the boat. We'll dine at nine." "Lid, darling, I have to do the show." "Oh, you've already done that. We'll expect you at nine." She is so very rich (hundreds of millions from General Motors), she doesn't realize the play goes on whether we have social obligations or not.

That opening night is also notable for Mrs. Horace Dodge's late entrance into the audience in the middle of the second act. She was wearing a white ermine coat lined with diamonds and her seat was in the middle of the fifth row. Half the row got up to let her in. She turned around to face the rest of the house, and opened her coat as she took it off. She got a hand.

The second week, someone in the first row starts to whisper during one of Celeste's speeches. Celeste stops her speech and waits until the whisperer realizes she's stopped the play. When she shuts up, Celeste goes on. Another night, someone starts to leave in the middle of a Celeste speech. She stops again and watches the culprit, following her with her eyes all the way out of the theater.

We should have been forewarned about that Palm Beach audience. It was classic. They were a hard-drinking society group, and it was said of them as an audience, "They are either pissed or going to."

Madly in Love is the fifth play I've tried to take to New York since *Anniversary Waltz*—and again it fails: *Memo*, which closed in Boston; a play at Cherry Point, Michigan, whose title I've completely forgotten; the play *Tin Wedding* with Maureen Stapleton at Westport for the Theatre Guild; and another one for the Guild at Westport, whose title also escapes me, as does the script. (The latter is somewhere in my garage and I keep looking for it.) It was written by Alexander Fedoroff and directed by Frank Corsaro and starred me and a newcomer named Ben Gazzara. It was and is a lovely play about a Jesuit novitiate in New Orleans (Alex had been a novice there). I was the head of the school, the master of the novices, and Ben played one of the novices who upsets the joy and tranquility of his whole class.

There are certain disciplines in the Jesuit order, particularly among the novices. Every novice, for instance must wear a chain around the leg for an hour, to teach him that, as a Jesuit, he must be prepared to bear pain and suffer for his God and his people. The novice played by Ben goes at his training with such an excess of zeal that he disturbs the attitudes of his fellows. He prays longer than the rest. He fasts more arduously. And he wears this token chain for three days and nights and is only discovered because he faints. The other novices begin to question their callings in the face of such excess of devotion. As the master of novices, I bring this character to the realization that his vocation is really being spurred on and fostered by a desire to escape from the real world. I point out to Ben's character that he must face the challenge of the real world first and come to terms with it before he is ready to become a priest. And I send him home.

It is a strong play, both spiritually and dramatically, and was well received by the Westport audience. I am irresistibly drawn to this theme because it subliminally echoes my own attitude toward work and toward my family. I tend to substitute blind work for coming to terms with the real world; it is the eternal pit that the addictive personality falls into. The essence of being a good Catholic is to balance discipline and freedom, to respond to situations appropriately rather than to work blindly—this is something I'm still trying to do.

The Theater Guild's Armina Marshall and Lawrence Langner had not read the play before Westport (it had been recommended to them by Tennessee Williams). They were apparently very anticlerical and when they saw it on the stage in the theater, they decided not to take it to New York, though it was a success. I still think it would have been a very successful play—and movie, for that matter. But now I can't find Alex Fedoroff and I can't find the play.

Tennessee Williams had the same agent as Alex. One night, Alex tells us Tennessee has just been arrested for being drunk in a small town in Georgia. The sheriff took Tennessee out of his car, handcuffed his wrist to the sheriff's leg, and dragged him into the jailhouse. To me, this is the most shocking revelation of the way homosexuals are being treated in our society. That image has stayed with me always—the picture of our greatest playwright being dragged along the ground into a cell.

When I am home in Los Angeles in 1965, there is a telephone call from Ted Corday asking me to do a soap opera. I am desperate. I can't get any decent movies and I can't get a successful play. Soap opera is considered a step down in the profession, but it is steady work and Ted makes it sound attractive. The show will be called "Days of Our Lives." It will be built around my character, Dr. Tom Horton, and his family. "But I warn you, Mac," Ted says. "You may be still playing this ten years from now."

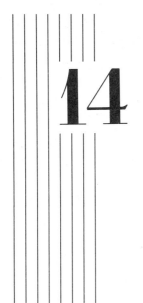

14

Twenty-five years have passed and I'm still playing Dr. Tom Horton on "Days of Our Lives." Ted has passed away, as has his wife, Betty Corday, who ran the show after Ted died. Ken Corday, their son, is now the head man.

I forget who the first Mrs. Horton was. She was good, but the chemistry between us wasn't right, so she was replaced by Frances Reid. I recently ran into the original lighting man on the show and he said they had to shoot the whole first week over because the lighting was all wrong in the beginning. Frances Reid, as Mrs. Horton, and John Clarke, as my son Mickey, are the only other members of the original cast who are still around today. The show is having a fantastic run. There are few other soap operas that can match it, for longevity.

Deciding to do "Days of Our Lives" is a funny trip psychologically. Not that I considered it a step down. Or did I? I had started out in radio doing soap opera under contract to NBC. My first radio soap, "Woman in White" in 1937, was written by Erna Phillips; now I am twenty-seven years older, a star on Broadway and in movies and nighttime television, and I am back doing a TV soap opera called "Days of Our Lives," written and conceived by the same Erna Phillips and again under contract to NBC. Am I stepping down, stepping ahead, or stepping in place? *Variety*, at the time, remarks that I am the first movie star to be doing a daytime soap. As I write this, twenty-five years later—fifty-two years since I started in radio—have I moved upward or onward? Maybe not on the surface, but now, certainly in the last nine years, I have. Because for the last nine years I have been sober. Any way you look at it, one thing I've always done is keep moving. Remember, it's hard to hit a moving target.

Now that I'm writing a book about the days of *my* life, a book about soap operas, a book about acting—at least this actor's acting—my attention is constantly being caught by the dissertations of other actors, most recently Charles Grodin and Frank Langella. Langella says acting is the search for attention and the dealing with fear. And of course I agree. He also says:

With each new role comes a test of heart, mind and spirit. Through the work an actor finds his place in society. Up against a task larger than himself, he can transform and overcome. More than everything, more than success, more than defeat, the work strengthens and illuminates, it calms the tremble. It steadies the see-saw.

As a child, I was always trying to get attention. Subconsciously, I always echoed my father's complaint, "No one ever listens to me." But when I got the attention, I never had anything to say. That's why I wrote plays and made up shows—once they were written down, they were the guarantee that I had something to say. Keeping busy also stilled my fears. The thing everyone growing up fears most is not being invited to play in the game—whether it's high school or college or life. Kids join gangs in the ghetto for the very same reason. The urge to be accepted, to be wanted and needed is very primal. Fear of not being accepted was the reason I started to drink and the reason I kept on drinking.

Fear drives you, too. Every actor knows what that shot of adrenalin does for you just before you go on. But to be a good actor, you need more than just drive and vitality. You need to be able to listen and react. To do this requires a special kind of passivity. So as an actor, even when I am passive, I want to be actively receptive, and in that way, in that moment of balance between acceptance and action, I find the truth I can share. Charles Grodin speaks of it as the moment when you're not sure what's going to happen next. You can't be sure in life and you shouldn't be sure in the theater. He says, "I strove to get myself again into a state of not anticipating what was next, of not knowing."

I remember at the University of Iowa, E. C. Mabie taught me this lesson when I played George Washington under his direction in Anderson's *Valley Forge.* I learned it when I learned the speech of Washington's that I used so successfully to audition in radio, theater, and television, the speech to one of the men in the Revolutionary Army, which starts, "Well, Master Teague. . . ." This is the essence of acting: to give the illusion that everything that's happening is happening for the first time and that you are saying the words for the very first time.

For me, Langella is right. It's fear and the desire for attention that drive me the most.

This is as good a place as any to point out that many actors are alcoholics (the stories of John Barrymore's drinking are legend), but most actors don't display their alcoholism if they work everyday. As long as I had a play to do, a movie or a TV show, I never completely succumbed to my alcoholism. There's no way you can do both—drink and act. Subconsciously, I knew this and always kept myself as busy as possible. It can be argued that my devotion to lessons and learning was another evidence of my addictive personality. Who knows? There was a lot more to my anxiety to keep busy, however—I really did want to improve as an artist.

Though I don't realize it, in 1965, when I start working in "Days of Our Lives," Betty and I are in the final crisis of our marriage. Newspaper stories from the preceding three years give a quite different impression: "Marriage for Keeps"; "Hollywood Father"; "Hollywood's Perfect Pop"; "Love in a Goldfish Bowl"; "Marriage Moral"; "The Private Life of Macdonald Carey"; "Stork Talk"; "Star in Your Home"; "Hollywood Marriage Morals"; "Hollywood Is Not So Wild, Says Macdonald Carey."

Wild or not, the last year we live at 812 Foothill, right before I start "Days," finds me really letting down my guard. I am drinking more and more and, though on the surface I'm functioning, I'm noticing less and less what is happening around me.

I don't even notice how strange our daughter Lisa is turning out to be. There have been small signs, of course, along the way. Lisa had always been a little eccentric. There had been that strange incident in Greenwich, Connecticut, when I was doing *Anniversary Waltz*, when six-year-old Lisa told us boys had made her take off her clothes and had hit her with twigs. Prior to this, she had had terrible temper tantrums, which I sometimes could coax her out of by getting her to laugh. She had never had many friends, she wasn't outgoing and sociable as our other children were, and she was moody. These were things I simply accepted about her.

But when we ask Eleanor Lee, our decorator at Foothill, to recommend Lisa for a finishing school Betty wants her to attend, Eleanor refuses, implying that Lisa is too odd. A girl's school, Santa Catalina, in Monterey, California, does take her, however, and, for the time being, unaware of how wrong the future would prove us, we fool ourselves into thinking Lisa is all right. Our other children seem to be going through the normal vicissitudes of childhood: Lynn going to school at Immaculate Heart in Hollywood; Steve at a Benedictine priory in northern California; and Theresa, Mac, and Paul still at Good Shepherd in Beverly Hills, where all our children had started.

By the last year at Foothill, Betty has her real estate license. We are beginning to live apart, but I don't recognize the fact. We're in the same house, we have the same tremendous king-size bed, but Betty's office is in one part of the house and my office-den-study—with a bed for me to sleep on if I come in late from work—is in another wing of the house. So physically, in a sense, we are more and more apart, and emotionally, intellectually, and spiritually, there is a complete rupture of relations that I don't consciously admit even to myself.

In her role as realtor, Betty finds a handsome apartment building on the corner of Charleville and Roxbury in Beverly Hills for us to buy and live in. This is thought of as an economy move. We can turn a small profit on our house on Foothill, and we won't have the heavy mortgage payments to deal with. The kids must feel some sense of dislocation and loss —there is no lawn at Charleville, no pool, and certainly less privacy—but they don't say anything. They aren't asked, of course.

From the very beginning, I never felt that our new apartment was my home. At our house on Foothill, we had rugs under our feet. As a sign of the impermanence I feel in our apartment, Betty never puts a rug down in our bedroom. I ask her to, but she still doesn't. Now we are sleeping in twin beds. I go to bed every night with the feeling I haven't really moved in yet and am not going to. A rug doesn't appear in the master bedroom until we are divorced.

I find it difficult even writing about anything that happened in the 1960s and 1970s. During that whole period, I am heavily into denial, but then denial and I are old friends. I never recognize all the warning signs of my alcoholism. Before Betty's and my divorce, I am still drinking, I am unhappy with Betty, and she is certainly unhappy with me. We're still together, we're still in the same house, we go to the same dinner parties, we play tennis with the same people, but each of us is operating on completely different wavelengths. From the day we met, there was always conflict between us, but there was also an abiding hope and faith in each other. Our faith is long gone, my hope is weakening, and I'm soon to find out that Betty has no hope for our marriage at all.

The whole period from the early sixties to the early eighties is one long trauma for me. The trauma doesn't destroy me completely. I am still a functioning human being and an actor. I do two nighttime series and seventeen years of a soap opera during this period, and, after I am divorced, I have relationships with other women. Nevertheless, it is all as if I were underwater. Even though I am functioning, I feel fragmented, as if I'm disappearing from life, from the living. I no longer feel myself a conscious, organized part of society and of the world. It's as if my worst childhood fears have been realized. Betty's rejection devastates me: I'm no longer accepted, wanted, or needed. I have two solaces, the same solaces I've always had—acting and booze.

The first years of my life had been a sort of preparation for these years of disappearance. I was no longer in contact with the people and the world I'd built around myself. Now I avoided people I had known. This dark and blurred part of my life was almost preordained. When I was a child, I first fell in love with acting, an urge within me fed by my dreams, and even by my drinking, during my early years. As a teenager, I fell in love with booze. And as a young man, as Rodgers and Hart put it, "I fell in love with love." In fact, it was

Marcy Westcott, whom I had such a terrible crush on, who first sang those lyrics to "Falling in Love with Love" in *Boys from Syracuse* on Broadway, with me in the audience:

Falling in love with love is falling for make-believe.
Falling in love with love is playing the fool;
Caring too much is such a juvenile fancy.
Learning to love is just for children in school.
I fell in love with love one night
when the moon was full,
I was unwise with eyes
unable to see.
I fell in love with love,
with love everlasting,
but love fell out with me.

This is a literal rendition of my life, before, during, and after Betty.

From the moment we are pushed into this world, we are asked to adjust. The climate is different and so is the very atmosphere around us. "What is all this air, this empty air, this food someone is poking into us?" A forever Pisces, I guess I spent the first sixty-nine years of my life trying to return to a watery womb or some ambience that was liquid. That it was liquor, that it was booze that, for the moment, made me feel safe, almost brought me to the tragic end so many of my friends and contemporaries achieved. Given my genetic background, my growing up in the days of Prohibition, and the fact that in the twenties in Sioux City, Iowa, the rite of passage to manhood was how much you could drink, my future could hardly have been stable and sober.

As I start "Days of Our Lives," I am well into my nightmare. I'm not doing well, I'm not doing well at all. Betty and I are hardly communicating. I have my own pretend world and "Days of Our Lives" becomes an extension of it. The show was only a half hour in those days, but I was in practically every scene every day, twenty to thirty pages of dialogue to learn nightly, and "Days of Our Lives" runs, as it does now, fifty-two weeks every year.

Like every actor first going into the soaps, I find it hard to learn the words. The first year I try every means to learn my lines. I have myself cued by friends and family. I write out the lines. I put my lines and/or my cues on a tape recorder. I try everything, and while I won't drink during the day, I'm still having cocktails before dinner at night. One time at the end of the second year, when I am relying on the cue cards and still fumbling my lines, Ted Corday calls my agent to complain. This shakes me up enough for me to cut down on my drinking, but I don't cut down enough and not for too long because now I am relaxing and beginning to sort of absorb the lines by osmosis. I'm not fighting them anymore.

Frances Reid, who plays my wife, divorces her husband that first year, a husband who drinks. Now she finds herself in the ironic position of working with a pretend husband who drinks and whom she can't divorce. On top of this misery, her former husband dies and she is daily faced with me, a bitter reminder of him.

Meanwhile, though there are nights when I get in late and Betty is already asleep, I'm not sleeping around. I am too busy drinking and I'm not the best candidate for an affair. I am too preoccupied with the drink, about which Shakespeare said, "It provoketh the desire, but it taketh away the performance." I am picked up by the police twice for being involved in a fight, which is absurd in itself because I only get more docile and happier with each succeeding drink.

I get a 502, which, for those of you who don't know, means driving under the influence. I was leaving a bar called Alberto's in West Hollywood, two blocks from the Motion Picture Academy, on whose board I was serving during soberer moments. I was following some drinking mates home for exactly what I didn't need—another drink. I was driving very slowly to be sure I didn't exceed the speed limit. Later, in driving school, I learn the sure sign of a drunk driver: a car going very slowly with all the windows down and all the lights on, even inside the car, and the driver with his head out the window. He is drunk.

The West Hollywood cops put me in a big cell with one other guy asleep on the bench on the opposite wall. I doze off only to be wakened by my feet being tickled. I kick the tickler away and tell him to move back to his side of the cell. He does and he lies on his side with his face to the wall. And he pulls his pants down. I don't doze off again. I don't sleep another wink that night for keeping my eye out for a move from this bum. Not a pleasant sight, one might say, a night looking at a bum's bum.

The whole experience was terribly humiliating, especially since the fact that I had been arrested for drunk driving was on the evening news. Paul Caruso gets me out of jail and takes me to Scandia for a comforting lunch with drinks. Of course, Betty is furious. People on "Days of Our Lives" go out of their way to let me know they're not embarrassed by what I've done. The incredible thing is that soon, neither am I. I drink away my shame to the point that I berate NBC newscaster Kelly Lange for having mentioned the episode and my name on the air.

Like a schizophrenic, I am escaping, or trying to escape, into my private imaginary world. Reality is more than I can imagine. It catches up with me at the point that Betty sues for divorce. The ups and downs of my own life continue to rival the plot of "Days of Our Lives."

15

Betty and I had each married someone we didn't know. We each wanted to pass our dreams onto our children, but we had different dreams. We both wanted fame and artistic success, but Betty's fame and artistic success included power, social and personal power. Mine didn't. These were not important to me. I believe that whatever you have—talent or material possessions—is never yours for eternity, never really yours, for that matter. It's only lent to you. With God's grace, you use it well.

There had been a game at the Heckscher table when Betty was a child. Papa Heckscher led the table in discussing current events that had occurred that day. Betty wanted us to play it with our family, too. But it never worked. Since there were always six kids at the table, at the very least three, what started out as an attempt to keep order ended up in chaos. It usually bogged down with Betty's former governess Anna, who was very bitter and violently anti-clerical, saying that politicians were all crooks and priests were all hypocrites.

The kids didn't defend the church. Betty didn't defend it. And I defended it, if I did, very ineptly. I always opted for peace at the table anyway. And Betty always called for order so we could play her family game. So the church—which was the one structured thing in the children's lives—lost, the children lost, and I lost. For me, it was like being in the jungle again during the landing at Mindanao. I was with my platoon and we were lost, but this time my two sergeants, Betty and Anna, were rebellious. They decided to take over the command and lead the patrol themselves—or so it seemed to me.

I never had enough command presence for Betty. I never went after power in the home because I didn't think one had to go after it. I didn't go after power in Hollywood either. I went after work, I went after leading roles, but I didn't go after stardom. I wanted to be a versatile actor, not a matinee idol. If that happened, okay, but I wasn't going to break my back for that—to me—meaningless laurel. Big money also never had a great temptation for me. I think I never became a big star because I never wanted it badly enough.

It seemed as if I could never do anything right for Betty. When I was still doing "Lock-Up," as a sop to her long-standing thirst for the stage and screen, I got her a part in the show. She was fine, but the part was less than memorable. She said, in essence, "I don't really enjoy it that much anymore and it's too little and too late." I also brought Lisa down to audition for a part, but Fred Hamilton, the producer, didn't think she was right. The fact that Lisa's shyness was hiding a troubled mind was one we all just swept under the rug, as we had Betty's disappointment and general dissatisfaction, and my alcoholism.

When I start "Days of Our Lives," the wildness of the sixties is underway. Our firstborn, Lynn, is unhappy at school. She's been kicked out of Marymount for not working hard enough and is now at Immaculate Heart, which is famous for its art teacher, Sister Corita. Too, the boys are discovering Lynn. As parents, Betty and I are learning that in this new decade, old values don't count anymore. While we are at Foothill, we give her a party for her sixteenth birthday, a party for twenty that turns into a party for two hundred—the number keeps growing. Lynn's birthday is on Halloween, which helps spread the word. Teenagers come from all over Los Angeles. Everyone seems to know the address.

At the party, one of the boys broke something. I told him to go in the sun room, forgetting there were a couple of big china pieces there—collectors' items. He then breaks one of these and I tell him to leave. He runs around the back of the house and breaks down the wooden gate we've just put up to shut off the driveway. I chase him into the street, where he joins a gang of about thirty kids. I suddenly realize there is nothing I can do or had better do, so I retreat to the safety of the house. Other parents start to arrive and the crowd breaks up.

The week before, in my capacity as a member of the board of the Catholic Big Brothers, I had lunch with one Mr. Whizzens, who has a restaurant complex in Agoura—a luncheon where he urges me to join him in setting up some kind of defense against the hippies from Haight-Ashbury, the drug culture he says is soon to overtake and overwhelm Los Angeles. The mob of kids outside my house on Halloween is a harbinger of the drug scene that soon takes us over. It is, at the very least, an augury of the unrest that characterizes the sixties.

Around this time, an actress named Regina Gleason is on "Days of Our Lives," and she tells me that on Halloween she is going to take her child to trick or treat away from Hollywood, where they live, to Beverly Hills, where the rich people live. She says so many people go there now on Halloween. She goes there armed. She shows me the knife she always carries in her purse to protect herself and her child.

237

A couple of years later, it is worse. The police are doing sweeps on the Sunset Strip night spots for teenagers who are out after 9:00 P.M. The Sunset Strip has become one long crash pad for hippies, and our daughter Theresa and her friends are hanging out there. The police call to tell me she's underage and should be home, and I go to pick her up.

Just about the time Betty began studying real estate, she and I took a Dale Carnegie course together. Betty was asked to go to the Midwest to give a speech in Sioux City, Iowa, my hometown. While she was away, Lent began, and I realized how excessively I was drinking. I went on the wagon.

Not that I hadn't tried before, but this time is to be the real thing instead of just for this one Lent. I am going to make it stick. I am on my fifteenth day of sobriety. I took the station wagon to go down somewhere in Nixon country to be with some other celebrities campaigning for a Democratic candidate. I told Betty I would be home early. She went out in the new Cadillac, which was nice and shiny and white. She had a date with a priest from Sioux City who had been on the platform with her when she was there making her speech. She prepared me for this date by telling me the priest remarked on how beautiful her head would look on a pillow, looking upward.

The night she sees the priest again, she doesn't get back until 2:00 A.M. and the car is muddied and filthy. She says they got stuck in the mud on Mulholland, a notorious necking spot. Priest or not, this is all I need to start drinking again. There doesn't seem to be any reason anymore to stay sober, my alcoholic mind tells me.

So round and round we go.

Over the twenty-six years of our marriage, I've been away on location or on the road practically thirteen years, if you add up all my absences for TV shows and plays, as well as movies. With my daily intake of cocktails, I haven't been entirely present even when I am there. Anna Bilcsik is always with us. She is really the behind-the-scenes arbiter as far as the children's problems are concerned. The household is run by this crazy triumvirate—Anna, Betty, and me. It's amazing that the children's psyches remain as healthy as they do. At rock bottom there is always tension in the household. My background and Betty's and Anna's are all different; we are forever at odds.

Anna has always been a servant. Some country priest in Hungary had made a pass at her when she was a child and that's why she despises the Catholic church. She'd been an immigrant to the United States and was taken in by the Heckschers in Philadelphia. The Heckschers were a Main Line family with Main Line WASP values. When Stevens Heckscher, Betty's father, died, Anna had had free rein, very free rein, in bringing up Betty. And Betty, of course, had yearnings for the stage.

Betty was a stunning girl: tall, lithe, full-mouthed, full-bosomed, slim hips, with flirtatious green eyes. Men were drawn to her. My marriage proposal was a bid not to just make beautiful music together but beautiful babies as well. Betty wanted a family, too, but she also wanted a career, which she thought I, as a rising young actor, would help her get. Many actor-actress marriages work like that. Ours didn't, and the one whose career was sacrificed was Betty's.

I was basically a middle-class boy with a middle-class background who had artistic intentions. Though I never admitted it, I was also a congenital alcoholic and the temper of the times and the customs of my profession reinforced the alcoholic tendency I had. I was as successful as I was because I was also addicted to work and to perfecting myself. I had a good voice and talent and a strong constitution—and I was lucky.

I know Betty tried her best to make our marriage work. She converted to Catholicism and tried hard to have successful pregnancies even to the point of staying in bed for long periods. She even suffered constant social jibes about being "a breeder." I remember Lady Sylvia Ashley, Douglas Fairbanks's wife, making an acid comment about Betty's having to go home early from a dinner party that was running into the morning hours: "Oh, is the poor dear preggy?" She also put up with my alcoholism. Not only that, she did not have the public recognition she wanted very much. One opening night, Tyrone Power, his then-wife Linda Christian, Betty in her mink coat, and I were in front of Grauman's Chinese Theatre in Hollywood. "Hey, turn around. We want a picture," a fan yells and tugs at Betty's coat, turning her around. "Oh, forget it. She's nobody," says the fan as he walks away. This sort of thing happened many times and it wasn't easy for her.

I tried, too. I tried to understand her flirtatiousness, her social code that allowed her to spend time with men and to be continually presumed innocent. I accepted Anna becoming part of our family and trying to teach our children prejudices that I didn't want them to share. Financially, I never begrudged Betty or the family anything, but I can see now that emotionally I was starving her. My response to her flirtations was to reaffirm my masculinity by having occasional one-night stands—and by drinking, of course. I never had a real affair as long as we were married because as much as we hurt each other, I always loved her. I never loved another woman. As a Catholic, I believed in our marriage, for better or for worse. But I was remote and I didn't even know it. Betty was emotional, and she needed me to be more responsive. I didn't understand that, so I didn't understand her. I'm sure now that her continual flirtations were a way of trying to provoke me into some kind of emotional communion with her.

Betty's interpretation of my basic behavior was that I was simply being servile—without fulfilling her needs or taking care of my problems. At a "Days of Our Lives" family picnic at a rented house on the beach, I was cleaning up after a dog who had dumped in the middle of the room. Betty leaned over to Frances Reid, who plays my wife on the show, and said, "That's Mac for you. Always cleaning up someone else's shit."

If Betty and I had been emotionally on the same wavelength, the differences in our backgrounds might not have mattered so much. As it was, the differences added to the friction between us. There was a basic imbalance in a marriage between Betty, a Main Liner with a pure Eastern seaboard family, and me, a small-town Midwesterner with a middle-class family of merchants, teachers, bankers, and newspapermen. The Heckschers were Episcopalians (a social choice), the Careys and Macdonalds Irish Catholic (a birthright). Though Betty was a Catholic convert, the religious awkwardness of the marriage was characterized by the historic fact that the Irish Catholics were only allowed in the back door in Philadelphia and Boston society.

The political backdrop of our real-life soap opera was turbulent too—analagous to our own mounting unrest. When President Kennedy was shot in 1963, my domestic life and my career were unraveling. Movies were few and far between and I was forced to spend more and more time on the road —eight plays, three musicals, and two tries for Broadway all in the same year. With Kennedy's death, my own life, my own marriage, began to pass away. Just as the idea flourished and passed that America was a group of people with a cause, the life of adventure that I had proposed to Betty—that we were to create a new, wonderful generation of people—this dream floundered on the insecurity of my jobs as an actor and the insecurity of my actions as a man. I was drinking too much to be a husband and father Betty could esteem.

It's no wonder we don't recognize each other even after twenty-some years of marriage. We go to psychologists. We go to hypnotists. I go on the wagon again. But it is too late.

My first awakening to the fact that the marriage might not succeed had actually been back at the rehearsal for our second wedding in Bryn Mawr, Pennsylvania, this one for Betty's family and friends. We'd been married a month.

We are in the Church of the Redeemer in Bryn Mawr. Mother and Dad have flown in from California. They are there at the rehearsal. Mother has taken her seat on the groom's side in a pew where a children's Bible class has been held that morning. She finds herself perched in a puddle of children's pee, and I am comforting her when I hear a clicking noise. It is Betty, snapping her fingers at me to get me in my place with the wedding party in front of the altar. I get put in my place. I should have grasped the terrible symbolism of that moment when Betty put me in line as the perfect metaphor for our marriage. In years to come, I certainly kick against the traces enough, but in a very stupid way. I just continue to drink too much and have my one-night stands.

When I started writing this book, I thought I could count the number of one-night stands I had had on one hand—or two hands, at the most. But now that I've gotten this far, I realize I was really a womanizer, if a half-hearted one. I had a lot of rules. One was that I wouldn't sleep with any of my leading ladies. Another was that there would be no emotional attachment beyond that one night. Also, I never set out to sleep with anybody, I never planned it. It only happened if I had too much—but not a great deal too much—to drink. Since I did have so many rules, I figured that when I was screwing around, I really wasn't because I certainly wasn't doing it as much as I could have if I didn't have any rules. Some people saw through my puritanical pose; for one, Ida Lupino, who called me "the Deacon." As secretive as I thought I was, it was apparently common knowledge that I played around, and the guilt I felt canceled out the pleasure factor. I was playing the archetypal preacher in *Rain*. In the end, it was just one more obstacle between Betty and me.

I have been Dr. Tom Horton, the faithful husband of Alice Horton, on "Days of Our Lives" for twenty-five years, almost as long as I was not-so-faithfully married to Betty in my real-life soap opera. Last night, I tried to write the stories of my occasional boozy infidelities, but there was a sameness to all of them. Routine seems to be built into my personal as well as my professional life.

When I'm written in the show, I go to work at NBC at 6:00 in the morning, having risen at 4:30 A.M. We block the day's scenes, and since I'm usually in first, I have time for a nap when mine are over. Then we block for camera at 8:30. At 11:00, we go to lunch. At about noon, we dress rehearse, and at 2:30 we start taping.

Today, I go to my dressing room after that first blocking and start to take my nap before I have to get back on the set at 8:30. I dream this dream:

I am in my dressing room. I lock it. I don't want to be disturbed. Lock it as I always lock it. I start to turn out the light. I suddenly see a comb, a corset, and several filmy, lacy things around the room. Someone has been in here. I lock the other door. The room suddenly has two doors. I hear a noise and there stands a new actress. She seduces me and we lie down on the couch, which is now a bed. Suddenly another actress appears and gets into bed with us. We object but she gets in anyway. There are now four doors in the dressing room. We pull the covers up over us as the four doors start to swing open. It is the cast, the crew, and the management. I never work again. I walk down the street and people avert their eyes. I accost one of them. He shakes me off, making a slurring remark. I swing at him and my fist goes right past his face. I try to hit him again. He doesn't move and my punch harmlessly misses him once more. I am stumbling as I pull myself up and try to keep walking. Everyone shuns me. My career

2 4 3

is obviously over, but I'm suddenly joined by a very short man (is this my agent, at last?) who says he will stand by me and get me back in the business. He accosts the same guy I had accosted, receives the same slurring remark, and he hits him. He knocks him down and I am back in the business. People give me jobs again.

I wake up to hear my name being called. It is time for camera blocking.

In real life, although there was always drinking involved, the bed didn't always materialize. Always when I actually did stray, word would get back to Betty and she would become more and more contemptuous of me. I suppose I set it up that way subconsciously, my way of trying to reach Betty and tell her how jealous she had made me. Betty and I are caught in a trap like the people in Ingmar Bergman's *Scenes from a Marriage*—she drinks because he is unfaithful, and he is unfaithful because she drinks. In our case, I drink because Betty makes me jealous and she disdains me because I drink. By the time I really make attempts to stop drinking, she tries to make me jealous, which makes me drink again. This is our pattern from the very beginning. We end up on a relentless merry-go-round until Betty asks for a divorce.

After a separation of several months during which we see psychiatrists, marriage counselors, and priests, Betty tells me she wants to go through with the divorce. I feel my life going out the window. The final indignity for me is having the lawyer from my own business management firm, EBM, set up the amount of money Betty should get in the divorce settlement. Once the divorce is a matter of fact, EBM, which handles a lot of people in the business, including Carol Burnett, Lloyd Bridges, and Gene Barry, immediately drops my account.

George Jessel, who was called the Toastmaster General because he attended all the show business funerals and gave all the show business elegies, saw me in Romanoff's five years before this (when I'd come home from doing a radio show in New York) and hailed me with this line: "When you walked in, Mac, I thought you were dead." This was not very cheering, as the worst thing you can be is dead in show business. Now, five years later, when my wife and then my business manager drop me, I have a feeling I'm really dead. EBM apparently thinks I've lost so much of my capital in the divorce that I'm not worth handling since their fee is always a percentage of one's overall income, including investments, a lot of which have been separated from me, as well as my being separated from Betty.

What's left?

When Ted Corday first called me about "The Days of Our Lives" in early 1965, he said, "I have a part for you. It's a young doctor with a family of five. He was a baseball player in his youth. The story is about his life in a small town in America and his family's adjustments to that life. That's you—Dr. Tom Horton." After more than twenty-five years playing Dr. Horton, the show is no longer just about me and the Horton family. It goes pretty far afield at times, but it always comes back to the Hortons sooner or later. Every day I always open and close the show with a taped announcement, an extra crumb (an extra fee, that is) Ted threw me to convince me to do the show: "Like sands through the hourglass, so are the days of our lives. This is Macdonald Carey, and these are the days of our lives. . . ."

We still have our traditional Horton family gatherings, particularly at Christmas, when my wife, Alice, played all these years by Frances Reid, guides the trimming of the family

Christmas tree and we hang the tree with the Horton balls. Each Christmas "ornament" (as we are careful to call them) is decorated with the name of a Horton. I think Addie, our only girl, is the only one who is dead, and she didn't go quietly. She was played by Patricia Barry and was dying slowly of leukemia—but there was such an outcry from the fans that she was snatched from the grave only to be run over by a truck and killed three months later. This was because a new story line had developed that had her husband Doug marrying a younger girl—my granddaughter Julie. Julie was the one who was caught shoplifting in our very first episode. She was Addie's daughter by her first marriage, so Doug married his wife's daughter. (See the "Days of Our Lives" family tree on the following pages.)

As you can see, it's been very hard for the writers and even the actors to keep track of the characters' relationships to each other. I remember the first Thanksgiving we celebrated on the show, I invoked God's blessing on our "daughter" Ben. Things really got confusing. Ben, of course, had been Addie's first husband, Ben Olson. There were other perils in putting on a soap opera. The first big story line of "Days of Our Lives" for me was an ecological story. The waters of the Salem River were being polluted and, as the head medical officer of Salem University Hospital, I was out to find the culprit and clean up the town. The story line had to be cut short because I traced the pollution to its source— the Salem soap factory. Our sponsors, soap makers all, quickly disposed of that idea.

As the years went on, my missing son Tommy was found in Russia, where he had been given another face by a plastic surgeon. He came back to Salem somehow, but he was suffering from amnesia and fell in love with his sister Marie. Her amour and about-to-be husband conveniently disappeared while, as the author said, "flying the hump" in India.

THE HORTON FAMILY

TOM HORTON **ALICE HORTON**

Alex Marshall aff **MARIE** m **CRAIG MERRITT**   **TOMMY** m **KITTY**   **MICKEY** m **MAGGIE SIMMO**

Jessica Blake   m **NEIL CURTIS**   **SANDY HORTON**
        m **JOSHUA FALLON**

JANICE   **MELISS**

THE JOHNSON FAMILY

HARPER DEVERAUX ←

Billy (Jack) Deveraux ←   **KAYLA BRADY** m **ST**

STEPH

THE BRADY FAMILY

SHAWN BRADY m **CAROLINE BRA**

ROMAN m **ANNA**   **KIMBERLY** m **SHANE DONOVA**

CARRIE   **ANDREW**

m **MARLENA**

ERIC   **SAMANTHA**

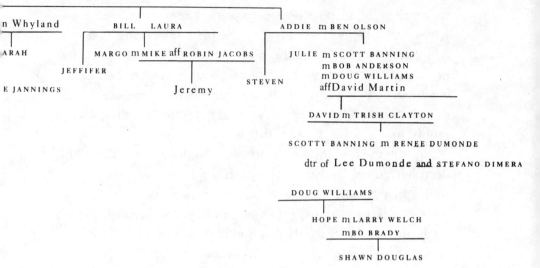

n Whyland   BILL   LAURA   ADDIE m BEN OLSON

ARAH   MARGO m MIKE aff ROBIN JACOBS   JULIE m SCOTT BANNING

JEFFIFER   m BOB ANDERSON

E JANNINGS   m DOUG WILLIAMS

Jeremy   STEVEN   aff David Martin

DAVID m TRISH CLAYTON

SCOTTY BANNING m RENEE DUMONDE

dtr of Lee Dumonde and STEFANO DIMERA

DOUG WILLIAMS

HOPE m LARRY WELCH
m BO BRADY

SHAWN DOUGLAS

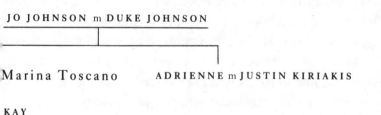

JO JOHNSON m DUKE JOHNSON

Marina Toscano   ADRIENNE m JUSTIN KIRIAKIS

KAY

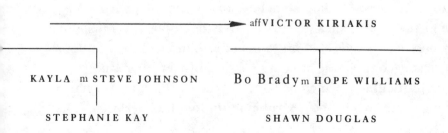

aff VICTOR KIRIAKIS

KAYLA m STEVE JOHNSON   Bo Brady m HOPE WILLIAMS

STEPHANIE KAY   SHAWN DOUGLAS

When Marie discovered Tommy was her brother, she became a nun. She was also a nurse in University Hospital and kept retiring to the hospital chapel to pray. I remember one scene when she took a call from Tommy on a telephone that was conveniently placed on the altar, but for the most part, the producers are very careful, at least as far as medical accuracy is concerned. We always have a registered nurse on the set to supervise all the hospital scenes, even though the Horton family has a habit of operating on each other.

Another fascinating plot line involved my son Bill (wonderfully played by Ed Mallory). Bill fell in love with Laura (played by Susan Flannery). Laura was a nurse at the hospital who had married my son, Mickey, the lawyer, played by John Clarke, the only original member of the cast who is still with us besides Frances Reid and myself. Anyway, Bill not only fell in love with Laura, he raped her in the hospital dormitory and made Laura pregnant with a baby that grew up to be Mike, now played by Michael Weiss. Mickey thought he was the father until I discovered Mickey is sterile, and Bill and Mickey and Laura—and everyone—find out, too. Laura, several years later, is now being played by Rosemary Forsyth. She becomes quite mad, only after Mickey has divorced her and Bill has married her. At present, she's being kept in a sanatorium in Chicago near where Bill is practicing medicine.

Meanwhile, Mickey catches that popular soap opera disease that is apparently in the Horton genes—amnesia. He gets lost somewhere in the countryside and ends up in a farmhouse being taken care of by a blind girl played by Suzanne Rogers. Mickey somehow discovers his own identity and takes her back to Salem and to University Hospital, where she is operated on to heal her blindness by a famous eye surgeon, who is of course assisted by brother Bill.

I particularly remember one operation Bill had. He has a long scene where he's scrubbing up for the operation. The lines are difficult. He doesn't have a firm grasp on them. So he (Ed Mallory) has carefully placed the lines in the sink he is scrubbing in; but when they start taping, they put real water in the plumbing. I am playing the scene with him. It is tragic to see those scraps of paper with Bill's lines on them swirling around in the sink and disappearing down the drain. It's a tribute to Mallory that the scene didn't go down the drain, too.

There are a lot of other stories I haven't told you about, like my great-grandson David Banning's interracial love affair with a black woman and the new con man in town, Alex Marshall, who, we discover, had been previously married to my daughter Marie—but then, lots of people come and go in Salem to make way for new characters. One new set of characters takes over for a while. Dr. Marlena Evans, a psychiatrist friend of Laura, and Roman Brady, the scion of the Brady family (they were old neighbors of ours), get married and the Bradys dominate a lot of the plot lines. The Bradys are a large group. Shawn, who sells fish, is the father, Carolyn, the mother. Their sons are Roman and Bo, who falls in love with and marries Hope, who is the daughter of Doug and Addie. Roman is a policeman with a black sidekick called Abe Carver. They have endless struggles finding the Salem Strangler and fighting the wiles of the international criminals Stefano DiMera and Victor Kiriakis, who turns out to be Bo's real father.

The Bradys' daughters are Kimberly and Kayla. Kimberly turns out to have been a prostitute who reforms and takes over the child abuse center. She marries Donovan, who is an international intelligence agent. Kayla has an endless romance with Steve Johnson, who wears an eye-patch.

Mike and Jennifer come back to Salem and have many adventures. Mike almost converts to Judaism for love of Dr. Robin Jacobs, but that story line doesn't work out and he falls in love with a young Chicana, but that never pans out as I send him to China because they need medical personnel after a big chemical factory explosion.

Through all this, Dr. Neil Curtis has married many different characters and had many adventures. We help him through and out of his alcoholism and addiction to gambling. Now he just has trouble with women.

Doug and Julie go to Europe, but now Julie is back and I understand Bo and Hope are on their way back, too. The Horton family is becoming the central story line again.

Of course, the real center of "Days of Our Lives" is and always has been Salem, a small town that might be anywhere but is certainly somewhere because you can reach it on an international flight from anywhere. You can also reach it daily on television. As Mary Cantwell wrote in the *New York Times* on December 20, 1989:

It is time to speak again of "Days of Our Lives," but then I am always speaking of "Days of Our Lives." "Did you tape the show?" my daughter asks on the days she's forgotten to set her VCR. "What happened?" I ask on the days when I've done the same.

I like this place, this Salem, where the dust never settles and the hospital never lost a patient except Rosa, whose drunken husband, Monty, pulled the plug on her respirator when the scriptwriters ran out of plot. A few blocks from my house, the drunks, whose home is the park at the corner, are settling down for the night, and the transvestite prostitutes who work the meat market are starting their stint, and uptown the children in the welfare hotel are trying to sleep while doors bang and voices whisper, "Smoke? Smoke?" But I and my daughter and millions of others are in Salem, and Kimberly—so faithless! so quick to drop her widow's weeds!—is cuddling up to Cal.

A few years ago I spent the day doing the rounds with a visiting nurse. All her patients were breathing their last.

But in every home a television set was flickering. Sometimes it was the health-care worker who was watching; sometimes it was the patient. Last week, near Times Square in New York, some men who'd tapped a street light for the electricity were watching television in their bed, a canvas-sided Dumpster. It was noon, and the show was a soap. I don't know if the welfare hotel has a television room, but if it does, I'll bet that set, too, was tuned to a soap—to "Days" perhaps, and to Salem, where complexions glow and diamonds glitter and death has no dominion.

As labyrinthine as the plot lines and the family trees of "Days of Our Lives" seem to be, we, like those in other soap operas, find time to touch on today's issues—ecology, environmentalism, nuclear and racial problems, alcoholism, mental health, homelessness, and incest, just to name a few. Television soap opera is the natural child of radio soap opera. I've lived through both, as well as my own personal real-life soap opera. How much I am steeped in its stoic philosophy is shown by the way I title my first three books of poetry: *A Day in the Life, That Further Hill,* and *Beyond That Further Hill.*

There is no basic difference between radio soap opera and television soap opera. In TV soap opera, the characters are more fully developed and a wider spectrum of people is touched in the stories and appealed to in the audience as well, but the plots are still about family, health, love, sex, passion, lust, and job or profession. Daytime soap opera, with its daily and serial quality, is like life in that it is concerned with birth, death, rebirth, and renewal—concerned on a daily basis.

It's Joseph Campbell's hero's journey in myth and folklore: birth, death, and rebirth. It is art imitating life imitating art. It is man's journey of shifting and timeless renewal. While the soap opera speaks in more plebeian terms, it addresses every age and every class because, underneath it all, it speaks of endless transformation and regeneration. People look at soap operas and keep looking, not only because soap operas show them different life-styles and mirror their own but because they give people hope that things do change. There is life after death in that there is rebirth. There's hope for us all.

Pragmatically, my soap opera supports me in more ways than economic. It bolsters my belief in myself and comes to my side when I finally realize I must change.

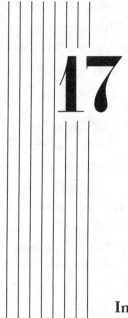

17

In 1966, when my marriage to Betty is on its shaky last legs, Lisa slips away from us and from sanity into a state wherein she hears voices. She was just about to graduate from Santa Catalina. By then, Theresa was there, too, in the next class, with Patty Hearst. It is a strict Catholic girls school, and the Dominican sisters who ran the place preached hellfire and damnation. Lisa starts hearing satanic voices. Schizophrenia is the final diagnosis and it makes her hide somewhere deep inside herself.

Besides her shyness and moodiness, we had many signs along the way that something was not quite right with Lisa. She was a beautiful, Dresden doll-like kind of child, blue-eyed and ethereally blonde, but that blonde hair had a coarse, wirelike texture that her pediatrician said was due to a glandular deficiency. When she went into her teens and started to grow, she grew startlingly, like a giantess. The doctor injected her joints with something to impede that growth. Out of her silences would come strange oracular pronouncements that were sometimes incredible. One night when she was a small child, I took her out to the patio, held her in my arms, and she reached her arms up to the night sky and said, "Daddy, the moon. The moon." I said, "What is it, Lisa?" She said, "I want to kill it."

No one knows what really causes schizophrenia, if it's genetic, if it's a chemical imbalance in the body, or whether it's drug or trauma related. One definition describes the schizophrenic as "a person who is born without the mental switchboard or filter we all have." Our minds act as switchboards that filter out all the sounds, sensations, and thoughts that we live with and that impact on us. The traffic outside my window, the hum of my furnace, the ring of my telephone, the sound of your voice, and what I think and dream I can separate, label, and put in their proper places in my mind. The schizophrenic can't do that. All of these bombard her at random. She can't separate them, and among all this artillery, she hears voices. She is in constant confusion.

When this happened to Lisa, it was the mid-sixties and we thought at first she'd taken some PCP or LSD. But she was seventeen, the classic age for the schizophrenia to manifest itself.

We take her to St. John's first, then to a sanatorium in West LA, for a year, then home. For three years I take her to a psychiatrist whose office is nearby on Little Santa Monica Boulevard. When he leaves town and she has another breakdown, I take her to Olive View Hospital, where she stays for almost a year. We get her out of there just in time before the earthquake of 1972 strikes and demolishes the place. God is handling something right for us.

For the next three years, Lisa is in a mental institution called Foothill Health and Rehabilitation Center. I then take her to Camarillo State Mental Hospital, where she improves enough to be put in a day-care home. At this point, she falls in love. She is nearing thirty, so, with the psychiatrist's approval, we allow her to live with the guy. They are in love, but they fight and he hits her. I'm there to supervise the domestic scene and I can't let him beat her, so I break them up and put her back in Camarillo. There she is put in a "carrot and stick" treatment group, created and administered by UCLA, and she shows marked improvement—at least a recognition of reality and a willingness to deal with it. She's also on a limited dosage of drugs.

About this time, California is under a Republican administration, with Reagan at the helm. The state with the best record in mental health in the United States begins a policy of dropping funding for state and county hospitals, which naturally includes Camarillo. I write Ronnie in protest and in pleading. There is no response but a polite letter.

I feel a complete sense of helplessness. A helplessness that every parent feels who has a mentally ill child, not just because she is your child, your own flesh and blood, but because there is little if anything that psychiatry or medicine can do, and now there's nothing that society itself will do to help.

My dear friend, actress Marsha Hunt, Mrs. Robert Presnell—I played tennis for years at their house and Bob was particularly wonderful to Lisa when I would take her out there with me—is a social activist and she gets me on the board of the San Fernando Valley Mental Health Center, where she is serving. For the past seven years, I've been on it, and through my connections there, I learn more of this disturbed and disturbing world of mental health.

The policy of sending the mentally ill back to their communities and homes to be taken care of there has not worked, in case anyone doesn't know it by now. When Ronnie becomes president and it becomes a national policy, it is no longer in the realm of social service but in the domain of lottery. Almost from the time that Lisa was improving at

Camarillo, our mental health problem—that of the state and the nation, as well as hers—was growing to the monstrous condition it has assumed today.

Of the three million homeless in the United States, at this point, 30 percent of them are estimated to be mentally ill. I know I can walk the streets of Los Angeles and recognize some of the mentally ill who are there as friends of Lisa from Camarillo or other mental homes. They will recognize me and say, "Hi, Mr. Carey. How's Lisa?" That Lisa is not there but being cared for in a "home" is owing to her luck in having a father and mother who see she is cared for. The others aren't so lucky. In fact, a good percentage of those whom we don't recognize as mentally ill are now mothers and children who are without homes. Is it asking too much of the state to care for its own homeless and mentally ill? The smallest percentage of that three million homeless is what the conservatives call "the professional poor," those who would be "all right if they'd get a job and not just collect welfare checks."

As I write this, things aren't getting better, they're getting worse. The county and city are dropping their funding for the mentally ill. We seem bound on developing into a Clockwork Orange society, composed of only the rich and the poor; or perhaps we are so in love with antiquity that we're willing ourselves back to the Middle Ages, with debtor prisons and jails and ghettos wherein the insane and the poor can be segregated and forgotten. I suppose we should be thankful we still have the humanity to turn our eyes away so we don't see the poor and the mentally ill; in the Middle Ages and in the early twentieth century, people used to visit the madhouses for a good laugh at the antics of the insane.

Through Marsha and the San Fernando Valley Mental Health Center, I discover a residential program where Lisa now lives with four other patients (or clients, as they call them) in a regular house and home. She, with the others, has household chores—washing dishes, making beds, doing laundry. From 10:30 A.M. to 2:30 P.M., she attends adult education classes, with time out for lunch. She has the rest of the day for social activities and physical fitness time in a conveniently adjacent empty Army gymnasium. She also has lengthy visits with a psychiatrist every week and regular medical care. Lisa is a pretty woman when she is well groomed and a good athlete who excels in volleyball, tennis, and swimming. She sketches well and is a good musician. She sings and plays the guitar and piano—her tastes range from Debussy, Bach, and Chopin to Bob Dylan and Joan Baez. There is a forty percent incidence of remission in cases of schizophrenia, and I will always have hope that Lisa will one day lead a normal life.

Helping me through the early period of Lisa's illness are my singing lessons with Alice Mack Rowe. Singing has always been a part of my life, and finding my voice again is very much a part of finding myself again. It's also part of being alive and staying alive. Only last year, I ran into John Raitt, who looks and sings better now than when he was doing *Pajama Game* on Broadway and I was doing *Anniversary Waltz* across the street. Johnny said, "You know the reason we both are as healthy as we are, Mac? It's singing." "We're the only ones who breathe these days," I said. And then we both say, "Look at how long those orchestra conductors live—they always have their hands and their chests up in the air!"

I still study singing with Alice every day that I'm not working. My daughter Lynn is a marvelous jazz singer and composer, and recently we've played a few gigs together. We're putting together an act. Lynn started out professionally in rock as one of the first women to have her own group, Mama Lion, which put out six albums on RCA. She is a beautiful blonde who now sings scat jazz and has a range of three-and-a-half octaves—a combination of Ella Fitzgerald and Janice Joplin, and that ain't bad.

2 5 9

Lynn is the first child, then Lisa, then Steve. He's the oldest boy and a realty lawyer. In one of my poems, I surmise this is how he got that way:

The Law

Why everyone is surprised by the Beverly Hills Police
Overreacting on Rodeo Drive on Van Cleef and Arpels
Puzzles me
When my oldest boy Steve was ten he stole
Three goldfish from the Beverly Hills Park Pond
On Sunset Boulevard

I told him to return them

The police caught him putting them back
And two squad cars picked him up
And took him to jail
I had to go downtown
To get him out. They'd locked him up.

It was a traumatic experience

He grew up to become
A Beverly Hills lawyer.

Steve is six-foot-four—in fact, all the boys are—and he looks at thirty-nine about the way I did except that he's taller and more muscular. There is a loving, affectionate relationship between us as well as between me and my other children. Amusingly enough, there's also an element of the classic father and first-son competition between us. When Steve was twelve and found out I was a liberal Democrat, he went right out and got a job distributing Nixon leaflets. He is now married to a beautiful actress named Indy Shreiner, with whom he was in kindergarten at Beverly Hills Catholic. We just celebrated the christening of their second daughter. I am Catholic but Steve, still my firstborn son, attends All Saints, the Episcopalian church, which is a block away from us Catholics at the Good Shepherd. The christening was held at All Saints. Perhaps Steve's defection to the Episcopalians is just another expression of the father–first son syndrome.

I guess it's like Ricky Hearst, one of Steve's friends, who told me when he was eight years old, "My mother and I just have a personality conflict." Steve will call me, though, when he's lectoring at All Saints and wants to discuss one of the readings. And I don't mean to suggest there's any conflict between us: we always greet each other and say good-bye, all my boys and myself, with an embrace and a kiss. This was a heritage from my father; the Careys were a very affectionate lot.

The next in line, Theresa, is a wonderful pianist. She was composing at age six and took lessons with all the other Beverly Hills brats—Jascha Heifetz's son, Johnny Green's daughter, and Jane Wyatt's son—from Mrs. Gold. Mrs. Gold was well along in years. I remember driving her back to her apartment in Hollywood on a block behind Grauman's Chinese Theatre, which has fallen into some disarray. I also occasionally drive the Guatemalan lady who does my cleaning to the same block. Many Central and South American immigrants now live in those apartments, some three or four to a room.

But, as they say, I digress, in this case from my story about Mrs. Gold and her husband, who had been first violinist with the San Francisco Symphony. One day, Pierre Monteux (the famous French conductor) arrived to take over the symphony. Maestro Monteux loved uniformity, homogeneity. Since his hair was black and he wore a mustache, he instructed—no, demanded—that every man in the symphony orchestra grow a mustache and color his hair black. Mrs.

Gold's husband was his own man, however. Rather than change his looks, he left his job. But he was afraid to tell Mrs. Gold, so each evening at seven o'clock, when he'd normally leave to go to the symphony, he'd kiss Mrs. Gold good-bye, walk out the door with his violin case under his arm, and go to the park and sit there alone until the time the concert was over. Then he'd get up from the bench and go home. After a month, Monteux found the orchestra not quite what it had been with Mr. Gold as first violin. Also the totalitarian sight of the whole orchestra with black hair and black mustaches was singularly unappealing to the audiences, so he telephoned Mr. Gold and begged him to return. He also told the orchestra they could go back to their own hair colors and clean-shaven selves. Mr. Gold returned and they all lived happily ever after. I think.

Mrs. Gold never discovered her husband's gentle solicitousness in not telling her until after his death. So I guess the Golds did any how—live happily ever after, that is.

Theresa never pursued her very possible career as a concert pianist. She had an exquisite touch and still plays when asked, but it's no longer her whole life. She married and had two little boys, Vytas and Aras. She is now a single parent and is an insurance agent for Northwestern Mutual—Charlie's company. Now that Charlie's gone (he died in 1988), she's carrying on the Carey name at Northwestern and has chalked up a surprising number of sales for her first year as an active agent.

Mac is my fifth child and at one time was not as close to me as he is now. The following is from *Beyond That Further Hill*:

Growing

My boys are all 6'4"
And into their own lives now

We don't see each other much anymore
I remember
We had a problem with one of them
He stammered
I kept trying to talk him out of it
(Speech is important to an actor)

The doctor said "Your voice is very
Threatening to an eight-year-old. Tell him
You don't mean to sound that way"

I told him about my being an actor and all
And he never stammered again

One night after that
We were wrestling in the living room
After dinner
And I let him toss me over his shoulder

"There" he said
"I threw the whole father"

Mac and his buddy Jay built and ran the Rocking Horse restaurant for seven years in Walnut Creek, California, a suburb of Oakland. Right now he is finishing his graduate year in math and physical education and is planning to teach. Quite a leap from hosting a restaurant and bartending, but I think teaching is what he loves the most.

Paul, the youngest, is in Napa Valley. He is a trial lawyer. He was brilliant at UCLA: not only did he make Phi Beta Kappa, he headed the debating team his last two years. He now has a successful practice in Napa. He was married in June 1989 to a very caring young woman, Sharon, and they are living in Napa. Paul is the sort of man who will sit up all night with you and discuss the number of angels on the head of a pin. Besides having a restless, inquiring mind and a love for the game of golf, like his uncles Charlie and Gordy, he sings in a barbershop quartet. And Napa is a beautiful part of the world. Not just the wine but the air itself is tasty.

Maybe I cherish my children all the more because earlier I was only intermittently close to them. In the years Betty and I were first separated—1967 to 1969—up to and including the time we signed a property settlement, an estrangement from my children began. The separation itself had an opening night. Betty and I were planning a party for two hundred people at Chasen's to repay our social debts. As we're writing out the invitations, Betty tells me she wants me out of the house. We have recently been seeing counselors and she says she'll continue going to them with me but she wants to be alone. I am numb with shock, but the fact that we have been fruitlessly going to counselors and talking to priests has somewhat prepared me. It hasn't prepared me for going through with the party, however. Betty, on the other hand, sees no reason to call it off. I can only guess that she sees it as some sort of coming-out party for herself. For me, it is a funeral.

It is a black-tie party in the new glassed-in section to the right as you come in Chasen's. A good proportion of the people we know socially in the business are there. The Watson Webb gang, Fred and Lily MacMurray, Ray and Mel Milland, Dinah Shore and George Montgomery, Henry and Skip Hathaway, the Bob Mitchums, the Bob Prestons, Howard Duff and Ida Lupino, Bill and Ardis Holden, most of the friends we know in and out of the business. The whole evening is one long horror for me. There's a small combo playing with a standing microphone. I watch Betty go up to the mike and make the announcement that she and I are separated. I'm getting numb as different people get up and make some kind of half-assed toast to us. I can't repeat what anybody said; if any part of my life has been blocked out, this evening is it. I remember being led up to the mike myself and saying something like, "May this be a celebration of a beginning rather than an ending."

Inside, I feel it is the end of my life. Betty is calling it a separation, but in my heart I know she wants a divorce, and I am right. The ensuing days see no more visits to counselors or priests. Betty says it's over. I am a Catholic and basically believe marriage is no casual tie but an eternal one. Never before has there been a divorce in the Carey or Macdonald family. It never occurs to me that all this drinking and infidelity on both our parts, but on mine particularly, could lead to divorce, but here it is and Betty makes it clear to me that nothing I could do or say at this late date will change her mind. I have been living in a fool's paradise where I always believed things between us would magically improve. I am now out of that Eden. For me, the breakup is not only traumatic from a husband's standpoint but from a father's as well. I'm losing my children, the one thing besides my career I've devoted my life to having. I'm also losing my self-respect.

There was always a duality to my nature: the outgoing, one-of-the-boys, good-with-the-girls, singing and acting extrovert and the introvert, sympathetic in childhood to my mother's being pushed out of her nest and believing that as an artist I must always have humility. I believed these diverse traits could exist alongside each other and that my marriage and family life would nourish them. Here I was being thrown out of the nest much more severely than my mother had been and suddenly I felt that neither part of me has any value at all. With the death of my marriage, a good part of me dies, and it's years before I find out who I am and if I have any validity.

In the soap opera of our divorce, there is no question who gets custody of the children. It is Betty. She has the house. She already has some income of her own, and now, according to our settlement, she has fifty percent of our investments and a sizable allowance from me for her and the children every month. And she has Anna to run the house. I turn out to be the extra man at my own house as well as at dinner parties around town.

When I move out of the house, I move into an apartment building in West Hollywood that I soon find out has been dubbed "Sin City." The atmosphere there is compulsively congenial, full of false heartiness, and just plain sex. My first night, there is a knock on the door. I open it to find two attractive women standing there with three glasses of scotch and soda—one of course for me. Practically everyone on board the Good Ship Sin City is newly divorced. Or just generally at their wits end—and everyone seems to drink a lot.

I meet a lot of people there, among them the fabulous Bricktop of Paris and Rome fame. She becomes a drinking buddy. She is black, red-haired, Catholic, and in her eighties, at least. She had run a famous nightclub in Paris circa 1920 to 1930. She was the first to sing many of Cole Porter's songs; he was there and wrote them for her. The same went for Noel Coward. Hemingway, F. Scott Fitzgerald, James Joyce, Ezra Pound, William Carlos Williams, and Picasso, among others, frequented her place. I go to a party in Sin City for Sam Bronston, who had been the producer of *John Paul Jones*. At the party, I run into Maria Cole, Nat King Cole's widow. I had met her before when she'd come to our house on Foothill with Benny Carter and his wife. Maria and I arrange to have dinner together. I lose her telephone number and ask Bricktop to get it for me. She gives me Maria's number but says, "If you're planning to date Maria Cole, both of you should think what you're doing. You're white and she's black." "But I think she's Catholic," I tell Bricktop. "Her daughter goes to Immaculate Heart with my daughter Lynn." I try to call Maria twice, but she never returns my calls. I'm lonely and obviously available.

The field is open for me to have all the one-night stands I

want, but now that I have the opportunity, I don't really want them.

After the divorce became final, I left Sin City and rented a shack at Trancas Beach, north of Malibu. It was far from town and I had to get up at 3:00 A.M. to get to "Days of Our Lives" in Burbank, but it was on the ocean and I made a little garden there. There was some sense of renewal going on. It is at Trancas that Henry Jones, a very good character actor who, in 1940, had lived in the room above me at 34 Beekman Place, introduces me to a uniquely attractive woman, Norma Dauphin, who soon becomes part of my life.

Norma was born Norma Eberhardt. She was an actress before she met and married the French actor, Claude Dauphin, best known for his work in French cinema and in the theater. She was also a model and very striking, to say the least. She has one blue eye and one brown eye and has been on the cover of *Life* three times. Norma is petite, wears her hair in a pigtail, and wears pinafores and very little girl dress-up clothes. She is a painter. I still have some of her work. Also, she is a gourmet cook—a graduate of the Paris Cordon Bleu. I will never forget those mousses. And she knows most everyone in the movies and in the theater in New York and London, in fact, internationally. She knows designers, painters, and writers. She is an education in herself and she introduces me to an entirely different life than I'd known with Betty.

Norma encourages me to write again. She not only does that, she gets a publisher for me, Bill Thompson, who at the time was at Doubleday in New York. She is wonderful with Lisa, and Lisa responds to her beautifully. She helps me a great deal when I need help. When I meet Norma, she is divorced, I am divorced. At this time, I'm not much of a practicing Catholic, so there is no impediment to our getting together. There are all sorts of coincidental acquaintance-ships we have: besides Henry Jones, there is Mac Mac-

Namara, the former publicist for David Selznick, now married to Eloise, who had been my neighbor at 620 North Cañon in Beverly Hills when she was married to Hans Habe, a European writer who had been blacklisted during the McCarthy years. MacNamara, Eloise's present husband, is a good painter whose house in Franklin Canyon is hung with his artistic forgeries. He is very good at doing the Impressionists. All his paintings are signed: Max Renoir, Max Cézanne, Max Picasso, Max Degas, Max Lautrec, and, as they say, many, many more. Mac (as he's called) is also a friend of Betty's and my old friends Jane and Bunty Lawrence.

I work every day on "Days of Our Lives," so it's hard to dignify the few evenings Norma and I go out by calling them a social life. Mainly, Norma and I are there with each other at home. For me, she is girlfriend, poetry critic, and a sign that my life is not over despite the divorce. I owe her a lot that I'll never be able to repay. She taught me a great deal and helped me through two very rough years. I think she knows what she has meant to me.

Norma and I broke up in 1979. The logical culmination of our relationship would have been marriage, but I didn't want to marry again. Marriage just doesn't seem to work for me, and way in the recesses of my Catholic mind was the thought that this would drive a wedge between me and my children.

It takes me a while, however, to realize I never want to get married again, and I'm afraid I put Norma through unnecessary pain dangling the possibility before her and then taking it away. When we separate, she goes back to New York almost immediately.

Norma and I remain friends, though, and her influence continues. Writing poetry becomes a new way of life for me. It is leading me back to some sort of integrity; it is helping me find myself. I take poetry classes with Robin Johnson at UCLA, with Holly Prado in Hollywood, and, mainly, with Peter Leavitt, a wonderful poet and teacher who opens me up to modern American poetry and introduces me to the LA poetry scene. That my poetry goes beyond simple therapy is my very good luck. In 1981, Norma's friend Bill Thompson, now at Coward-McCann, sends out an editor, Jason Schinder, who has just edited Allen Ginsberg's most recent book of poems, to work with me. A year later, 1983, my first book of poems, *A Day in the Life*, is published by Coward-McCann.

I am introduced to the mysterious world of publishing. I correct the proofs and there are still mistakes in the printing—not just errata in the text, but my name is misspelled on the cover: MacDonald Carey instead of Macdonald Carey. I wonder what they'll do with my tombstone. Maybe I should put a codicil in my will instructing my survivors to plant tall grass around the plot, like the actress who tells her survivors to plant moss on her tomb in a way that her birthdate will be obscured.

Although *A Day in the Life* is received well critically, I realize that I still haven't found my "voice," as they say. I find another poetry teacher at UCLA, Jack Grapes. Jack gets to me by simply making me do what he makes all his students do—sit down and write two pages every day of what he calls "straight talk," a narrative review of the day in the first person. Gradually, I find my identity and I find myself in the midst of my poems. It is liberating and wonderful to experience. In finding my voice, I find myself, and "myself" is what I used to put myself down for: I'm common—and the very commonness of me makes me more accessible to people who read my poetry. It's like acting, I find; it all has to do with truth and simplicity, and it's like singing; it all has to do with "letting go." It has to do with what Monet said painting should be: "Like a bird sings."

I keep taking classes from Jack. His pupils make up their own books at the end of each term and, through him, I publish a small chapbook, *That Further Hill*, with Bombshelter Press.

In 1979, I met a wonderful lady, Lois Kraines, whom I see

faithfully for more years than we like to count. We are still the closest of friends—perhaps she is my closest friend. We met, of all places, at Hugh Hefner's Playboy mansion, where I was a judge for the tennis matches and was emceeing the raffle for an organization called "Tennis and Crumpet," which was started by Mrs. Spencer Tracy to help deaf children. Tennis was still very much a part of my life, not just judging but playing; I never came close to being the tennis player my father was, but it was as much a part of my life as my drinking. And soon Lois is a part of my life, too.

How many times by now have I talked about my drinking? How many times have I said I have a drinking problem and I don't know it? How many times have you asked yourself in reading this how the hell could I have not known it? Isn't it about time he found out? But you see, that's just the point. There are an infinite number of ways an alcoholic can delude himself and tell himself he's not an alcoholic, and I used every one I could lay my hands on. An alcoholic has to hit bottom before he recognizes that he has a problem. Nobody can say what anybody else's bottom is. It happens when it happens.

At the beginning of 1982, I had an epiphany, of sorts. One day, I had a drink before I went on in "Days of Our Lives." This worried me. I've always told myself that when I start to drink on the job, that would be it. I suddenly get the brilliant idea that I am a drunk and that I have to do something to stop it.

This coincides with the reappearance of another woman I had dated once, years before in Las Vegas. I take her out to dinner. She doesn't automatically fall on her back with arms outstretched but instead tells me she is in Alcoholics Anonymous and that I might just possibly consider that this is the place I belong.

Then I get a call from my boy Steve, who says he is having trouble with his drinking. This convinces me that this is the time to try AA, particularly since I'll be helping Steve. So I

270

call one of my friends who lives in the valley. He has been suggesting AA to me for years but hasn't plagued me with attempts to convert me.

On January 8, 1982, my life begins. I admit I'm an alcoholic. I go to my first AA meeting in the valley, and I haven't had a drink since, nor will I ever.

To think that I had to live through all this—and more— to reach this point:

1. I thought Mother had psychic powers. She always knew when I'd been drinking. How could she miss? She'd find my vomit in one of the loving cups that littered the house.

2. Boozy party at the Martin Hotel (the girl in the dark room).

3. Spiked beer and Templeton rye—Prohibition days drinking.

4. Incident at the University of Wisconsin (rain and Rush Week and bed-wetting).

5. Getting kicked off the freshmen crew for drinking beer.

6. Not allowed to act at Iowa until I gave up Cedar Rapids binges.

7. Drinking sherry before "The First Nighter" shows.

8. Shakes at my Twentieth Century–Fox movie audition.

9. Shakes at my Marine physical exam.

10. Shakes on *Shadow of a Doubt*.

11. Drunk on parade in the Marines.

12. Drinking overseas in the Pacific.

13. Pattern of drinking and hangovers in LA after the war.

14. Jail in Beverly Hills—we're all drinking and a neighbor misses me with gunshot.

15. Jail for a 502 (drunk driving).

16. Boozy one-night stands.

17. Divorce.

18. Van Heflin asks me if I have blackouts. I pity his overindulgence in booze.

2 7 1

19. Wendell Corey's death.
20. Bill Holden's death.
21. Brod Crawford's death.
22. Dan Dailey's death.
23. Drinking with Norma.
24. Drinking with Lois.
25. Drinking on the job.
26. Woman from Las Vegas turns up and turns me down for a date, saying I should join AA.
27. I join AA.

I am an alcoholic, a recovering alcoholic, and I will be one for the rest of my life. So far, from that miraculous night on January 8, 1982, life has been an endless, never-ending joy. My health has improved; the eternal shaking has gone away. I don't have arthritis. My hair is darker. My nails are stronger. My acting is better. My singing is better. My relationship with people is better. My former wife Betty and I have a civilized relationship. I'm reconciled with my children. We share each other's lives. We are all together on every holiday. Christmas day they are at my house.

Steve, by the way, doesn't show up after the first month for AA meetings. I call him a few times until I finally realize that he just pretended to have a problem to help me join AA.

There are two things one must do if one joins AA. First, admit you're an alcoholic; second, accept as fact that there is a power higher than yourself. It follows as night the day that I would go back to the Catholic church. I am an usher, a lector, and a Eucharistic minister. I not only carry communion every Sunday to the sick and to people who can't attend Mass, I also give communion at the altar rail with the priest. What that means to this altar boy you can't imagine.

And my poetry is better. It is certainly clearer and more accessible, and I'm still studying. I keep working with Jack Grapes, and I've been a student in seminars of Clayton Eshelman and many of the current poets—from C. K. Williams to John Ashbery—who come to my house where we hold the seminars. When Pope John Paul visited the United States in 1988, Bill Wilson, our first ambassador to the Vatican, suggested that I be asked to go to Columbia, South Carolina, to do a two-and-a-half-hour show preceding the Pope's arrival to meet with all the heads of the U.S. Protestant churches.

I go with Richard Thomas, Michael Keaton, Jane Wyatt, Bonita Granville Wrather, Helen Hayes, and Martina Arroyo. Father Jerome Vereb, the priest who wrote the script for us and for the Pope, befriends me. He has been with the Pope in the Vatican for seven years and is about to take a chair in the arts at the University of South Carolina. He gets my third book of poetry, *Beyond That Further Hill*, published in 1989 by the University of South Carolina Press.

As I have said, the fourth step of the twelve steps in AA is doing a complete inventory of your life and asking for forgiveness. My editor told me after my first draft of this book that I was still into denial—that I was leaving something out. She was right, and in rewriting the book, I interviewed everyone near me whom I had possibly hurt. The last couple of weeks have been filled with interviews, long talks with Norma Dauphin, talks with my children Steve, Theresa, Paul, Mac, and Lynn, talks with Betty, talks with Frances Reid and Lois. The news was both good and bad. As I now view my past, the picture is not as blurred.

Betty agrees with me that we did our best to kill what we had and that we spent a good part of our time together hurting each other. "But I hurt you more than you hurt me," she observes. She agrees, too, that we constantly misunderstood each other; we were like two countries trying to communicate with different codes. She waited for me to assert myself and stop her flirtations, and I never did; they just drove me further away. She remembers being mad if I drank too much; I also remember her being mad if I drank too much but being equally mad if I stopped. Drinking was a social necessity to her and, in those less-AA-oriented days, she didn't understand my alcoholism; me, I was just an alcoholic.

Talking with Frances Reid, my soap opera wife, I realize I put her through hell. Being married to an alcoholic as she was in real life, and coming to work with one during the day was horribly painful for her, more than anyone should have to bear, especially after she divorced her husband and he died alone, his body not found for three days. The fact that the two of us have been able to portray two people in a happy and enduring marriage is a testament to Frances's forbearance and to the craft of acting and the show itself.

Norma Dauphin remembers that during her time with me I fell into terrible rages many nights, but I never struck anyone. I was angry, but I was angry at my fate and my failure. Angry at me.

My anger didn't start with my divorce from Betty. Lynn tells me that before the divorce, after we had moved to the apartment house on Charleville, I had gone into her room and the other children's rooms late one night, doing my own version of Joan Crawford. I woke them up and insisted they empty all the wastebaskets. Most of the time, they only knew about my drinking because they were told to keep quiet when they were playing near my window as I was sleeping off a hangover.

But with all I drank, why was I alive? How did I continue to live when so many of my contemporaries were dying of alcoholism? God knows I drank enough; even Bill Holden told me I drank too much, and think how Bill went.

Norma tells me, and I think she's right, it was because of my enormous consumption of vitamins along with my enormous consumption of booze. In my way, I was a health nut. I took vitamin B-complex, B-12, B-6, and B-1 orally and intramuscularly. Even when I went on location in England, I gave myself shots in the behind, watching my rear in the mirror. I carried little four-ounce bottles of rubbing alcohol for the hypodermic needles. I was very neat and economical. I'd save those little empty plastic bottles and fill them with vodka—one hundred proof. From 1966 to 1982, I was never without liquid vitamin B and C and never without vodka, and after an hour's sleep, I'd wake up and eat massive sandwiches patterned after my diet during my struggling radio days—sandwiches of whole wheat bread, peanut butter, mayonnaise, lettuce, and lots of milk. I didn't take barbiturates; I used nonbarbiturate sleeping pills and calcium pills and herbal sleeping pills and got back to bed. And I'd play tennis every day I wasn't working.

The other thing I wasn't without was good genes—longevity and hardiness run in both sides of the family. As despairing as I ever got, I never really lost my faith. In Ireland, instead of saying, "Have a nice day," they say, "Keep the faith." I obviously did. It, more than the vitamins, genes, and exercise, pulled me through. Now, of course, I have AA.

My sober hours I worked and I worried about the children, especially Lisa. I worried about all of them, wanting them to become that better class of people I'd asked for from Betty —literate, kind, socially responsible, and, above all, loving.

The children were of course aware of the awful example I was giving them. But even Betty says, and they say, they never thought I didn't love them. I was always there for Lisa, as I still am, visiting her, taking her wherever she needs to go, a constant part of her life, preserving her sense of being part of the family. One thing I never harbored is the terrible guilt so many parents feel when they have a mentally ill child, a guilt that often translates itself into shame. As I write this, I have just moved Lisa from a place she has been in for six months, which was too structured yet too understaffed to handle her. While she was there, I didn't see many parents visiting. The same is true at other places Lisa has been, and those number more than ten; if parents do show up, they don't come in, they park outside and let the child come to them. The one exception is Clontarf Manor Artesia in Artesia, California, where Lisa is now. CMA encourages parental visits and councils parents in how to handle their attitudes.

Norma was wonderful with the children, and Mac and Paul and Lisa adored her. One thing they all remember is the house I rented at the beach and in particular, my roaring at them to be quiet one night. We were toasting marshmallows and some had dropped to the floor, and they all started sliding around on them, pretending they had skates.

When Norma first moved in with me, I rented a little house in Beverly Hills off San Ysidro from a well-endowed actress called Karen Steele (who later starred in "Flipper"). I remember she had letters from several well-known stars in her storeroom, letters vowing temporal if not eternal love, that Norma found just lying there in an open box. John Clarke (my son Mickey in "Days of Our Lives") helped me move in. The house was almost bare. We had two sets of stainless steel cutlery in the kitchen, some paper plates and napkins, and a crate for a table in the living room. There were three or four books. One was Antoine de St. Exupery's *Little Prince*, another, a book by Teilhard de Chardin.

Norma designed bunk beds, which a carpenter friend put together, big wooden coffins with drawers I could store my belongings in. There were four of these, as I remember. We bought foam rubber pads to serve as mattresses. Two of the coffins could be put together to make a double bed; the others were in another room. Norma was not living with me yet and the other beds were there so the kids, if they visited, would have a place to sleep. The house was on the top of a hill and was surrounded by a wire mesh steel fence. A gate of the same material guarded the driveway. Deer would occasionally leap the fence and, surprised, find themselves penned in an enclosure. I'd have to swing open the gate to let them out.

After Norma and I split up, I would cablegram my poetry to her. She tells me she has boxes of poetry I sent her. Bill Thompson, the editor to whom she introduced me, received the same flood of poetry. I would cablegram it to both of them. I would cablegram my poems to anybody who showed any interest in them. Norma says some cablegrams were a yard long. I will be forever grateful to her and to Bill and to Jason Schinder. It was their help that got me into print. To think I was still drinking when my poetry book came out in 1982. Unbelievable. I actually got good reviews.

Norma also tells me there was a time when I passed out face down in my dinner plate, a comedian to the last.

But, of course, even then I hadn't hit bottom. There were to be more years of drinking before I finally joined AA. Lois, who was my companion during these years, says an average evening's drinking for me would consist of two or three cocktails, martinis or old-fashioneds, wine with dinner, and a liqueur or just straight scotch and water after. Then we'd go on to the Little Club, have a few scotches there, and close the night at the Polo Lounge or at Alberto's on Melrose with another couple of drinks. The total was stupefying. The question is, who drove the car? How I got through those years with only one 502 and never killing anyone, I don't know.

Joining Alcoholics Anonymous and rejoining the Catholic church are stepping-stones in my happy recovery. They've helped me find and face my "shadow." I was Dr. Jekyll and Mr. Hyde; deep in the hide of me, there was, oh, such a hungry yearning, burning inside of me. It was my shadow crying out to be recognized. Inhibited, it drank potions of alcohol. Besides its primal urges, it was snobbish and uppity.

Once I realized I am a *human* being with a weakness who was putting on airs, and I reconciled this part of my intro-

2 7 7

verted side with my extroverted side, I was on the yellow brick road to happiness. In answer to that old question, No, I don't think I'm the Queen of Romania. I'm me.

Montaigne says, "The journey, not the arrival, matters." Thank God, I am still journeying. Everyday since I became a declared recovering alcoholic provides psychotherapy for me. Last Sunday, one of the people I take communion to is a lady to whom I have been taking it for the last month. This time, she answers her doorbell to tell me she doesn't need it, she is going to Mass. She hasn't been sick, she's just been staying home to dodge a process server.

This would be enough laughter for the day, but then I drive out to Lisa's new home in Granada Hills. I bring her some new tennis shoes, Reebok's, with some extra socks in case the shoes are too big for her, but the shoes do fit, and she fairly dances across the carpet as she tries them out, walking, almost skipping back and forth across the room. Two of her housemates are there and praise her basketball playing the day before. One of them says, "You're the best basketball player I've ever seen. How come you never miss a basket?" "I just don't plan it," says Lisa.

> There is a story that is told by actors since
> There was a Hollywood and there was an
>   East Coast
> Two actors leave the Middle West to find fame
> And fortune
> One goes to Hollywood and one to New York
> Neither one after ten years is working
>   very much
> In search of greener fields one
> Gets on a plane and flies east
> One gets on a plane and flies west
> As they pass they yell to each other
> Go back! Go back!

I'm trying to go back today
But back somewhere else
Back to the Middle West
Today I'm trying to write a poem
Of meanness and hate of revenge and despair
I'm digging tunnels to tunnels of resentment
And cravings and fears in my past
It ain't easy
Because
It is today and I have hope

But you can go home again if you try
There are ways

I am a child again at the boat club
In Sioux City. A boy of nine
I stand on the bank of the river and watch
A man tumble from his boat into the
        muddy water
I run for help but
No one comes. No one ever comes.

I dream of that man to this day
But even in my dreams I never find his body
In the muddy water that rushes past
And in my dream
Sometimes I'm in the water searching for
        him groping
And sometimes in my dreams I'm that man
        in the
Water and I know no one will ever find me
That's the way it is with me—the boy lost on
        the bank
The man lost in the water

I am both
Or

I am a boy again on Jackson Street in Sioux
    City
A boy of ten
I watch the car hit my dog
I run to the dog and yell at
The car which speeds on its way
I yell for someone to help me
Someone to help my dog
But no one helps me
No one comes
He dies there as I hold him
I dream this dream to this day too
Sometimes I'm the boy and sometimes I'm
    the dog
And sometimes I am both

This week my daughter
Is beginning to come out of her madness
She can take the bus herself now
And no longer cuts her wrists
Today she said "People aren't really
    marionettes, are they
They're really real people aren't they?"
I tell her yes, Lisa, yes they're really real people

Yesterday my daughter came late to therapy
Class and gave a wild cockamamie excuse
The doctor said "You're lying aren't you Lisa"
My daughter said "Well what do you know
I could have sworn I was telling the truth"

The wonderful thing about sobriety is that "on a clear day you can see forever"; reality and normalcy become quite palatable once you get used to them. I suddenly have a relationship with the world. The simple constant joy that each day, each moment, brings me is more than I can describe. Oh, there are frustrations, there are disappointments. But in the overall frame of every day, they are minute, miniscule. I am a living example of a man who's been closed off from society, finally accepting responsibility by working for others, not just myself. Everything I can do for the church, for mental health, for people, enriches me. For the first time in my life, I'm honestly happy.

I thank God. A painting of Sister Corita hangs on the wall in front of my desk. The legend on it says:

TO BELIEVE IN GOD IS TO KNOW THAT THE RULES . . . ARE FAIR AND THAT THERE WILL BE . . . WONDERFUL SURPRISES.

Call Back

A wardrobe's not enough at all
To get you through God's cattle call
And sadly youth and looks and charm go
They keep you warm in winter snow? No!
Your sidewalk star held by no eternal mortar
Despite raves from "The Hollywood Reporter"
Disregard that columnist chatter
Fame dies for guys
And dolls for that matter

It's age, survival pays the rent
No agent worth his ten percent
Can get you this
It's heaven sent

So kiss the tortoise, forget the hare
Who cares
Who really cares
My dear
Your dreams came true, you got the part
Who gives a flying flowering fart?
It's how you finish
Not how you start

Macdonald Carey

APPENDIX:
The "Days of Our Lives" Family

THE HORTON FAMILY

Alice and Tom Horton

CHILDREN

Marie Horton
- Married to Craig Merritt.
- Married to Dr. Neil Curtis.
- Had affair with Alex Marshall. They had a child, Jessica Blake.

Mickey Horton
- Married and divorced Laura Spencer.
- Through an affair with Bill Horton, Laura had Mike, raised by Mickey.
- Married Maggie Simmons.
- Janice was their foster child.
- Legal guardians of Melissa Anderson.
- Maggie had Sarah, with Evan Whyland, the biological father.

285

Bill Horton	• Married Laura Spencer.
	• They had Jennifer Rose in addition to son, Mike Horton.
Addie Horton	• Married to Ben Olson.
	• They had a daughter, Julie Olson, and son, Steven Olson.
	• Married Doug Williams.
	• They had a daughter, Hope Williams.
Tommy Jr.	• Married Kitty. They had a daughter, Dr. Sandy Horton.

GRANDCHILDREN

Mike Horton	• Married Margo Anderman.
	• Had a son, Jeremy, by Dr. Robin Jacobs.
Jessica Blake	• Married Joshua Fallon.
Hope Williams	• Married and divorced Larry Welch.
	• Married Bo Brady.
	• They have a son, Shawn Douglas Brady.
Julie Olson	• Had a son, David, whom she gave up for adoption, through an affair with David Martin.
	• Married Scott Banning, who had adopted David.
	• Married Bob Anderson.
	• Married and remarried Doug Williams, now divorced.
Melissa Anderson	• Married and divorced Pete Jannings.

David Banning

- Married and divorced Trish Clayton.
- They had a son, Scotty Banning.
- Married Renee Dumonde, who was the illegitimate daughter of Lee Dumonde and Stefano DiMera.

THE BRADY FAMILY

Caroline and Shawn Brady

CHILDREN

Roman Brady

- Married and divorced Anna.
- Carrie Brady is their child.
- Married and widower of Marlena Evans.
- They had twins, Samantha and Eric.

Kayla Brady

- Briefly married to Jack Deveraux.
- Now married to Steve Johnson.
- They have a daughter, Stephanie Kay.

Kimberly Brady

- Married to Shane Donovan.
- They have a son, Andrew.

Bo Brady

- Son of Caroline Brady and Victor Kiriakis, with whom she had an affair.
- Bo now married to Hope Williams.
- They have a son, Shawn Douglas.

THE JOHNSON FAMILY

Jo and Duke Johnson

CHILDREN

Steven Earl Johnson
- Married to Marina Toscano.
- Now married to Kayla Brady.
- Their daughter is Stephanie Kay.

Adrienne Johnson
- Married and divorced Justin Kiriakis.

Billy Johnson
- Adopted by Harper Deveraux, now known as Jack Deveraux.
- Married briefly to Kayla Brady.

FILMOGRAPHY–
MACDONALD
CAREY

FILMS

Year	Film	Director	Co-Starring
1942	*Dr. Broadway*	Anthony Mann	
1942	*Take a Letter, Darling*	Mitchell Leisen	Rosalind Russell Fred MacMurray
1942	*Wake Island*	John Farrow	Brian Donleavy Robert Preston William Bendix
1942	*Star Spangled Rhythm*	George Marshall	
1943	*Salute for Three*	Ralph Murphy	
1943	*Shadow of a Doubt*	Alfred Hitchcock	Teresa Wright Joseph Cotten
1947	*Suddenly It's Spring*	Mitchell Leisen	Fred MacMurray Paulette Goddard

289

1947	*Variety Girl*	George Marshall	
1948	*Hazard*	George Marshall	Paulette Goddard
1949	*Dream Girl*	Mitchell Leisen	Betty Hutton
1949	*Streets of Laredo*	Leslie Fenton	William Holden William Bendix
1949	*Bride of Vengeance*	Mitchell Leisen	Paulette Goddard John Lund
1949	*The Great Gatsby*	Elliott Nugent	Alan Ladd
1949	*Song of Surrender*	Mitchell Leisen	Claude Rains Wanda Hendrix
1949	*South Sea Sinner*	Bruce Humberstone	Shelley Winters
1950	*Comanche Territory*	George Sherman	Maureen O'Hara
1950	*The Lawless*	Joseph Losey	Gail Russell
1950	*Copper Canyon*	John Farrow	Hedy Lamarr Ray Milland
1950	*Mystery Submarine*	Douglas Sirk	Marta Toren
1950	*The Great Missouri Raid*	Gordon Douglas	Wendell Corey
1951	*Excuse My Dust*	Roy Rowland	Red Skelton Sally Forrest

1951	*Cave of Outlaws*	William Castle	Alexis Smith
1951	*Let's Make It Legal*	Richard Sale	Claudette Colbert
1952	*My Wife's Best Friend*	Richard Sale	Anne Baxter
1952	*Count the Hours*	Don Siegel	Teresa Wright
1953	*Hannah Lee*	John Ireland	John Ireland Jo Anne Dru
1954	*Malaga*	Richard Sale	Maureen O'Hara
1956	*Stranger at My Door*	William Witney	Patricia Medina Skip Homeier
1956	*Odongo*	John Gilling	Rhonda Fleming
1956	*Edge of the Law*		
1958	*Man Or Gun*	Albert Gannaway	Audrey Totter
1959	*Blue Denim*	Philip Dunne	Marsha Hunt Carol Lynley
1959	*John Paul Jones*	John Farrow	Robert Stack Bette Davis
1962	*Stranglehold*	Lawrence Huntington	
1962	*Devil's Agent*	John Paddy Carstairs	

1962	*These are the Damned*	Joseph Losey	Shirley Anne Field Viveca Lindfors
1963	*Tammy and the Doctor*	Harry Keller	Sandra Dee
1965	*Broken Sabre*	Bernard McEveety	
1977	*End of the World*	John Hayers	
1980	*American Gigolo* (Cameo)	Paul Schraeder	Richard Gere Lauren Hutton

TELEVISION SERIES

Year(s)	*Title*
1956	"Dr. Christian"
1958–1959	"Lockup"
1965–1990	"Days of Our Lives"

FILMS FOR TELEVISION

Year	Title	Director
1955	*Miracle on 34th Street*	Robert Stevenson
1958	*Markham*	Jules Bricken
1958	*Natchez*	
1963	*Last of the Private Eyes*	Marc Daniels
1965	*The Green Felt Jungle*	Irving J. Moore
1972	*Gidget Gets Married*	E.W. Swackhamer
1973	*Ordeal*	Lee Katzin

1975	*Who Is The Black Dahlia?*	Joseph Pevney
1977	*Roots*	Gilbert Moses, John Erman, Marvin Chomsky, David Greene
1978	*Pressure Point*	Hubert Cornfield
1978	*Summer Of Fear*	Wes Craven
1979	*The Rebels*	Russ Mayberry
1980	*Condominium*	Sidney Hayers
1980	*Top of the Hill*	Walter Grauman
1981	*The Girl, the Gold Watch, and Everything*	William Wiard
1981	*Buck Rogers in the 25th Century*	Michael Caffey
1984	*Access Code*	Mark Sobel

TELEVISION SHOWS AS GUEST STAR

"Alfred Hitchcock Presents"
"Ben Casey"
"Bing Crosby"
"Burke's Law"
"Checkmate"
"Daniel Boone"
"Dick Powell"
"Fantasy Island"
"Mr. Novak"
"Murder, She Wrote"
"Rawhide"
"Run for Your Life"
"Thriller"
"Wagon Train"
"Zane Grey Theater"

LIVE TELEVISION

"Alcoa Theatre"
"Alfred Hitchcock Presents"

"Celanese Theater"
"Climax"
"Kraft Television Theatre"
"Lux Theatre"
"The Magician"
"Owen Marshall, Counselor at Law"
"Philco TV Playhouse"
"Playhouse 90"
"Playwright's Theatre"
"Pursuit"
"Studio One"
"In Times Like These"
"On Trial"
"U.S. Steel Hour"
"Your Show of Shows"

Broadway

Anniversary Waltz, opposite Kitty Carlisle
Lady in the Dark, opposite Gertrude Lawrence

Broadway Tryouts

Madly in Love, opposite Celeste Holm
Memo
Tin Wedding, with Maureen Stapleton

Musicals

Guys and Dolls
Music Man
Take Me Along
Trial by Jury

Summer Stock and Road

Calculated Risk
Getting Married
Marriage Go Round
Oh Men, Oh Women
Take Her, She's Mine
Thousand Clowns

INDEX

3 0 3

3 0 5

309